Praise for O

"Don't pick up *Off the Road* expecting some dry, religious treatise on this famous pilgrim's route. . . . You'll learn something and enjoy yourself just as Hitt did on this fabulously entertaining journey."

—*The Vancouver Sun*

"This is an unusual and immensely entertaining travel memoir."

—*The Toronto Star*

"Jack Hitt's *Off the Road* is an inspiring addition to tired old travelogue. He retraces the Pilgrim Route from France through Spain in a wise, funny and touching book."

—*The Observer*

"It's a pleasure, in a world full of trash, to rave about the perspicacious . . . writer Jack Hitt, who has brought us a delightfully cynical and irreverent story of modern pilgrimage, *Off the Road*."

—*Newsday*

"What Jack Hitt has wrought with *Off the Road* is a funny, informative book which wears its learning as lightly as the author bore his travails."

—*The Washington Post*

OFF THE

SIMON & SCHUSTER PAPERBACKS
New York · London · Toronto · Sydney

JACK HITT

ROAD

*A Modern-Day Walk
Down the Pilgrim's Route
into Spain*

SIMON & SCHUSTER PAPERBACKS
Rockefeller Center
1230 Avenue of the Americas
New York, NY 10020

Grateful acknowledgment is made for permission to quote from
the following book: The Pilgrim's Guide to Santiago de Compostela
and Gazetteer by Annie Shaver-Crandell, Paula Gerson, and Alison
Stones (London: Harvey Miller Publishers, 1994).

First Simon & Schuster paperback edition 2005

SIMON & SCHUSTER PAPERBACKS and colophon are registered
trademarks of Simon & Schuster, Inc.

For information about special discounts for bulk purchases,
please contact Simon & Schuster Special Sales at
1-800-456-6798 or business@simonandschuster.com.

Manufactured in the United States of America

10 9 8 7 6 5 4 3 2 1

Library of Congress Cataloging-in-Publication Data

Hitt, Jack.
   Off the road: a modern-day walk down the Pilgrim's Route
into Spain/Jack Hitt.—1st Simon & Schuster Paperback ed.
      p. cm.
      1. Spain, Northern—Description and travel.
2. Christian pilgrims and pilgrimages—Spain—
Santiago de Compostela. 3. Hitt, Jack—Journeys—Spain,
Northern. 4. Santiago de Compostela (Spain) I. Title.
DP285.H58 1994
914.6'10483—dc20   94-18984 CIP

ISBN 978-0-7432-6111-1

For Lisa

CONTENTS

ACKNOWLEDGMENTS

There are a lot of people I would like to thank for a good deal more than this book: Ellen Abrams, Kevin Baker, Geraldine Brooks, Charis Conn, Ira Glass, Penelope Green, Tony Horwitz, Geoff Kloske, David McCormick, Ann Patty, Michael Pollan, Jonathan Rabin, Stephen Raulston, Ron Suskind, and Paul Tough.

There are many others, but they'll have to wait. This book owes way too much to one man. If you know him, you know why. A great teacher: Tom Spaccarelli.

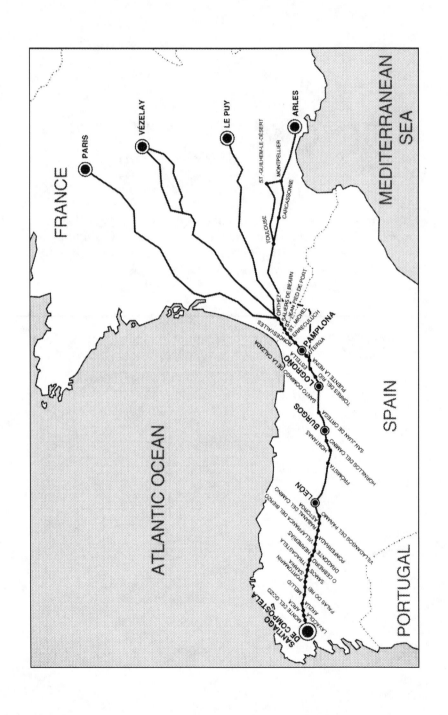

FRANCE

PARIS

VÉZELAY

LE PUY

ARLES

ST-GUILHEM-LE-DÉSERT

MONTPELLIER

CARCASSONNE

TOULOUSE

MEDITERRANEAN SEA

ORTHEZ
SALIERS DE BÉARN
ST-JEAN PIED DE PORT
ST-MICHEL
RONCESVALLES
ESPINAL
EZKIROZ
ZARIQUIEGUI
PAMPLONA
ITERGA
PUENTE LA REINA
ESTELLA
TORRES DEL RÍO
SANTO DOMINGO DE LA CALZADA
LOGROÑO

BURGOS
MONTAÑAS
SAN JUAN DE ORTEGA
HORNILLOS DEL CAMINO
FRÓMISTA

SPAIN

ATLANTIC OCEAN

LEÓN
ASTORGA
VILLAFRANCA DEL PÁRAMO
EL GANSO
VILLADANGOS DEL PÁRAMO
PONFERRADA
VILLAFRANCA DEL BIERZO
O CEBREIRO
TRIACASTELA
SARRIA
PORTOMARÍN
PALAS DO REI
MELIDE
ARZÚA
ARCA
LAVACOLLA
MONTE DEL GOZO
SANTIAGO DE COMPOSTELA

PORTUGAL

OFF THE ROAD

INTRODUCTION

Like many my age, I effortlessly cast off the religion of my parents as if stepping out of a pair of worn trousers. It happened sometime around college back in the 1970s and therefore was done with the casual arrogance and glibness famous to that time. I remember lounging in the last row of my required religion class. Professor Cassidy was making some relevant point, and I popped off that I would happily sum up the closed book of Western religion: The Jews invented god, the Catholics brought him to earth, and the Protestants made him our friend. Then god suffered the fate of all tiresome houseguests. Familiarity breeds contempt. With that, we dragged him into the twentieth century to die.

Afterward, the other sophomores and I ran off for the woods, read aloud the poetry of Arthur Rimbaud, and lit one another's cigarettes with our Zippos.

Let me say that my general attitude about religion has mellowed since then into a courteous indifference. On most days I side with the churches and synagogues in the everyday political battles that are called "religious" by the papers. My libertarian bent tilts enough against government that I don't get too excited about people who want to pray in schools or erect crèches or Stars of David in front of City Hall. And yet, if I'm angry or have been drinking, I am quick to say that when it comes to goodwill on earth, religion has been as helpful as a dead dog in a ditch, and that in this century it's been little more than a repository of empty ritual and a cheap cover for dim-witted bigotries.

So, imagine the reaction of many of my friends and relatives when I announced that I was going on a pilgrimage. And not some secular skip up the Appalachian Trail, but an ancient and traditional one. I intended to retrace the famous medieval route to Santiago de Compostela, Spain. Tucked into the northwestern panhandle of Spain on the Atlantic, Santiago is a few miles inland from Europe's westernmost spit of land, Finisterre. As its name implies, it was the end of the world until 1492. The road began in A.D. 814 when a hermit in the area stumbled upon the body of Saint James the Apostle. Since then, the road has been walked every year—in the Middle Ages by zealous millions; in more recent times by curious thousands.

For most of the late twentieth century, pilgrims to Santiago followed the shoulder of a blacktop highway paved by Generalissimo Franco. Then in the early 1980s scholars based in Estella, Spain, reacted to public concern after at least four pilgrims had been run over by trucks. Using old maps and ancient pilgrim accounts, the historians recovered vast sections of the original footpath still serving as mule or cart routes between the hundreds of poor villages along the way. Sections of the road were also intact in France, but once a modern pilgrim crossed the Pyrenees into Spain, there it was: a slightly wrinkled beeline of eight hundred authentic kilometers due west, following the setting sun by day and the streak of the Milky Way by night—over the craggy hills of the Spanish Basque territory, into the wine valleys of Rioja, across the plains of Castille, through the wheat fields of León, over the alpine mountains of Galicia, and finally into the comfort of the valley of Santiago. Depending on where I started, the walk could take two months, maybe more. Since pilgrims are supposed to arrive in town just before James's feast day on July 25, the idea I had in mind could not have been more simple and appealing. I would fly to Europe and spend the belly of the summer walking to the end of the world.

Despite my many, obvious disqualifications for being a pilgrim, I have long had an interest in the tradition of walking the road. After all, one could dress it up with all kinds of rationales and ritual, but stripped down, a pilgrim was a guy out for some cosmically serious fresh air. So in the beginning, it was the very simplicity of the idea of pilgrimage as a long walk that attracted me. Little did I know.

The medieval argument for pilgrimage held that the hectic routine of daily life—with its business obligations, social entanglements, and petty quarrels—was simply too confusing a pace for sustained thought. The idea was to slacken that pace to the natural rhythm of walking. The pilgrim would be exiled from numbing familiarity and plunged into continual change. The splendid anarchy of the walk was said to create a sense of being erased, a dusting of the tabula rasa, so that the pilgrim could consider a variety of incoming ideas with a clean slate. If escaping life's hectic repetition made sense in the Middle Ages, when time was measured by the passing of day and night, then it seemed to me reasonable to reconsider this old remedy now that we schedule our lives by the flash of blinking diodes.

This idea was a lot more than a Saturday hike or weekend outing. A pilgrimage would mean subletting my New York apartment, quitting my job, and resigning from my generous health plan. I would live on foot, out of a backpack, among old pueblos—some unwired for electricity, others abandoned centuries ago to become stone ghost towns. My long-set routines would be shattered, and my daily responsibilities would evaporate. I'd walk out of the pop-culture waters in which I had spent a lifetime treading and onto a strange dry land. I'd be far, far away from the AM hits that leak from cars and malls and dorms. I'd be at a blissful remove from CNN headlines and last night's news. I wouldn't have an opinion on whether the wife was justified in shooting her husband or whether the cop thought the ghetto kid was reaching for a knife or whether the woman had consented before the rape or whether the nanny had accidentally dropped the baby from the window . . . because I wouldn't know a single fact. My mind and attention would be cleansed of all that, and I could discover what topics they turned to when so generously unoccupied. A long walk. A *season* of walking. As it happened, I had just reached the Dantean age of thirty-five. What better way to serve out my coming midlife crisis than on a pilgrimage?

I quickly found, though, that one cannot discharge a word like "pilgrimage" into everyday conversation and long remain innocent of the connotations that drag in its wake. I had spent the last decade working as a magazine writer and then as an editor at *Harper's Magazine*. When I began to speak of my idea to associates throughout the media, I sometimes encountered polite interest. More often, I'd hear a bad joke. "Yo, Jack Quixote." A famous New York agent told me that if I found god, to tell him he owed her a phone call.

Those who were interested enough to keep talking would sometimes pinch their eyes as if to get a better view. Their lips crinkled in apprehension. Their fear, of course, was that I might return from Spain with an improved posture, a damp smile, and a lilac in my hand.

As a Western practice, pilgrimage is not merely out of fashion, it's dead. It last flourished in the days of Richard the Lion-Hearted, and it was one of the first practices Martin Luther felt comfortable denouncing without so much as a hedge. "All pilgrimages should be abolished," were his exact words. As something to do, the road to Santiago has been in a serious state of decline, technically speaking, since 1200.

The problem with pilgrimage is that, like so much of the vocabulary of religion, it is part of an exhausted and mummified idiom. We know this because that vocabulary thrives in the dead-end landfill of language, political journalism. Senators make pilgrimages to the White House. The tax cut that raises revenue is the Holy Grail of politics. Clean-cut do-gooders such as Bill Bradley and John Danforth are saints. The homes of dead presidents are shrines. Any threesome in politics is a trinity. Mario Cuomo doesn't speak, he delivers sermons or homilies. Dense thinking is Talmudic or Jesuitical. Devoted assistants are apostles.

The connotations of what I was doing hadn't deterred me because, before I went public, I had decided to walk the road on my own vague terms. I didn't foresee how much the implications of this word would overwhelm my own sense and use of it. In America, for whatever reason, any discussion of Christianity eventually gets snagged on an old nail. As a Christian, you are forced to answer one single question: Do you or do you not believe that Jesus the man was god the divine? If you can't answer that question easily, then you'll have to leave the room.

It is strange—and I say this without cynicism or bitterness—how *little* that question interests me, especially as a pilgrim. In fact, the weighty topics of theology intrigue me no more today than they did in Professor Cassidy's class. I realize it is apostasy as a pilgrim to admit this. But all those ten-pound questions—Does god exist? Is faith in the modern age possible? Is there meaning without orthodoxy?—bore me. The reason they wound up as running gags in Woody Allen's movies is precisely their hilarious irrelevance to the lives of many of us.

I think one reason religion has become so contentious when it is expressed as politics (abortion, death penalty, prayer in school, etc.) is that the answers to those Big Questions can't keep any of us awake. Thus, we turn to the hot-button questions about how other people should live their lives. Religion has become a kind of nonstop PBS seminar on ethics, conducted in a shout.

The result is that other unarticulated notions and yearnings once associated with religion have become intensely private. And that is why I wanted to walk to Santiago. At times it seems that the average American feels more comfortable discussing the quality of his or her orgasm on live television than talking about religion. I wondered: What are these hankerings that are so intimate they cause widespread embarrassment among my peers?

For me religion was always bound up with a lot more than graduate school theology and those incessant Protestant demands to believe in the supernatural. I grew up Episcopalian in Charleston, South Carolina. My family attended St. Philip's Church, the oldest and most prestigious church in a town that prides itself on being old and prestigious. I served eight years there earning my perfect attendance pin in Sunday school. And every time I walked through St. Philip's twelve-foot mahogany doors, I passed the same ten full-length marble sepulchers. Those nineteenth-century vaults contain my great-great-grandparents. Inside the church, our family always occupied the same pew and has, according to lore, since those folks in the white graves sat there. Fixed beside the altar is a brass ornament honoring a Charlestonian who died for his country. That man's name is my name.

So, overthrowing the religion of my parents was not merely a theological affair. It was tangled up with my own ideas about the transmission of tradition, about honoring past communities, and about forging new ones. I began to wonder just what else went into the drink when I so handily gave religion the heave-ho. Now that I was thirty-five, the vagaries of religion didn't seem quite so irrelevant as they did while I was refilling my Zippo with lighter fluid. More than anything else, I needed to take a long walk.

Since I was troubled about overthrowing the past, my long study of the even older tradition of Santiago seized my attention. The road had an Old World sense of discipline that I liked. A pilgrimage is a form of travel alien to the American temperament. We colonists like to think of ourselves as explorers, path blazers, frontiersmen always on the lam and living off the cuff. Our history is an unchartered odyssey, a haphazard trip down the Mississippi, of unscheduled stops along the blue highways. When Americans are on the road, we don't really want to know just where we are going. We're lighting out for the territories.

But a pilgrimage doesn't put up with that kind of breezy liberty. It is a marked route with a known destination. The pilgrim must find his surprises elsewhere. I hadn't the slightest idea what this would eventually mean, but I liked the idea of searching out adventure in the unlikely place of a well-trod road. There was even a sense of gratitude, in that to keep my days interesting, I would be relieved of the usual devices of wacky coincidence or deadpan encounters with the locals.

I also came to realize that my word was offputting precisely because it retained a grubby literalism. A pilgrimage was about sweating and walking and participating in something. The word still had enough of its medieval flavor to suggest that one was submitting to a regime, a task, an idea whose ultimate end would be discovery, even transformation. "Pilgrimage"—those gravelly Anglo-Saxon consonants rolled around in the mouth and came out ancient. It was evocative, imaginative, and suggestive, I think, precisely because it was something so definable. For example, if I had announced that my intention was to sweep through Europe to "study heaven," no one would assume I had in mind a distinct piece of real estate. But once upon a time, people did. The medieval worldview held that the blue sky above us was a plasmatic skin literally separating us from heaven. The engineers of the tower of Babel had nearly climbed up to it and were punished. Today, the word has lost all but its symbolic meaning. Heaven is a spent metaphor.

For many people, the entire language of religion is symbolic in this way. Even as I was growing up, god was being refined out of literal existence. In St. Philip's parish hall, the psychedelic banners declared in letters cut from curving felt, "God is Love."

Metaphor is a powerful literary device, but only if it is grounded to a literal meaning. Pure metaphor is corrosive and enfeebling. Think of Prince Charles.

I understood that I was assuming a vocabulary that had this medieval ring to it but had retained its breadth and complexity long after that age had ended. Chaucer rightly suspected that a pilgrimage would easily serve as the stage for the hapless circus of the entire human comedy. The passengers on the

Mayflower adopted this word because they were convinced that they would transform themselves and the world, and they thought the word could adequately contain such ambition. In the Romantic period, "pilgrim" was one of William Blake's favorite words because of its multiplicity of connotations. According to legend, Samuel Coleridge awoke from a nap to compose "The Rime of the Ancient Mariner." Not coincidentally, the book he was reading when he fell asleep was titled *Purchas: His Pilgrimage*. In the post–World War II era, only John Wayne and Kurt Vonnegut seemed to have preferred its ring.

As a tenderfoot pilgrim, the more I tried on this awkward word, the more I liked its ill fit. Heaven may no longer be literally above our heads, but the road is still beneath our feet. And until we invent our way beyond ground transportation, the word will retain its express sense of action. A pilgrimage is both inescapably metaphorical and literal, and I wanted to walk them both.

But why settle for the road to Santiago, instead of the far more prestigious routes to Rome or, especially, Jerusalem? My preference for Santiago has to do with my own rank qualifications for such a trip. In 1981, just after college, I had walked the asphalt simulacrum paved by the generalissimo. Since then I've kept up my reading on the history of Santiago and have grown to admire the road's patron saint. I appreciate him because whatever flaws I have, James is no one to talk.

In old Spanish the name *Iago* dates to the collapsing of the Latin name *Jacobus,* who after canonization became "Santiago." In English this linguistic journey turned "Jacobus" to James. As a man, James is always described as a major player among Jesus's apostles, one of the top three along with his brother John and Peter. James was present for the transfiguration, when Jesus turned into a column of light. He was among the three intimates invited into the garden of Gethsemane for the agony when Christ begged that "this cup pass from me." Despite this privileged status, the Bible isn't very forthcoming about him. James's character is sketchy. He almost never speaks. But in the scattered clues, he slowly comes into focus.

James's mother was Salome, said to be Mary's sister, making James a first cousin to Jesus. Salome had money and reportedly funded a lot of Jesus's work, including paying for the Last Supper. She was also the Holy Land's version of a stage mother, constantly promoting her sons to Jesus.

In the gospels, James always appears alongside his brother John, and the two of them come across as dim-witted sycophants who snaked their way into the boss's confidence but didn't know what to do once they got there.

On one occasion, Christ is confronted by skeptics. James and John tell Jesus just to give them the word—wink, wink—and they will eliminate those doubters by calling down a thunderbolt from above. In the words of Luke 9:54: "Lord, wilt thou that we command fire to come down from heaven, and consume them?" Christ shushes them and says, "The Son of man is not come to destroy men's lives, but to save *them.*" During this exchange, the reader senses that Jesus is beginning to understand just what kind of men James and John are. According to Luke, Jesus "turned" to them and said, "Ye know not what manner of spirit ye are of." This line is from the King James version, the most elegant English translation of the Bible. One can't help but wonder what Christ *actually* said. Later, Jesus starts calling James and John by a nickname—Boanerges, or "Sons of Thunder." Correct me if I'm wrong, but I believe Jesus is being sarcastic here.

Another time, James and his brother pull Christ aside from the other apostles. Quietly they ask if they can occupy the most important seats in heaven—at his side, one on the right, the other on the left. Even in the King James version, Jesus's annoyance survives the shellacking of a high-minded translation. According to Mark (10:38), Christ says, "Ye know not what ye ask." Jesus goes on to say that they cannot expect to sit beside the throne. "Can ye drink of the cup that I drink of?" he asks. James and John, never quick to take a hint, immediately answer, "We can." Jesus stumbles at their audacity but gets out of this uncomfortable situation by saying, it "is not mine to give."

The other apostles were jealous of James and John for several reasons—the two were cousins of Jesus's, their mother had money, and they were incorrigible lickspittles. When word got around that the twosome had asked for the prime seats in heaven, the other apostles fell into a dark mood, according to Mark (10:41): "And when the ten heard *it,* they began to be much displeased with James and John." What is interesting about this story is not that James is once again revealed to be an apple-polisher, but it would appear that Jesus had really grown to dislike James and his brother. Applying the methods of investigative journalism to the Bible might not be fair, but consider: Who leaked the brothers' secret request so that the other ten apostles would be unhappy? Chances are it wasn't James or John.

Yet James served his leader unfailingly to the end. After he proselytized around the Holy Land, the last we hear of James (Book of Acts) is his return to the realm of King Herod, who welcomed him home with martyrdom. And that's the end. It's a pretty good story but inadequate to the demands of pilgrimage. Ironically, that's what made him perfect for the job of patron. James was as highly ranked as Peter or John, yet he was merely an outline, a skeletal character. There was a lot of room for embellishment. In the ninth century in northern Spain, one began to hear some extra-biblical tales.

One story explains that James had come to Spain just after the crucifixion of Christ to convert the Roman citizens of Hispania. He utterly failed, winning over fewer than a dozen new believers. James then returned to the Holy Land where King Herod beheaded him and threw his parts outside the city wall to be eaten by wild dogs.

Devotees of James collected his head and corpse and carried them to the beach. Two of the associates placed the body on an empty boat, and miraculously it set sail, piloted only, it is said, by the love of the Virgin Mary. The ship navigated eastward to Gibraltar and then north along the Portuguese coast to the end of the world, Finisterre. When James's disciples landed, they tied the bowline to a stone stele, which still stands on the shore. For centuries, the diaries of pilgrims who visited Finisterre mentioned a stone boat marooned on the beach. (A

Flemish pilgrim named Jean Taccouen, who walked the road in 1512, reports that he saw it resting on its side. The locals told him that only a Christian who had attained a state of grace could move it. Mr. Taccouen adds wryly, "I have not spoken to anyone who has budged it.")

The disciples brought the body ashore and laid it on a stone slab, which went soft like wet clay, leaving a bas-relief of the apostle. The ruler of this area, a vicious pagan queen named Lupa, greeted her visitors in a diplomatic way and sent them to see a man named Beleth, whom she knew would kill them. When Beleth jailed the disciples, an angel released them. When Beleth's knights chased them across a river, the bridge collapsed and drowned the pursuers. Queen Lupa then dispatched them to a mountain range she knew to be inhabited by dragons and wild bulls. When the disciples arrived, a dragon spit fire and charged, but a quick sign of the cross split him in two. The wild bulls charged, but another sign of the cross reduced them to complacent beasts of burden. When the disciples returned with the wild bulls pulling their cart, Queen Lupa awakened to the inadequacy of her creed and converted at once. The bulls slowly dragged their heavy load another few miles and suddenly stopped at a temple to Bacchus. The pagan statue immediately disintegrated. The disciples mixed the dust with water to make the cement for a shrine. They called this place Santiago de Compostela—the city to which I am headed.

In death, though, James had no better luck in Spain than in life. The conversions still numbered no more than Queen Lupa and a few others. After these and the disciples died, the body was left in a cave and forgotten for nearly eight centuries.

In A.D. 814 a hermit named Pelayo lived in the northwest corner of Spain, eating insects and scavenging for honey. One evening he looked into the night sky and saw a series of strange lights near the river Sar. They seemed to be indicating a direction, growing smaller and smaller as they approached earth until they were nothing more than spangles of light dancing in the brush. Pelayo followed them and heard the singing of angels. He informed the bishop, Theodomir, who dispatched a crew of men to hack through the dense undergrowth. They came upon a cave. Inside was a sepulcher and papers declaring that it contained the body of Saint James. Theodomir told the pope, and soon Rome declared an official pilgrimage to the site. The apostle was instantly elevated to a new status.

For the Catholic Church, the discovery of James's body was conspicuously timely. In the previous century, invading Moors had conquered all but the hardscrabble northern strip of Spain—precisely where the pilgrimage route is located. Arab soldiers stood poised to breach the Pyrenees and take Christendom. They had already crossed the mountains a few times, most famously repelled in 732 by Charles the Hammer at Poitiers, France.

The Church, which had no army and had a divine commandment forbidding killing, found the site a good way to lure men, money, and arms into northern Spain. But the pilgrim's trail turned out to be much more useful than just a boot camp for a holy war. Without knowing it, the Church had also stumbled upon a new way of generating great wealth. The continual ebb and flow of skilled and unskilled people created what residents of Florida or California would recognize as a tourist economy. For the next five centuries, Santiago would draw enough men and goods into Spain not only to defeat the Moors but also to power the Spanish Empire's economy until New World gold could take over.

James, once a clumsy yes-man, was now a poster boy who was always changing costumes to meet the changing needs of a medieval Catholic bureaucracy. His earliest images were of a simple pilgrim. The first polychromatic statues show an earnest fellow in a cloak and hat. He is almost always depicted as a man on foot, eternally about to take that next step. But as the pilgrimage drew millions of people, the road developed different meanings and uses. And so did James.

In the early ninth century, for example, the Christians were routinely being slaughtered. The Moors had all the physical advantages of men, horses, and arms. But they also had the arm of Mohammed, said to be in a vault in the south of Spain. One of the benefits of such a divine possession was that their messiah appeared in the sky on a charger and led them into combat. Mohammed would not be alone up there for long.

At the battle of Clavijo in 845, James appeared in his first major conflict. He was now a giant in the sky, riding upon a horse and swinging a sword. He killed sixty thousand Arabs that afternoon, according to reports. James's appearances as a fighter against infidels became so common that it earned his new image a nickname. Always mounted—sword in one hand and a bearded head dripping gore in the other—he was simply Santiago Matamoros: Saint James, Moor-killer.

It was a remarkable transformation. None of the other roads has adapted itself so nakedly and so successfully to changing times. Despite the pilgrimage's status as the most tired of clichés, the traditions of Santiago have quite effectively subverted and survived them all. That, too, is why I wanted to follow this road.

In the heyday of religious peripeteia, the three great routes to Santiago, Rome, and Jerusalem bound the world of Christendom with a belt of serene traffic—Santiago to the west, Jerusalem to the east, and Rome in the center. In some ways, they were competitive. Each had its own emblem. Santiago promoted the scallop or cockleshell. Pilgrims to Rome wore a small key on their cloaks and were called romers. Those going to Jerusalem laced a swatch of palm in their clothes and were called palmers.

But even among the big three, Santiago was distinct. Pilgrims to Rome or Jerusalem could go for any number of reasons. Jerusalem had prestige and Rome was a political center, so any pilgrimage there was practically a junket. But Santiago had little appeal beyond that plain idea of a long walk.

Dante Alighieri favored Santiago's simple clarity. "In the wider sense," he wrote in *La Vita Nuova,* a pilgrim is "whoever is outside his fatherland," but "in the narrow sense, none is called a pilgrim save he who is journeying toward the sanctuary of Saint James of Compostella." Among lesser routes, pilgrimage typically had to provide some other draw, such as supernaturalism. Pilgrims to Lourdes in France *expected* a miracle and were disappointed if they didn't get one. Although miracles were associated with Santiago, this was never the only attraction. Most pilgrims of St. James came and went without any cures, or with the standard minimum (at that time) of signs and wonders.

I don't hold myself out as much of a pilgrim, what with my cloudy motives and facile past. But even as I sat reading at my desk in New York, my failings became encouragement. Among the ancient documents that survive are reports that during the Middle Ages many "others" walked the road, including Moors, then the very stamp of libidinal mustachioed infidel. A twelfth-century document from the pilgrims' shelter in Roncesvalles declares: "Its doors are open to all, well and ill, not only to Catholics, but to pagans, jews and heretics, the idler and the vagabond and, to put it shortly, the good and the wicked." I believe I can find myself in that list somewhere.

ONE
SAINT-JEAN
PIED DE PORT

Where does the road to Santiago begin? It was a question my medieval predecessors never had to consider. In those days, a pilgrim simply stepped out of his hut and declared his intention. Then he might report to a cloister and receive a signed letter to serve as proof of intent. Afterward, the pilgrim walked west until he picked up any of the established routes in Europe. From the east and south, the pilgrim followed any of four established roads that fanned like fingers across France and converged at the palm of Spain. A few miles inside the Pyrenees, they formed a single unified road shooting straight across the breadth of the country.

I lived a few doors off Washington Square Park in New York City and an ocean away from my destination. I couldn't just walk out my door. For reasons of symmetry and authenticity, this bothered me. I thought I would toss a coin onto a map of France and proceed from there, but this seemed too haphazard. It felt wrong to begin this trip with such an American sense of abandon. I studied a map of France to see if any of the cities had a personal significance. I checked my family's records to see if any ancestors a few centuries back might have had some interaction in this part of Europe, but according to all available information, one branch was too busy fleeing Prussian law while the other was stuffing a sheep's stomach for a weekend of haggis. Arles, Montpellier, Carcasonne, and Toulouse were not likely vacation spots for Teutonic horse thieves or Scottish presbyters.

One Saturday I happened upon a brochure that offered a solution. Not only could I walk out my front door, I could take the New York subway. I boarded the A train, immortalized by Duke Ellington, and took it almost to the end, where the Metropolitan Museum of Art maintains a branch called the Cloisters. The museum is an assemblage of ruins from four medieval cloisters, dating from the Romanesque and Gothic periods, and once located on the road to Santiago. I resolved to spend a quiet afternoon among the weathered columns and begin there.

The most beautiful—the cloister of Saint-Guilhem-le-Désert—is covered by a plastic dome. Fat gobs of New York City rain fell the afternoon I visited, making a bass-drum thump that left me feeling strangely dry. Instead of the customary central garden, there is a marble floor, giving the space the linoleum acoustics of a grade school cafeteria. My attempt at meaningful silence was carefully monitored by a suspicious security guard who understood museum policy and the slight reach of his power only too well. At one point he chased a camera-toting teenager in a ludicrous race around the columns after a disagreement over competing interpretations of the flash-attachment policy. Packs of schoolchildren snickered and laughed at the often lewd capital carvings, and the guard's echoing shouts of "Quiet!" were louder still. In a moment of pure museum irony, a man who had been there quite a while was asked to leave because he was loitering.

After the rain broke, I went out back where a stone porch opened to a view of the Hudson River and the New Jersey Palisades. It all fell into place: I would begin here, fly to Saint-

Guilhem-le-Désert in France, visit the original site, and take up the walk from there.

The cloister is, like a pilgrimage, the literal representation of the same idea. On a pilgrimage and in a cloister, the longer journey of three score and ten is reduced symbolically to something much smaller—a few months of walking or a stroll around the cloister's four-sided garden. Both have a beginning, middle, and end. Both force upon the visitor a number of encounters—on the road, these are random events; in the cloister, these are sculpture. And both offer a finale of redemption. On the road, it is the physical exhilaration of arrival. At the cloister, it's the walk into the direct center, a place the monks called *paradeisos*. So I thought a visit to a monastery cloister would be appropriate.

The idea of a monastery grew out of the thinking of a hermit named Benedict who lived in the sixth century during the declining days of the Roman Empire. He had committed himself to the reigning idea of his day—a life of utter solitude in the wilderness. This idea had been imported from the Holy Land, where hermits pursued different fashions of isolation. The stylites sat on the top of a pole. The dendrites carved a hole in a tree and lived inside. For his effort, Benedict isolated himself in Italy at the mouth of a cave not far from Nero's summer house. He clothed himself in animal skins, which his biographer reports frightened the local shepherds. He ate berries.

But the call of the hermit's life was not attracting too many Europeans. It was a bad time to be alone in the woods. The sixth century saw the continuing collapse of Roman order, opening the door to the invading Huns, Visigoths, and Longobards. From time to time, the barbarians would drop down to cut the tongues from women and disembowel the men. This was the era when the famously airy architecture of Roman atriums and columned porticoes closed up. Castles were built, moats were dug, drawbridges were engineered. It would not be long before the religious orders sought a similar kind of protection. Benedict is credited with solving these problems. His innovation offered isolated monks a sliver of companionship and physical protection: a monastery.

Like all good ideas, Benedict's was not immediately embraced. His first collective of monks didn't appreciate his harsh rules and tried to murder him. But others liked the idea, and eventually Benedict wrote a strict code of monastic living called *Benedict's Rule,* which is still observed today. Reading *Benedict's Rule,* though, one can sense a yearning for utter solitude—not the minimal society of the monastery, but the pure singularity of the desert, far from the corruption of man, alone in nature. To stand in a cloister, even sky-lighted in plastic and teeming with riotous schoolchildren, is to feel the architectural memory of Benedict's original idea. The cloister is a patch of that wilderness, imported and mod-ified to the demands of society. It is a bit of desert, open directly to the original skyward view of the hermit, secreted away in the center of the monastery. The cloister is not the perfection of an idea, but rather a constant reminder of its compromise. The cloister is nostalgia. It is an original plan fallen short, a vestige of an older and purer sense of purpose. Like my own effort, the cloister is somewhat corrupt, an acknowledgment of failure.

As I began to read up on these particular cloisters in New York, I marveled at how perfect they were for my beginning. The reason they're in Manhattan and not on the road to San-tiago is because of a desperate American sculptor. At the turn of the century, Robert Barnard made his rent money by buying medieval artworks from guileless French rustics and selling them for impressive profits. He began with small statues but eventually was buying entire monasteries. When the French government found out that the nation's patrimony was being shipped off to serve as lawn ornaments in the front yards of American millionaires, a huzzah went up in Paris. Just days before December 31, 1913—when the French parliament out-lawed Barnard's hobby—he packed 116 crates of his precious cargo, each numbered and cataloged, and sailed for New York on the next boat.

For a while, Barnard ran his own museum in Manhattan, but when money problems arose again, he offered to sell his medieval cloisters to some Californians for use in an amusement park. A cry went up among the Fifth Avenue set in New York, and the call for a white knight was heard.

John D. Rockefeller, Jr. was a curious savior from West Coast tastelessness. Among his architectural achievements, he had spent millions erecting his idea of "colonial America" in Williamsburg, Virginia, where women in Betsy Ross dresses and men in breeches escorted tourists to the town stockades for a wry photo opportunity.

With his new cloisters, Rockefeller ran through a number of plans. At one point he wanted to create a feeling of lost grandeur he associated with abandoned castles and King Arthur, but the most sophisticated architects of the day cautiously explained the logistical *difficulty* of using religious carvings from France to construct a secular castle from England. Rockefeller caught on and soon realized that what he had purchased was the emblem of the solitary search, that desire for monkish isolation, Benedict's idea. Rockefeller grew obsessed with the Cloisters and demanded daily briefings. He had notions of his own.

Across the Hudson River, seen from the parapet of the Cloisters, are the vast cliffs known as the New Jersey Palisades. This state park extends from the George Washington Bridge all the way upriver to the state border. One might assume that this preservation was the result of some antidevelopment politician. Actually John D. Rockefeller bought that thirteen-mile stretch. He wanted to preserve the quiet contemplation of his Cloisters—to carve out of the thickest clot of American urbanity a bit of nature that straddled a river and gave almost no hint of the presence of man. Rockefeller understood the idea of the cloister. He imported that ancient yearning for the desert, via Benedict, into New York City. I had found my place in America to begin.

The only duty remaining was what to wear. I am not being coy. Pilgrim fashion is not a glib subject. Throughout the Middle Ages and Renaissance, the clothes a pilgrim wore became a style as widely known in its symbolism as a king's crown. Parliaments met and debated pilgrim's clothes. Their sale was licensed and regulated by bureaucracies. Underground markets for certain pilgrim items flourished at times. Kings corresponded on the subject. Some legal scholars argue that pilgrim fashion created its own brand of law. Any person—peasant or noble—wearing the official pilgrim's garb was exempt from the laws of the country through which he was passing and was judged instead under a special collection of statutes written expressly for pilgrims—the first international law.

This outfit became so recognized that pilgrims en route to Santiago had to wear it if they expected to receive the benefits of the road—free lodging, food, and respect. Obviously, with such perks available, the clothing had to be regulated. Four popes issued decrees, backed up by excommunication, outlining the rules and regulations for the sale of the pilgrim's outfit and even its duplication in souvenirs. In 1590 King Philip II issued a decree restricting the donning of this apparel in Spain to a narrow corridor running the length of the road from the Pyrenees to Santiago.

A pilgrim wore a dashing full-length black cape to serve as protection from wind by day and to provide a blanket by night. On his feet were strong boots. To block the sun and rain, he wore on his head a fetching broad-brimmed black hat. He carried a staff for protection and tied to it a gourd for carrying water. At the waist was a small satchel called a crip for carrying money, a knife, and toiletries. On the cape or hat, or hanging around the neck, or fastened almost anywhere, was at least one scallop shell, the symbol of the Santiago pilgrim.

Once I got familiar with this classic image, it began to appear everywhere, even in New York. Walking to the Spanish embassy one day, I passed Saint Bartholomew's Church on Park Avenue. A giant stone Saint James, fully dressed, stands beside the front entrance. As I did my homework, I discovered the pilgrim in the paintings of Bosch, El Greco, Rubens, Ribera, Murillo, and Raphael. Either as the main subject or in the background, the wayfaring pilgrim in trademark apparel can be seen drifting through centuries of European landscapes.

By the late Middle Ages the Catholic missal included a "prayer for the walking stick," which stated that as the pilgrim's third leg, the staff represented the trinity. There was also a "blessing of the backpack," which taught that the "backpack is made of the rawhide of a dead beast" because "the pilgrim ought to torment his own depraved and lusting flesh with hunger and thirst, with great abstinence, with cold and destitution, with punishment and hard labor."

The thought of dressing up this way and tormenting my own depraved, lusting flesh didn't really fit in with my plans. I grew up Episcopalian after all. Yet wouldn't it be a more authentic experience if I were to wear the clothes described in the medieval documents?

Then I asked myself, Did the pilgrims take along a staff because they wanted that three-legged symbolism? Or did they carry a sturdy piece of oak to beat wild dogs in the head? Did they tote the rucksack because they wanted something abrasive to give them blisters and rashes? Or did they originally carry their food in it? Wasn't all this gear—the hat to block the sun, the cape for warmth at night—originally meant to reduce suffering? These other meanings were imposed. Which came first: the backpack as a device to ease portage or the backpack as a tormentor of depraved and lusting flesh? I set off immediately to a shop called EMS: The Outdoor Specialists.

The manager quickly discerned that I was not a rock-climbing hound who'd come to learn the latest advance in titanium carabiners. He knew what he saw: a gold-card-carrying desk jockey with a head full of distant vistas. He signaled a scattered pack of wilderness consultants, and they surrounded me.

When I was a teenager, camping gear was sold at the Army-Navy store. The place was located uptown, in a marginal neighborhood, and was operated by a chunky old man with thick glasses and a consumptive cough who dreamed of one day opening a gun shop. I still have in a closet at home an old green rucksack with *U.S. ARMY* stamped on it and long straps pinched with metal tips. I have my felt-covered canteen with a chain to hold the cap, now missing. The mess kit is in a plastic bag, blackened by its first and last use over a campfire. My bowie knife, in its handsome tooled-leather sheath, is in a drawer. As a boy I used to carry it on camp-outs, but it was soon retired since it was too big to use around a campfire and too small for the woods. A bowie knife is best for wrestling gators and killing nightstalkers, problems that never came up.

I briefly considered gathering up my old goods and flying to Europe. If it was authenticity I wanted, there was something exceedingly real, in my imagination, about this equipment. But my wilderness consultants knew better. By the time I left the store, I owned

- Lycra boots, "not waterproofed because you want your feet to breathe and not sweat."
- two-ply hiking socks, with thin tubing up the ankle to create a "capillary effect" for "chiropodic aspiration."
- a backpack with an interior frame bent into a "parabolic twist" to fit my spine.
- a sleeping bag that weighed about a pound.
- a tent, about two pounds, with magic poles connected by thin shock cords. Unfurl, shake a little, and the tent practically snapped into position in one minute. Neat.
- a poncho the size of a fist that nearly floated in air.
- an air mattress that self-inflated.
- a toilet bag, "a state-of-the-art advance over the old shaving kit," that unzipped and tumbled open to a three-tier set of tidy pouches and a dangling mesh net pocket to keep a toothbrush aerated.
- a Swiss Army knife, with a sharp saw that cut down trees (and it does).

I bought it all, of course, and tossed in a green rubber snakebite kit and a tube of something called Instant Fire.

Only one piece of the traditional equipment called for special consideration. The shell was the sole item of dress that served no utilitarian purpose.

The shell was purely symbolic. According to one of the Finisterre legends, when James's disciples carried his sepulcher from the stone boat, they interrupted a pagan wedding. The sight of them spooked the groom's horse, which bolted into the sea where both drowned. James's first European miracle took place shortly thereafter when the horse and groom—both alive—rose majestically from the breaking waves, trailing garlands of seaweed laced with dozens of scallop shells.

This association of the shell with renewed life dates even further back to John the Baptist, who used a shell in his surfside christenings. Many baptismal fonts to this day take the shape of the scallop shell. It was a symbol of rebirth, the very task of the pilgrimage specifically and Christianity generally.

Other genealogies go back to images of pagan fertility—a symbol not of rebirth but of birth itself. The hinged scallop opens and reveals something new, a meaning connected to the scallop's physical similarity to a vagina. Botticelli's *Birth of Venus* shows the goddess taking her first step onto the land from a giant Santiago shell.

Another Spanish interpretation holds that the fingered scallop is the hand of Saint James, outstretched in the open-palmed expression of comfort and encouragement. Hung around the neck, the shell taps gently with each step at the pilgrim's heart, a soft metronomic patting from James's hand that heartens the pilgrim to keep on.

Here is a symbol that transcends the road itself, with a meaning that has survived from primitive man's desire for fecundity through Christianity's idea of rebirth to the Hallmark card sentimentality of a hand tapping the rhythm of the pilgrim's heart. I had to have one.

The problem is, for the modern pilgrim, the shell no longer holds much significance. In Spanish and French cuisine, there is an elegant appetizer called vieiras de Santiago or coquille St. Jacques, literally "Saint James's shell." The only other surviving reference is a proofreading mark in French called a *coquille*. It is a circle with a line through it like a veined scallop and—omen or no—signifies a mistake.

Where was a modern pilgrim to find a shell? The medieval pilgrim could borrow a shell from a neighbor or a relative who had walked the road. Or a pilgrim might buy one from the local clergy or, during the road's peak, from itinerant shellmongers. This was one problem I couldn't solve in America. So I flew to Madrid, bought my train ticket to the town nearest Saint-Guilhem-le-Désert, and spent my few days in Spain's capital reconnoitering for shells.

I'm not sure what was going through my mind when I flew into Madrid. Did I think the Spaniards would have shell shops? Or that humpbacked peddlers on the street would open their coats and show off a selection of scallops, large and small?

Moreover, once I made the commitment of actually flying to Spain, the embarrassment of calling myself a pilgrim consumed me. An idea that had seemed so suggestive as I scanned the New Jersey Palisades shriveled upon my arrival, into something small, dark, and stupid, and it sat in my gut like lead. When I landed at the Madrid International Airport, I began to ask myself once again: What in hell am I doing here? I stood at the baggage conveyor, moronically hypnotized as the arriving luggage piled up and spun round and round, hundreds of bags, skis, suitcases, and trunks—each plastered with a yellow bumper sticker announcing Madrid's airport abbreviation in big black letters. Eventually my backpack belched from a hole and rode around in a circle, mocking me in agreement with the other packages: MAD, MAD, MAD, MAD, MAD.

I resolved to end my shell crisis practically. I talked to people I knew in Spain. The only good advice was to find a gourmet food store that might specialize in the finest cooking accessories since vieiras de Santiago were cooked in the shell. The department store, Corte Inglés, usually carried them, but since they weren't in season, the clerk told me no one would have them. He was a nice man, a seafood connoisseur. When I told him why I really wanted the shell, he plopped his beefy arm on my shoulder, snorted witheringly, and pointed in the direction of the store's gag and novelty section.

I checked my train ticket to France. No question about it, unrefundable.

The novelty shop did offer the modern pilgrim a wide selection of shells. There was a monstrous scallop practically the size of a head with hand-painted wooden figurines sloppily glued inside to form a crèche. There was a glass lamp full of shells. Another objet d'art was a shapeless glop of shell sculpture, either of the Dada school or evidence that shells, mucilage, and LSD do not mix. It was selling for twenty dollars. I opted for a handmade model of Columbus's caravel, the *Santa María*—a hull of plastic with sawed-off pencils for masts and three scallop shells serving as billowing sails. I spent my last afternoon in Madrid with a bottle of nailpolish remover carefully ungluing and unshellacking my little ship, transforming a new souvenir into an old one.

In Montpellier, France, everyone knows the little town of Saint-Guilhem-le-Désert, but no one except an odd man with a car for hire can remember the location of the old cloister. My driver is friendly with the cheerful habit of answering every question, *"Oui."* After a thirty-minute ride, he deposits me before a small stone edifice, all that Robert Barnard has left to the locals of the once great monastery.

For a thirteenth-century ruin, it is simple and well preserved. I step back among the olive trees to take in the ancient yellow stone. The ground has linear features. I make right-angled gestures with my hands and try to conjure where the cloister once stood. I amble down to the building itself, walking around the corners, trailing a finger along the forlorn, ancient stone until I come upon a small dirty window set in a corrugated steel door. I wipe away some dust and peer in to discover that I am contemplating the ineffability of a garage housing a rusting Citroën.

My driver is slightly embarrassed at my architectural prowess and, grinning maniacally and honking many a *"Oui"* through his nose, makes several other attempts to locate the scarred site of the old cloister. At the center of Saint Guilhem-le-Désert, I set off on foot. But I find that each local points me farther and farther out of town to another set of scattered stones. Hell, I am pretty sure I did find it. I'm just not certain which of the many piles of stones belonged to the old monastery.

It begins to rain. By the time I return to the car, I am agitated for the less-than-noble reason that I have spent $50 to get rained on in a quaint French village. In the meantime, the driver has made some inquiries on my behalf among the locals at a bar. He and his new acquaintances are waiting by the car, and he is enthusiastic to make his report.

"Eh, *Americaine,* the cloister you are looking for?"

"Yes."

"It is in New York!"

I board the next train out of town. I don't exactly know why. I guess it's cheating. But I am wasting money, and I feel lacking in basic pilgrim skills. When it comes right down to it—and major experts will back me up here—I don't really know what I am doing.

I disembark in Orthez, France. It is only a few days' walk from an important village, Saint-Jean Pied de Port, where two of the French trails converge before threading into the Pyrenees and then to Spain. When British pilgrims crossed the English Channel by boat in the Middle Ages, they often drifted south to towns such as Orthez. Then they would gather to cross the Pyrenees in huge groups for protection against—as every history book says—blackguards and highwaymen. I figure this is a more fitting place to *really* begin.

The way out of Orthez is a narrow industrial highway and a favorite of amphetamine-powered, speeding truckers. Ten minutes into my first (true) steps of walking as a pilgrim, it begins to rain. I struggle into my lighter-than-air poncho. Each passing semi cracks a whip of stinging droplets against my legs and face. How serendipitous. Now I don't need to flagellate myself.

Everything mocks me this morning. All my doubts about this pilgrimage find expression in this valley. The roar of each truck is a chorus of humiliating laughter. The billboards continuously advertise a soft drink called "Pschitt." The otherwise serene French countryside is populated by stubby pine trees, each branch ending in a tight fist of dark green needles from which shoots up, like a taunting obscene gesture, a single finger of tender growth. The pathetic fallacy is getting on my nerves.

The danger of the speeding traffic reaches critical mass when one truck passes another beside me. Suddenly a truck rattling at eighty miles per hour is kissing my elbow. The air foil at that speed slugs me with the force of a body blow, pitching me into a drainage ditch. I brush myself off. My shoulder is sore. The rain quickens its pace to a full gallop.

As I enter the village of Saliers de Bearn, I consult my map carefully. The next two days are nothing but trucking highways, danger, Pschitt ads, and certain death. But after Saint-Jean Pied de Port, the road is less traveled, more pilgrimesque. A short note on my pilgrim's map mentions that in Saint-Jean there lives an old woman named Madame Debril who has been greeting pilgrims for decades. Here is authenticity. The tradition of the humble volunteer who lives on the road to help pilgrims has a long historical pedigree. In the account of his 1726 pilgrimage, a French pilgrim named Guillaume Manier wrote admiringly of one Mme. Belcourt of Bayonne who lived "in the first house on the right, which has a sign of Santiago applied above her door. There all pilgrims coming and going rest. This woman is known on the four continents of the world for that." Madame Debril and Saint-Jean sounded like a proper beginning for a modern pilgrimage.

I sit on a public bench, consider the prospect of two days on a truckers' highway, and remind myself of the rich tradition of human frailty associated with the road.

I think about Benedict and his monasteries, and about Saint James, and about the very origin of the road itself. The first "proof" the early promoters of the road cited of Saint James's presence in Spain came from the writings of a man named St. Beatus. He lived fifty years before the discovery of the tomb, and he had heavily publicized Saint James's association with Spain (the "most worthy and holy apostle, radiant, gold-glittering leader of Spain"). Beatus used a simple list of the apostles and the places where they had proselytized as an original source of James's visit to Spain. This list had been copied by an anonymous scribe who mistakenly wrote that James's territory was "Hispaniam," or Spain, rather than "Hierosolyman," or Jerusalem. So the pilgrimage to Santiago de Com-

postela—which has been credited with forging Spain into a
nation, defeating the Moors, sending Arab learning into central Europe, bringing light to the Dark Ages, sparking the
Renaissance, fashioning the first international laws, and con-
juring the idea of a unified Europe—owes its origin to a typo.

I hail a cab.

TWO
THE PYRENEES

By late afternoon my cab pulls up at an inn. Saint-Jean is an ancient town with a medieval fortress and retaining barricade at the center. New bars and homes spill out past the flaking crenellated walls and down the slope of a hill. In the distance are the Pyrenees, some storm clouds snagged on their peaks. Madame Debril, the governess of pilgrims, lives among the older houses on narrow cobble streets within the wall, number 44, rue de la Citadel. On her shutter is a plaque declaring *"Centre d'études Saint-Jacques de Compostelle."* A knock on the door brings the lady herself, dressed in a bright flowered blue dress. Her gray hair is swept back recklessly from her face. Spectacles sit at the lowest possible point on her nose. A single long front tooth rests on her lower lip. Red blossoms beam from her cheeks.

"Oh, God," she says through a mouthful of food. I have only said "Hello," but it is enough for her to realize she has an English speaker at her door.

"I am eating dinner," she says, half in French and English.
I am all apologies.

"I am fatigued?" she adds. Her insecurity about English usage turns statements into questions. "I have seen many pilgrims?"

"Oh, I will come back in the morning, then."

"No, no, no, no, no," she says, opening the door wide.

Madame Debril's office is a clutter of Santiago memorabilia. An old 3-D topological map of the Pyrenees hangs beside the door. She is wearing a scallop shell around her neck. On her desk is a silver shell presented to her by the people of Pamplona. Clay shells hang from posts and on the wall and are draped over the edges of cabinets. A dozen real shells ride the chaos of papers on her desk. Rolled-up posters, photo albums, and an old typewriter occupy a small bed against the wall. At her foot is a teenager's boom box. The wall behind her is an enviable library of books about the road. I am directed to a caned chair that rides so low to the floor that my nose barely peeks above the desk.

"You are pilgrim to Saint James?" she asks, looking down at me. Her teeth are laced with baguette.

"Yes."

"Where did you come from today?" she asks officiously.

"I came from Orthez, but—"

"That is a lie," she declares. "You could not walk from Orthez to Saint-Jean in one day." A truly menacing look slowly fills out the rustic features of this old woman. The metamorphosis is werewolfian. She waves a few promiscuous strands of hair away from her face. Medusa rises from her chair.

"Well, to be honest, Madame Debril, I took a taxi from Saliers de Bearn because—"

"Taxi? You are not a true pilgrim. Why do you come here?" Madame Debril says.

I begin to tremble, half in undeserved rage and half from fear. She is revered on the road, mentioned in the guidebook. She is legendary. She is *authentic*. Her schoolmarm looks ignite an old guilt. I've been caught cheating on my homework.

So I did give up on Saint-Guilhem, and I didn't like the road from Orthez to Saint-Jean. Well, I wanted to get the project going.

"You do not look like a pilgrim," she says.

Oh, that hurt. It's true that I had washed up at the inn and put on my one pair of nice slacks and dress shirt I had packed for special occasions. But attire was one aspect of the trip I had thought through. Yet, seated on Madame Debril's cane chair, I realize that regardless of what circuitous route I took to arrive at my tastefully and WASPily restrained sense of pilgrim attire, it won't matter to Madame Debril. I look like a preppie tourist out for a constitutional, which in her eyes is exactly what I am.

I tell her I am writing a book, certain that she will want to flatter me to insure a good mention.

"We don't need another guidebook!"

I bow to her integrity (a quality in short supply on this side of her desk).

She rants that the road is being debauched by false pilgrims. True pilgrims, she explains, are those on foot or on horseback. Those others on bikes, or in cars, or in *taxis* simply don't count. The ancient trust is being abused.

She waves a card in my face. "This is a *carnet?*" she says. It is a small folded card that serves as a pilgrim's passport. They are stamped by monks or civic officials along the road, validating the pilgrim's journey. At the cathedral in Santiago, the *carnet* is exchanged for a "diploma," testifying to the pilgrim's walk. Without the *carnet,* she says, the journey is pointless. Staring down her nose through her spectacles, she insists I will not get one because "you are not true pilgrim?"

It is strange how much I want this old woman's approval. Somehow I suspect that I am not the first person to prop his nose on her desk and seek her blessing. Being a true pilgrim is no longer a matter of medieval clarity. Only a few pilgrims on the road would confess that they believe the actual corpse of Saint James rests beneath the altar of Santiago's cathedral. The modern pilgrim has to look elsewhere for verification. We long to believe that the very act of going somehow substantiates

our status. How prosaic of Madame Debril, I think, to reduce
the walk to a matter of the proper papers.

Nevertheless, I can see that the stamp bears her name and
address. This may be validation of the most perfunctory kind.
But I want it. So I decide to beg.

Of course, *this* works. She calms down. Not long after, I
spot on her shelf a copy of an ancient book I have read in
translation. The *Codex Calixtinus* is the first book ever written
on the pilgrimage, in 1160. It has reports on the inns, the food,
the quality of the rivers, the character of the people. Devotees
of the road call it the first tourist guide. Madame Debril is
impressed that I know this work and hands me her ancient
copy. I turn the crisp yellow pages and coo.

We are getting along now, and she gives me some advice on
walking (look out for bees). Then she mentions a questionable
American who passed through her house not long ago.

"He is Utican?" she seems to say.

"Utican?" I ask

"No, he is just?"

"Just?"

"No, he is wheezy?"

"Wheezy?"

"He is juicy?"

"Juicy?"

"No, he is juicy?"

"Jewish?"

Madame Debril understands that I now understand. She
waves her hand in the air and makes a sour face. I recognize
this expression. In my native South, a private discussion of,
say, blacks can culminate in a tiny slight from one speaker
punctuated by this face. The listener is invited to return the
expression, and then both are free to advance the conversation
to more clandestine topics. It is a kind of code. But I am in no
mood to bond, anti-Semitic-wise, with Madame Debril. I want
the damn card, but not at this price. Who am I to judge a Jew
walking the road to Santiago?

I return a stone face, and Madame Debril reads me clearly.
She sets aside the official *carnet* and stamps a torn piece of

note paper. That's all, it seems, I will get. On the way out the door, I try to reintroduce more pleasant topics in order to bring this encounter to a less than dismal end. I ask Madame Debril how many times she has walked to Santiago. Her face grows dark.

"When I was young, I was too busy, and now that I am old, I am too tired." Her eyes REM with anger. Clutching my rag of paper with her stamp, I glare with incredulity.

"You mean, you have never walked the road to Santiago?"

"No," she says, and shuts the door.

The next morning, I take a big breakfast at the local inn, hoist my backpack, and walk straight out of town. Actually I backtrack a quarter mile so I can begin beneath the fifteenth-century pilgrim's arch, a stone monument at the mouth of town. All the locals said this was the official thing to do. Being a pilgrim with a cab receipt in my pocket, I leap to any confirming tradition I can find. When I reenter town, I come upon Madame Debril in the street, a baguette in one hand, a hammer in the other, and a mouthful of nails. She is walking with a carpenter and about to step into a crumbling plaster house.

"One day this will be a pilgrim's shelter," she says.

"Very good."

"Pilgrims will stay for free," she says.

"Excellent."

"Only if they have the proper papers!"

The way out of town is straightforward, and as the last curve leads the pilgrim into the countryside, a simple burnt wood sign says "Santiago" and points left.

According to my map, I should soon come upon a hamlet, Saint Michel, then the road should turn right and begin an acute climb into the Pyrenees. I do reach Saint Michel, but the road merely bends right, slightly right, yet there is nowhere else to go. Overhead is a canopy of oak and pine. A hill rises to my left. Crashing along my right is a swollen river. The road on the map indicates a sharp uphill ascent, but my road is flat, meandering, easy. I slouch forward, anxious to feel the weight of my pack shift from my waist to my shoulders, and I lock my ankles into the painful angle that signals an uphill climb. But the road won't conform to my hallucinations. It just unfolds, flatly, around another deceptive curve. This river, I notice, is flowing with me, that is downhill, a fairly convincing piece of evidence that I am not walking uphill and shouldn't expect to be doing so any time soon.

The woods grow dark after black thunderheads move in and threaten all morning long to unburden themselves in a mighty release. Instead, they leak all day. The hot June sun, a gray blister behind the clouds, gives the air a thick texture. My view of the allegedly beautiful French country is seen from between the blinders of a poncho's cowl and then through the treacly drizzle. It is a holiday of some kind in this valley. No one's seen me walk by, except a vigilant turkey at one farm. He sits alert upon a post, wattle tossed rakishly, juking his neck absurdly as I pass. The few shops along the way are closed. The farmhouses appear abandoned; everyone is off to Grandpa's for the big meal. I can't help thinking they heard I was coming.

I press on down the road for nearly an hour and a half. Despite every indication to the contrary—instinct, the position of the sun's occasional wink, compass, *gravity*—I stubbornly believe that the road will translate itself into the right one. Around a (descending) curve, a lone farmhouse appears in the crotch of two sloping mountain faces. Two dogs race out to loudly inspect my boots.

A timid knock brings a young man to the door. Soon the entire table assembles on the porch for the grand event of a stranger in the yard. I explain that I am a pilgrim on the road to Santiago and fear I am heading the wrong way. They are delighted. Directions, I quickly learn, are a great way to jumpstart a conversation. It immediately locates you in the ditch of ignorance and puts the stranger upon the heights of knowledge.

A young man steps forward proudly and points toward a set of receding mountain peaks, but he is shouted down. This small crowd of French Basque farmers and their wives, daughters, and cousins spill off the porch into the front yard. Each has his or her own theory, and all of them involve a different direction and separate mountain ranges. An elderly man ends

the arguments with a motion and announces—half in untrans-
latable French, half in the international language of exaggerated gestures—the best way to Santiago. He suggests I head to
a village named Saint Michel and take a left. He points in the
direction I have come. I can't really understand the details of
what he is saying, but I am certain it ends with the Basque
equivalent of "You can't miss it."

I retrace the same slow curves of the morning, once again
taking in the boarded shops and closed farmhouses. The
turkey is at his post and watches me pass. He is perfectly still.
His garden-hose head musters a slightly superior tilt.

The repetition of the walk is interrupted only by a young,
excitable pup, who explodes from a tangle of mountain laurel
and joins the walk. She is a cute mutt and loves to walk at my
feet. A sweet image floats into view—arriving in Santiago,
hand-carved birch staff in one hand, a gamboling puppy
beside me. She is all chaotic tail between my legs and a delight
until I am brutally reminded that with a pack stiffening my
back, I am as agile as a hod of bricks.

At Saint Michel, near a bridge, I see a small paved road that
lurches straight up and out of the village. How did I miss it?
And there is a yellow arrow painted on a post—the *flecha
amarilla*. The yellow arrows are said to be painted especially
for pilgrims at every small intersection between here and Santiago. Seeing my first arrow summons a child's pleasure of
joining some secret guild. People in cars wouldn't even notice
these crude glyphs of yellow paint—three quick splashes on a
fence post or tree or the back of a road sign. They awaken a
warm intimacy with the hundreds of millions of pilgrims who
have walked this road in the last millennium or so. Surely
these yellow arrows would come to mean something powerful
to a pilgrim. I jot down in my notebook, "Yellow arrows and
metaphor?" and walk on.

When the arrows cease to appear, even momentarily, a dis-
may settles in. And the longer they refuse to appear, the more
impending feels the doom. Not far up this hill, fear and ignorance compel me into the driveway of a rural cheese farm. The
drizzle has temporarily stopped. My leaping pup is with me. A

cheesemaker and his daughter approach, both of whom have happily squished their way out front in their yogurt-stomping boots. From behind their legs, a dog the size of a grizzly bear gallops out. His eyes are blazing straight for my puppy. The farmer yells out in French, something along the lines of "actually very friendly, loves children."

I drop my pack and begin the stutter step of a guard blocking for his quarterback. The bear blows me aside like a bug and dives into the yin-yang tumble of a dogfight. The cheesemaker's dog sinks his teeth into the hip of my pup. And again—crunch—into her neck. From the blur of confusion, I can see my little dog, her eyes wide with fear and, so it seems to me, betrayal. Seconds later the victor saunters off, wagging his butt with a bully's confidence. In the distance the cheesemaker waves and says something to the effect of "wouldn't hurt a flea, bark worse than his bite." My pup bolts into nearby woods. I call after her. My whistles are carried off by a slight, humid breeze.

I envision a shady oak beneath which the little pup finally drops, licking her wounds, cursing her stupidity for leaving her territory, until death overtakes her. But just who is outside his territory if not me? Only a few hours into the pilgrimage, here is another fabulous incident brimming with significance. I reach for my notebook.

This is the problem with the road. Despite its literalness, the idea of the pilgrim's journey is a metaphor bonanza. Everything that happens on the road seems to translate itself instantaneously from what it *is* to what it *means*. I get lost! Yellow arrows! Fleeing dogs! Metaphor? Friend, I'm slogging through it. The road itself *is* the West's most worn-out palimpsest and among our oldest tropes. The obvious metaphors click by. The high road and the low, the long and winding, lonesome, royal, open, private, the road to hell, tobacco, crooked, straight and narrow. There is the road stretching into infinity, bordered by lacy mists, favored by sentimental poets. There is the more dignified road of Mr. Frost. There is, every four years, the road to the White House. There is the right road. And then there is the road that concerns me most today, the wrong road.

This wealth of cliché was one of my motivations as well. The world I left behind is obsessed with new metaphors, new ideas, new vocabularies. I took up the pilgrimage because of its contrarian possibilities. I wanted to traipse through one of the oldest junkyards of Western metaphor.

Then again, maybe I should calm down. Instead of trying to tickle meanings out of every curve (it's only noon of my first [true] day), maybe I should adopt a more conservative attitude. Maybe a dogfight near a cheese farm should remain a dogfight near a cheese farm. So I close my notebook and head up the hill in the direction the cheesemaker sends me.

Almost two hours after I leave the cheesemaker, it's the middle of the afternoon. The yellow arrows have completely disappeared, and I am plunged into despair. According to the sketchy map drawn by the cheesemaker on the back of a crumpled envelope, I should continue on this narrow paved road until I hit Spain. Around a curve the towers of a town rise into view. My guidebook says this town could be a Basque village called Untto, cut into the side of the mountain, or possibly Erreculuch. Whichever, the place is certainly flourishing, having overgrown its mountain slope and surrounded a river. I spot an old farmer hoeing a few rows of corn in his side yard.

"Greetings, sir," I say expansively. "I am a pilgrim to Santiago. Can you tell me the name of this town?"

"That one?" he says, pointing.

"Well, yes," I say, looking around at the otherwise undisturbed forests surrounding us.

"That's Saint-Jean Pied de Port, a famous town on the road to Santiago."

What can I say? Suddenly I can make out the crenellated walls of the old fortress. There is Madame Debril's street. From this slope, I can see that I am about twenty minutes from the burnt wood sign at the edge of town. My eyes water, and the farmer seems amused at the funny dance and high-pitched noises made by his visiting pilgrim.

An hour or so later I have reclimbed the mountain to a simple intersection where the cheesemaker's map had indicated a right turn. Of course, there is a yellow arrow on a rock, pointing to the left, as obvious as the one at Saint Michel. How could I have missed it? I take some comfort in knowing that the turkey on his post in the valley is no witness to my afternoon's effort.

From the top of the peak, the work of my first morning comes into focus. I have traced a rambling circle from Saint-Jean Pied de Port to the Basque farmhouse, back up and over a mountain, and again to Saint-Jean—a bowed triangle of walking. I am tempted to bring out my notebook and jot down a sublime note or two. If I am in search of Big Meaningful metaphors, here's a beauty. I am going in circles. But it is late afternoon and I have the Pyrenees ahead of me and, after that, the entire breadth of Spain. My first day out I have circumscribed a huge loop. This is often the gist of the last chapter of travel books—ending where one starts. Now that I have that out of the way, I am ready to begin.

All maps distort the land they describe. Most of us learn this in grade school when the teacher explains that Greenland is really shaped not like a fat arrowhead, but more like a pointed lozenge. For a pilgrim, a map is a constant disappointment. Over and over again, I learn that maps were invented for people in vehicles. Regardless of the era—ancient ships, modern cars—maps are for those who can engulf vast distances. A wrong turn in a car just means spinning around and heading back. It's just a few minutes. The same mistake on foot can cost you an afternoon or a meal.

Villages that should be far away suddenly appear. And landmarks allegedly close at hand show up late, unexpectedly, or not at all. A map is a reduction in scale, and a pilgrimage is about just the opposite, a sort of airing things out to an original measure. A map takes the rambunctious chaos of man's roads and nature's formations and then straightens it all into an efficient line that fits on a page. I bought mine near Madame Debril's house, and it is more about convenience than accuracy. My pilgrimage has been crammed onto pages measuring four by sixteen inches, made to fit my back pocket. On each tall page, a red line worms up from the bottom—

wriggling a bit to retain the look of "roadness"—past ruined castles, small villages, and peculiar outcroppings. Each page takes about a day to walk. So I'll be arriving in Santiago, including the preface, by page seventy-three.

Much to my relief, the yellow arrows are now appearing with warm regularity. It is this other map splashed in secret places at every intersection on which I will primarily depend. I pull the book out for color commentary on the pilgrimage. The pages tell me, for example, that just now I will ascend a peak known to the Basques as Itchasheguy, then one called Hostateguy, and then Urdenarri. But I am guided by the arrows, and I've gotten better at spotting them. If the road turns near a pole or diverges by a misshapen boulder or splits at a fence, I anticipate the comforting confirmation of the arrow. I am beginning to think like an arrow painter and have a sense of where to look before I get there.

Compared with earlier pilgrims, I have it easy. In the late Middle Ages, there were no maps. Each intersection was marked by a small pyramid of stones called a *montjoie*. A 1425 English itinerary noted: "Here beginneth the way that is marked and made with Mont Joiez from the land of Engelond unto Sent Jamez." Half a century later, a French pilgrim walked this part of the road and explained in his diary a difficulty I can only imagine: "We used to stab our staffs repeatedly in the snow in order to see if there were any montjoies; when we didn't find any, we recommended ourselves to god and we continued walking; when we heard that our stick had hit, we were more at ease because we had found a montjoie."

Deep into the Pyrenees, the road narrows into a rugged single lane of worn macadam, no more than six feet across, just enough to fit the buzzing Citroëns of the Basque shepherds who speed by en route to a flock. At this height and distance in the mountains, I am far from any village, far from a simple house. At Untto (six houses and a water spigot), the map says, "You will not find another inhabited dwelling until Spain."

To my right, there is nothing but meadows slanting upward. To the left is a fatal drop so acute the trees grow nearly parallel to the ground in their stretch toward the sun. From time to time I tiptoe through a herd of cows plopped on the road who follow me with blank sad stares, or I approach a flock of sheep who scatter amid a cacophony of ludicrous bleats. At last I am on the very path cut through the mountains by proto-Spaniards, the Celtiberians. Later the Romans improved it to accommodate their strip-mining of precious metals in Spain. This is the same road taken by Charlemagne to avenge the murder of his nephew Roland, a homicide that inspired the French national epic. And this is the road that millions of pilgrims have followed into Spain.

But is it really? I wonder if I am on the *true* road. Did the Celtiberians, the Romans, Charlemagne, and the pilgrims really walk on this very dirt, through these same meadows, or have I been hoodwinked by my long thin guidebook, local folk brimming with color, and their confederate, history?

Only yesterday it wouldn't have mattered. I didn't expect to ask these questions. Is this the *true* road? But my conversation with Madame Debril has preyed on my mind. I have spent the day reliving every line, every assertion, every blank silence, and every awkward pause. This tape loop plays over and over. By late afternoon I have reentered Madame Debril's door a thousand times. In one fantasy, I argue with the brevity and wit of Socrates. In another, I swagger through her foyer in full pilgrim drag, cape and floppy hat, mugging like José Ferrer. In yet another, I stumble to the door, covered in sweat, my visage the very stamp of pilgrim suffering.

My encounter with Madame Debril has left me rethinking the beginning of this pilgrimage. And let me say that if I had to do it all over again, I'd do everything differently. I'd contact the proper authorities. I'd find a monastery deep inside France and perhaps contact a group. I'd look into broad-brimmed hat sales. My entire effort feels corrupt, maybe ruined. All those oh-so-arch schemes, ranging from the Cloisters to the taxi, don't really sit well with purists like Madame Debril. Or me.

By late afternoon I am heaving up the Pyrenees, sweating in a poncho. The thunderheads still squirt fine rain, blasted into nettlesome pellets by a mountain gust. I haven't eaten all day because I never did find a store that was open. I fear to touch the few provisions in my bag. A strange lightness cushions my brain. I occasionally burst into laughter for no reason. The steep defile always on my left advertises a warm lush valley far, far below. How quickly I could get there if I wanted.

I mull over the origin of the word I have adopted. "Pilgrim" comes from the Latin phrase *per agrum,* or "through the fields." *Peregrinus* was used by Romans in more or less the sense we use "alien" or "stranger." To be a *peregrinus* was to be the fool who left the security of the village and wandered off, literally through the fields, into the wilderness.

Yet even here, on the windy edge of the Pyrenees, the road doesn't seem to lead me away from civilization. My medieval predecessors were in a much more frightening wilderness. They walked a road literally built for walking. They were days away from the next town, the next meal, first aid, the warmth of a fire.

Today's road is different. This thin macadam strip doesn't lead me into the wilderness. Every half hour or so, a Basque shepherd or a truck or a tourist passes by, reminding me that modern roads *are* civilization. They are corridors of culture connecting one town to another. I am always a short jaunt from help, and I am always connected to the world I left. This morning's breakfast in Saint-Jean was bought with my American Express credit card.

My exile is not geographical because I am never really all that far away, as much as I (and Madame Debril) want to think that way. The modern road makes everything within reach. The Roman road, Charlemagne's road, the pilgrim's road—built for them and their purposes—no longer exists for me and mine. It has been paved over, yielding to the demands of trucker and tourist.

As a pilgrim, I am an anachronism. Fittingly I can't even make myself walk *on* the road. The strong winds roaring up from the valley have the same Doppler effect of a car approaching from behind. I instinctively find myself hugging the side of the road. Even the architecture of the modern road, slightly buckled at the median for rain off-flow, makes the pilgrim list toward the edge. A pilgrim can no longer walk in the center. He's forced to walk just off the road.

By nine P.M. the slanting yellow light is thin and pale. The temperature drops considerably—it's nearly freezing—and the clouds open with a gushing rain. A Basque shepherd stops to tell me that Roncesvalles is just down a dirt road through a forest. After he drives away, I come upon the boundary of France and Spain. A simple metal gate bears the word *España* painted above another yellow arrow. My map marks this spot, which gives me enough of a bearing to realize that I am still five or six hours' walk to the next town. Roncesvalles is just over there, the shepherd said. Of course it is. *By car.*

I have been walking on the more dangerous edge of the road near the cliffs. My head is extremely light from lack of food, so I shift to the other side to keep from slipping off the mountain. Several times I find myself staggering and simply sit down in the rain and mud to gather my ebbing faculties. I wonder if I shouldn't retreat to the paved road and beg the next shepherd to take me somewhere, anywhere. But human instinct doesn't acknowledge danger until it sweeps over you. So I push on into the deep dark forest.

The road in the woods is normally damp dirt. Wheel tracks show the frequent passage of shepherds. With the rain, the damp ruts become gushing canals of mud. Getting twenty feet down the road is becoming difficult. When the sun pops behind a mountain, darkness sets in as quickly as hitting a light switch.

I find the least damp hummock on the side of the road among a dense knot of trees. There has been some logging farther up the mountain, so the mud is shifting around my little hill. But this spot seems safe enough. The decision, however mournfully taken, is to make camp rather than to walk on in the dark. I hang my shell on a nearby tree to claim my place. Of the hundreds of millions of pilgrims who may have passed this way, maybe one of them had to camp in this spot in the rain as well, wrapped in his cape, his head on his crip, his broad-brimmed hat resting on his face.

I feel a boyish excitement amid the cold and suffering. Those tent poles snap into position as effortlessly as advertised.

Madame Debril floats into view. "You are not a true pil-

grim." Shivers consume me, yet my doubts about being a true
pilgrim and worrying about my clothes, my shell, and my con-
victions are easier to assuage after a day of such intense labor.
The historical pilgrimage shouldn't be the model, as it is for
Madame Debril. No pilgrim can make sense of the road if he
reduces it to mere reenactment. I can't be a medieval pilgrim.

I can't consider myself an exile in the etymological sense of
the word *pilgrim* because that meaning, like the etymological
meanings of so many other words, has become quaint and out-
of-date. I haven't left the village, walked through the fields,
and wandered far from my home because the road is always
an outpost of the place I have just left behind. I have my American Express card. Even here, were I to succumb to hypothermia, I would be found the next morning by a passing
shepherd—curled into a large blue fetus. I would be choppered
out and taken to Madrid. Eventually I would wind up back
home. A little brain damage, they would tell my mother. And I
would assume my destiny as one of Charleston's glorious
eccentrics, a supernumerary from a Tennessee Williams play.

What the modern pilgrim is exiled from is not a place but
velocity. I haven't left the world of the city; I have left the
realm of the car. What distinguishes me is not that I am out of
town but that I am on foot. My predecessors were outcasts
because they left the security of the village. I have left the
world of technology and speed. I can't pretend to be that other
pilgrim. Nor can I try to breathe sense into the meanings we've
inherited from the people who were. I can't wear the cape any
more than I can believe in the contents of the shrine. I am a
pilgrim on the road to Santiago or, rather, a pilgrim just off the
road. I am more like Thor Heyerdahl, the man who sailed the
Atlantic in a prehistoric raft of sticks. I too am trying out a
neglected conveyance, not to reexamine the old meanings that
have trickled down to us, but to see if I can't recover one or
two that we've lost.

The temperature outside is plummeting. Inside the tent,
inside my sleeping bag, inside my coat, inside all my clothes, I
arrange my small supply of goods and examine my pantry: one
orange, one five-inch chunk of baguette, a jar of mustard, and

a tube of condensed milk. The rain sounds like a shower of marbles. Despite having trouble focusing on objects, I feel a child's sense of safety in this tent. I peel the orange and savor each wedge. A twelfth-century chronicler, after arriving more or less to this same spot, wrote: "How many thousands of pilgrims have died [here], some lost in snow storms, others, more numerous still, devoured by the ferocity of the wolves." The orange is the most delicious one I have ever eaten.

The baguette smeared with mounds of mustard flares my nostrils until they hurt. But the pain reawakens my senses, and I feel my equilibrium ebbing back. The questions of where to begin and how officially to get started now seem serenely irrelevant. I feel as if I have been on this road half my life. Madame Debril drifts away. I have other things on my mind just now— the likely sound of approaching wolves, the final thoughts of snowbound pilgrims, the symptoms of hypothermia, and the width of Spain. I grip the tube of condensed milk with my fist, put the aluminum teat in my mouth, and squeeze with all my strength.

THREE
ESTELLA

On a bend in the last mountain of the Pyrenees, a slight
dip in the road leads up a hump until a hazy green valley lowers into view like a card on a stereopticon. All appears peace-
ful in Spain today. The chimneys from the scattered farms feed
thin columns of gray smoke into a blanket of drifting white
mist. I feel restored this morning and ready for my descent into
Roncesvalles.

A marker tops the ridge, with a dozen wooden arms pointing chaotically in all directions. I expect to read outrageous
distances—New York, 8,000 kilometers; Buenos Aires 11,000 k;
Tokyo, 16,500 k. But I am entering Navarra, the land of the
Spanish Basques. They are not a people famous for irony. This
sign is just a sign pointing to nearby hamlets with long,
unpronounceable names. All of them should be within view,
but I see nothing except boulders spilling down a deep gorge
into the valley.

Roncesvalles is a famously mysterious place and has been

since the eighth century, just before the pilgrimage began, when it became the most notorious killing field of the Middle Ages. At the time, the giant armies of Islam had come to Christian Europe, so the scene was set for a cataclysmic encounter. The Moors had invaded Spain in 711 and by the end of that century were in control of all but the ribbon of desolation in the north that would become the road. Meanwhile, in Europe, Charlemagne was uniting the continent. This era would culminate on Christmas Day A.D. 800, when the pope crowned Charlemagne the first Holy Roman Emperor.

But Charlemagne's reunification of the Roman Empire and of Europe would come at a cost, paid at Roncesvalles in 778 and hymned forever in the greatest medieval epic, the *Chanson de Roland*. So the story goes, Charlemagne had entered Spain to liberate the local Christians but after some time had decided to make a prudent peace with the Arabs. As the poem opens, he is trying to settle a dispute between his nephew Roland and his brother-in-law Ganelon (also Roland's stepfather). Both are vying to be the king's emissary to win peace from the Arabs.

Ganelon won the argument, but his jealousy over Charlemagne's apparent preference for Roland drove him to treachery. While sitting in the silken tents of the Arabs (known as Saracens in poetry), Ganelon betrayed Charlemagne's route back into France as Roncesvalles. He explained to them that the rear guard, led by Roland, would be most vulnerable when it began to file into the narrow gorge that cuts into the Pyrenees, where I now stand.

> *High are the hills, the valleys dark and deep,*
> *Grisly the rocks, and wondrous grim the steep.*

On the late afternoon of August 15, 778, Roland and the rear guard were ambushed here. As the fighting spilled into the valley, Roland's best friend, Oliver, begged him to call Charlemagne for help by sounding his horn. All manly symbols in the *Chanson de Roland* have names; the horn's is Olifant. But rather than blow Olifant, Roland cried out for immediate battle. He goaded his men to fight at once and claim their honor. In the early exchange, no Saracen was safe from Roland and his mighty sword (Durendal by name). Roland's dispatch of the Saracen dandy Chernuble, whose "unshorn hair hangs trailing to his feet," is horrific even by our standards of violence:

> He spurs his horse and goes against Chernuble:
> he breaks the helmet on which rubies gleam;
> he slices downward through the coif and hair
> and cuts between the eyes, down through his face,
> the shiny hauberk made of fine-linked mail,
> entirely through the torso to the groin,
> and through the saddle trimmed with beaten gold.
> The body of the horse slows down the sword,
> which, seeking out no joint, divides the spine:
> both fall down dead upon the field's thick grass.

As the battle raged, Oliver pleaded with Roland to call Charlemagne, until it was too late. When the fighting turned against his men, Roland gave a blast on Olifant so powerful that his temples burst. In his death throes Roland cracked Durendal on a stone so no Saracen could carry it in triumph, and then he fell. After Charlemagne hastened to this ridge, he saw red pastures below, drenched in his men's gore. The enemy had vanished. Charlemagne sank to his knees and so moved the heavens with his plea for revenge that the late afternoon sun, it is said, held its place in the sky and lit the Spanish plains until Charlemagne caught the Saracens and carried out a final furious slaughter.

For pilgrims, the story was important, and vice versa. Along the road the song was performed by itinerant musicians called jugglers, and it became enormously popular. The pilgrimage and the song also introduced new ideas into Christian thinking at this time. The constant skirmishes with the Moors just off the road to Santiago had put the pilgrims, and subsequently Europe, in contact with a novel Arab concept—the jihad, or holy war.

After three hundred years of pilgrimage and fighting Moors, the lessons were learned. This new idea tried on different accommodating theologies until it became a Christian virtue. The Arab jihad was Europeanized into the Christian

Crusade. In 1095, Pope Urban II called on Christians to retake the Holy Land from infidels. Four years later Rome's flag flew in Jerusalem.

On the field in the valley, a stone marker announces the spot where Roland and his men engaged the Saracens. A nearby highway provides a short walk into Roncesvalles. This little village—no more than a hundred people—is a few houses, two bars, and an Augustinian monastery. A knock at a door of the chapterhouse puts me in the orbit of Brother Don Jesús. A short bald man with a quick chaotic air, he is in constant motion.

"Pilgrim. Pilgrim. What a surprise. How good this is," he says in fast, clipped Spanish. He herds me into his private office and eases me into a comfy chair. From somewhere he produces a clipboard and shoves a questionnaire in my lap. I am being polled. The monastery wants to know about the pilgrims who pass through. I am asked where I am from, where I started, how I heard of the road. The critical, final question asks my "motive" for walking the road. I am provided four possible answers:

- religious
- cultural
- historical
- other (explain)

That fourth option looks so sad and out of place alongside the first three. I check this box and write in Spanish, "I'd have to write a book to answer this question." Don Jesús reads it, laughs, and playfully snatches the clipboard from me. Apparently he doesn't care for polls.

"You are a pilgrim. We have been welcoming you for a thousand years!" Father Don Jesús throws his arm around my shoulder and squeezes my neck.

At evening, he says, the church still rings the bell, the last call for pilgrims to find their way out of the mountains and into the shelter of the monastery. I ask him if he has any pilgrims' passports lying around.

"Of course. We have no problem. They are here."

I tell him that I had met a Madame Debril on the other side of the Pyrenees and that she had told me it was pointless to walk without one. Don Jesús looks up at me through caterpillar eyebrows with a pair of warm, conspiratorial eyes. He pulls out a fresh passport and makes a show of applying an intricate stamp the size of a silver dollar. Sometimes I can't understand his fast Spanish, but just now our few words flow with all the elliptical intimacy of two old buddies.

"Ma-dame De-bril," Brother Don Jesús intones slowly. He smiles.

"Madame Debril," I say, and smile.

"Madame Debril," Brother Don Jesús says.

"Madame Debril," I say.

Slipping his arm through mine, Don Jesús escorts me out of the chapter house and into the open air. I tell him that I am especially interested in the story of Roland. There, he says, indicating an eleventh-century funereal chapel, that is where Roland blew Olifant. The shrill winds that whip through the mountains and valleys here are said to be echoes of Roland's ancient blast. He points to an open area and says that this is where Roland broke Durendal on a rock and where he died. A large tourist bus pulls onto the gravel near Roland's resting place and crunches to a halt.

Don Jesús drops me off for a coffee and some breakfast at a restaurant next door. Trying to be polite to the waiter, I tell him how enchanted I am to be in the place where Roland first suffered at the hands of the Arabs and Charlemagne turned the road to Santiago into a European phenomenon.

"Arabs?" muses the waiter.

"Yes," I say, baffled at his confusion. "Arabs. *Chanson de Roland*. Road to Santiago," I add, hoping my collection of Spanish phrases makes sense.

"There were no Arabs here."

I never know how to handle this. When one is convinced one speaks with authority on a subject, there is the tricky business of imparting this obvious (on your part) superiority without coming across as supercilious.

I tell him I had just read the *Chanson de Roland*. He smiles to congratulate me on doing my homework but ignores the arrogant implications.

"Roland did not die in an ambush of Arabs," he says. I decide to play along.

"So who killed him?"

"We did."

"You?"

"The Basques killed him."

Everyone in Spain issues warnings about Basques, and I had heard plenty before arriving here. They are a notorious people—most recently for a terrorist guerrilla war against the Spanish government. But, historically, they have always been enigmatic and work hard at perpetuating their cultural reputation. Linguists who have mapped the intersecting landscapes of language cannot place Basque anywhere on the map. Its origin remains a mystery.

A sardonic Englishman named Richard Ford published an account of his 1845 visit to this area. He found the Basque people inscrutable and their language outrageous—a people who write the name "Solomon" but pronounce it "Nebuchadnezzar." Ford tells the legendary story of the Devil, who studied Basque in order to corrupt these people, but he abandoned his effort after seven years because he had mastered only three words.

I look at my waiter and automatically screw up a dismissive look, but he stops me.

"When my father returns, he will tell you. He knows the whole story. We are the only people who tell the truth. The French, the Spanish, the Arabs, all lie about Roland."

Not long after, the waiter's father arrives. He is a short, stout man with a warm, inviting face. On several occasions he stresses the depth of his knowledge of America.

"I know who Nelson Rockefeller is," he says with a wink of braggadocio.

He owns this inn but was a teacher in Pamplona for most of his life. Before I can pose a question, he's launched into an excited explanation of where the Basques originated. I had read theories alleging that the Basque might be of ancient Celtic origin and another that suggested possible commonalities with old Hungarian. But both of these apparently are wrong.

"Originally, we were Japanese. Thousands of years ago a group of brave warriors were banished from Japan. They wandered the earth and arrived here."

"Really?" I pipe up, not able to disguise my incredulity even behind the thick blanket of a foreign language. I look again at my new acquaintance—an old white man a bit broad in the beam, his hair still showing traces of brown, his eyes as round as coins. "How come you don't look Japanese?"

"Diet."

He'd prepared for that one.

"Several Japanese scholars visited here not long ago," he continued. "One of them was a language professor. We were both amazed at how much of our language we could understand. For example, the word for mother in Basque is *ma*. That also happens to be the word for mother in Japanese as well." He nods his head significantly.

I don't want to tell him that "ma" is the word for mother in nearly every language on earth, since it's typically the first consonant-and-vowel combo a baby can pronounce. I also realize there is a bit of ethnic trendiness going on here. If, instead of the Japanese, the group with the reputation for hard work, intelligence, and cunning were Micronesians, somehow I suspect I'd be hearing tales of rafts rounding Tierra del Fuego and coming ashore on the beaches of Santander. When I change the subject to Roland, he immediately picks it up as if he'd been talking about it all along.

"The truth of the matter is confused," he says. "Charlemagne did not come here with the purest of motives. You will hear that he entered Spain to liberate Christians suffering under the rule of infidels. Charlemagne had other ideas—to expand his empire. He crossed the Pyrenees, but nothing worked out as he intended. This is Spain! This is Basque Spain! He tortured the Basques of Pamplona and allowed his men to have a little too much"—and he says this phrase in

English—"rest and relaxation with our women. When he was preparing to cross the Pyrenees, the Basque shepherds who lived around here heard about what had happened in Pamplona. And Basques are the best shepherds. We can talk to animals. Basques can talk to wolves. Our shepherds and the wolves slipped into the woods up near the steep pass when the time came. They blew their *irrintzi* [horns made of wild oxen]. And then we killed them." He grins.

He points to my paperback copy of the *Chanson de Roland* and says with a sneer, "You won't find much truth in that." He explains that none of the protagonists at the time wanted to tell the truth about Roland because no one was served by it. The French didn't want to admit that the death of Roland was the result of Charlemagne's un-Christian intentions. The Spaniards didn't want to tell the truth because they welcomed French propaganda (and assistance) in the war against the Moors. And the Arabs? In the Basque version, they don't figure into the telling. In the *Chanson de Roland,* they become the most feared people on earth.

That evening, Brother Don Jesús takes me to the third floor of the monastery's sleeping quarters. I pass a dozen doors marked with the names of the other brothers. I never see them or hear them. Each door warns me in Spanish not to disturb. On the top floor the pilgrims' quarters are several rooms with rough-hewn wooden bunks built three beds high into the wall. On a thin mattress I lay out my bag and turn on a flashlight. I pull out a new copy of the *Codex Calixtinus,* the twelfth-century tour guidebook I had discussed with Madame Debril. Among the Roland ashtrays and plastic Olifants, the monastery's gift shop sells a fresh edition of the pilgrimage's first *Baedeker.*

The *Codex* is attributed to a French cleric named Aimery Picaud. The book is amusing because the author's pro-France/anti-Spain bias is the most comically exaggerated in history. His critical reviews of the towns and food along the way are filled with crazed invective. France is all elegance, and Spain is a country of poisoned rivers, granite bread, and lethal fish.

Naturally Picaud has an opinion of the Basques. As a

gumshoe errant, I can't help but wonder if his writing in 1160 wasn't influenced by the same rumor I heard this morning, because it is for the Basques that Picaud saved his most ornamental condemnations. Picaud says the Basques of Navarra are a thieving people who force strangers to take down their pants. Their language sounds like the barking of dogs. They eat with their hands. In a bit of etymological overreaching, Picaud traces the origin of the region's name, Navarra, to the Latin *non verus,* the land of liars. But once Picaud really warms up his pen, the reader can't help but suspect that his loathing of the Basques reflects the French memory of what really happened in 778:

> This is a barbarous people unlike all other peoples in customs and in character, full of malice, swarthy in colour, ill-favoured of face, misshapen, perverse, perfidious, empty of faith and corrupt, libidinous, drunken, experienced in all violence, ferocious and wild, dishonest and reprobate, impious and harsh, cruel and contentious, unversed in anything good, well trained in all vices and iniquities, like the Geats and Saracens in malice, in everything inimical to our French people. . . . In certain regions of their country, that is, in Biscay and Alava, when the Navarrese are warming themselves, a man will show a woman and a woman a man their private parts. The Navarrese even practice unchaste fornication with animals. For the Navarrese is said to hang a padlock behind his mule and mare, so that none may come near her but himself. He even offers libidinous kisses to the vulva of woman and mule. That is why the Navarrese are to be rebuked by all well-informed people.

I am developing suspicions, especially since while I'm in the Basque region, everyone—shopkeepers, bankers, priests—all tell me the exact same story. I bring up the subject, and the locals speak of 778 as if it weren't so long ago. I feel like a detective arriving on the scene 1,200 years late to solve an old crime. Who killed Roland?

The next morning I walk out of Roncesvalles and I wander into the village of Espinal. A sign on a gift shop invites me to ring the bell if it is closed. A buzz produces a shadowy presence in the rear of the shop, a woman about fifty years old. Stepping around the corner of the counter to open the door, she runs her hand through a tangle of hair and whips the belt of a thick bathrobe into a knot.

On the left is a wall of religious objects, crucifixes, crèches, Virgin Marys. On the right is a wall of the local drinking jugs, called *botas*. Their long, tapered spout, which protrudes acutely at the base, allows locals to pour the wine—often at a distance—directly down one another's throats without swallowing. But these *botas* are novelty gifts, delivering their contents through some potter's best-slung rendition of a penis. In the position of a *bota* spout, the penises appear extremely cheerful and pose a bizarre contrast to the wall of suffering Jesuses on the other side. The woman shows me some of her other naughty merchandise. Each time she bends over to unlock a showcase, an errant breast tumbles out. She replaces it giddily. Spain has certainly changed since Franco died. I ask her about the recent murder of the Frenchman they call Roland. She laughs.

"We killed him, the Basques," she says as if all history had taken place in the last couple of weeks. "We threw out the French then and now we're trying to throw out the Spanish."

It turns out the Basques aren't the only ones with a story. One pilgrim version ended with Charlemagne walking to Santiago as the official First Pilgrim. Since Roland died in 778 and Santiago's body was discovered in 814, this makes Charlemagne's pilgrimage not merely the first, but quite likely the slowest. But what's a little discrepancy among epic poets?

The local priests too had their *Chanson de Roland,* built on a juicy piece of eighth-century gossip. It was widely whispered in those days that Charlemagne's libido often targeted his own sisters. This variation on the story made Charlemagne's lust the source of the evil and Roland's death inevitable since he was in fact Charlemagne's incestuous son. This rendition certainly gives Ganelon's bitterness and treason a sympathetic gloss. Since he was married to Charlemagne's sister, he was, in effect, the future Holy Roman Emperor's beard. How Ganelon must have seethed at the prospect of being humiliated by Roland—the product of his ongoing cuckolding by Charlemagne.

Other variations of the Roland story can be found throughout the continent, and even the epic cycle of King Arthur and his knights of the Round Table is said to be an Anglo-Saxon response to compete with the intoxicating tales of Charlemagne and his counselor chevaliers.

The more I looked into the case, the better it got for my Basque innkeeper. For example, Charlemagne's official historian, Einhard, never mentioned Roland in the written record until after the emperor's death. Then, Roncesvalles gets only a small mention—probably to refute the stories of humiliating defeat and cowardice circulating orally around the mountains. Einhard delicately notes that in the Pyrenees, Charlemagne had no real problem to speak of "except for a reverse" at Roncesvalles owed to little more than *"Wasconiam perfidiam,"* literally "Basque treachery." In the list of the dead, Einhard mentions several nobles and other worthies, among them a man with the unusual name Hruodlandus. Look carefully at that mouthful and you will see the orthographic ancestor of Roland. Then Einhard adds an astonishing kicker: "Nor could this assault be punished at once, for when the deed had been done the enemy so completely disappeared that they left behind them not so much as a rumour of their whereabouts."

So Charlemagne did not return to Spain at all. He left his nephew/son's body to rot in the future bus parking lot of Roncesvalles.

What had I stumbled onto here? If Einhard's reluctant admissions are true, then what does that make of the *Chanson de Roland?* A cover-up? The poem's not only wrong, but magnificently wrong, intentionally wrong. Could the *Chanson de Roland* be a brazen reversal of the truth, such as we often see in modern propaganda? Could France's national epic be the first use of the Big Lie?

• • •

Over the intervening 1,200 years, historians who admire Charlemagne have gone to heroic ends to spin the events in Charlemagne's favor. One nineteenth-century British historian, who signs himself J. J. Mombert, D.D., grunts with regret that this story has "two or three particulars which few readers of this history might care to have suppressed." He offers a dozen excuses for Charlemagne's cowardice in Roncesvalles but finally throws up his hands at the end of one paragraph in italic exasperation: Charlemagne "doubtless *tried* to win, although he only came, saw—and *went*." Something's going on here, so I continue looking.

The irony of my investigation is that for most of history, despite so many competing versions of the story, everyone knew that the Basques had something to do with killing Roland and that Charlemagne had fled. But more recently, other extenuating circumstances allowed an "authentic" French version to become preeminent. In the early nineteenth century, the fierce nationalism that gripped Europe had ripple effects everywhere. In literary circles this impulse manifested itself with the encyclopedic task of collecting a culture's great works in one book called an anthology. A country's fiction— assembled in one place—became an epic story on its own, with a beginning, a middle, and an end (always gloriously continued). A country such as England, for example, could proudly open its national anthology and find itself to be an island of constantly flowering talent whose blossoms could be plucked backward in time until one came upon the original bud—the tightly written, ancient work called *Beowulf*.

And the French? Where to "begin" French literature? For a while it was a problem. Then, in 1835, a graduate student discovered a manuscript of the *Chanson de Roland* in (of all places) a library in Oxford, England. This specific version of the story was elegant, probably the work of a troubadour hired by a French aristocrat so the poem could be read aloud on holidays. Specialists refer to the manuscript, for arcane reasons, as Digby 23, giving it all the charm and mystery of a distant quasar.

In it, Roland blows the Olifant, Charlemagne storms back into Spain, the sun stops dead in its tracks. We all know this story, because it is the *one* we all know—the classic tale of slaughter and righteous revenge. Throughout the 1800s, the French heavily promoted this version of the tale, and it became the First Work of French literature. It was internationally anthologized. French children were required to read this version in high school and still are. In translation by Dorothy L. Sayers (Penguin Classics) or by any other translator, this version is the *only* one available in bookstores.

This *Chanson de Roland* imposes on the past a dramatic and flattering story. Few people probably care that much about the story of Roland, so there aren't many who would want to challenge the *Chanson de Roland* as the first great work of French literature. But there are a few far-flung places where the cruel savagery of 778 continues.

In the rarefied world of academic textual critics, there are those (mainly French) who insist that the *Chanson de Roland* is the first great work. They say that the poem is an original work of art written by a single artist named Turold, who is mentioned in the last line. For these scholars, Turold is a real person who sat in his garret timing out the iambs of heroic verse. They say he is an epic poet whose talents compete with those of Homer and Virgil.

The other school of criticism mocks all this. They say that Turold is nothing more than a scribe who wrote down one version of the poem. At best, Turold polished a well-known work so that it had a sophisticated sheen. The original bards who sang the poem along the road and throughout Europe altered it to suit each particular audience and happily added names, changed events, or altered outcomes. In France these minstrels emphasized French honor. Elsewhere, his Christianity was paramount. In Spain the treachery of Arabs was key to their propaganda. In the Basque version—and there is one—it is a story that confirms their legendary ethnic ruggedness. The story of Roland is a collective effort, formed by slow accretion of plot and details.

French critics can get quite exercised when told that their

nation's First Great Work is not the achievement of a lone
genius, but rather is the collaborative work of hairy itinerant
peasants who played out their themes of violence according to
the moody applause of beery serfs.

For a pilgrim troubled by doubts of authenticity, the theory
is restorative. The idea that no one person wrote the *Chanson
de Roland* dates to the work of Albert Lord, who studied the
only oral epic poets to survive into our time. In the middle of
this century he traveled to the isolated mountains of Yugo-
slavia, where the last heirs to the juggler still carried on the
tradition. And he made discoveries that, when considered next
to the *Chanson de Roland,* make the French apoplectic.

Lord called the poet of oral tradition a "singer of tales" and
described him as an illiterate man with a talent for strumming
a simple instrument and singing many lines of verse, upward
of three thousand. Where we might hear his song and think
the peasant had done a good job of memorizing a very long
poem, Lord discerned an odd characteristic to prove otherwise. From performance to performance, the singer changed
the song—shortening or lengthening it by hundreds of lines,
changing the order of events, altering the names of the characters, playing out some scenes, abbreviating others. No two
performances were ever the same.

The singer of tales had not memorized a poem, nor was he
improvising each performance. Rather, Lord discovered that
each singer of tales had learned hundreds of phrases, called
formulae, that allowed him to compose the song spontaneously and differently every time he sang it. To Lord, this talent was comparable to learning another language. Where we
might learn words and compose the ordered sentences of standard human conversation, these singers learned formulae and
sang long narrative songs. When Lord asked some of the
singers to tell him what a "word" was, they could not answer
him. They thought in phrases only. *We* think in words. This
was not merely another form of expression. It was a different
way of thinking. Among those illiterate singers who were
taught to read, for instance, Lord witnessed the fading of the

singer's capacity to compose spontaneously. It seemed as if the
two modes of expression were not compatible.

What Lord was implying with his discoveries was a bomb-
shell in the tiny world of epic scholars. The poems handed down
to us were not merely mementos of another era, but a different
way of expressing the truth and telling history. "Our real difficulty," Lord says, "arises from the fact that, unlike the oral
poet, we are not accustomed to thinking in terms of fluidity."

Our literate, word-plagued minds demand a point of origin,
a single beginning, the *real* story—in the case of Roland's
assassination, a lone-swordsman theory. But, Lord adds,
"Once we know the facts of oral composition we must cease
trying to find an original." The mystery of who killed Roland
not only can't be solved, it's not even the right question. Each
"performance is an original." To us, "it seems so basic, so logical, since we are brought up in a society in which writing has
fixed the norm of a stable first creation in art, that we feel
there must be an original for everything." But in oral composition, "the idea of an original is illogical." Lord warns that we
who are reared in the ambiance of the printed word are troubled by a longing "to seek an original, and we remain dissatis-
fied with an ever-changing phenomenon."

The singers of tales continue to speak to the modern pilgrim.
Their stories shouldn't be studied for the facts, but listened to
for other melodies. Don't read history, say my illiterate hairy
muses, listen to it sing.

History and tradition plague a pilgrim at night when a break
in the day's labor grants enough time to worry about them and
maybe read up. Otherwise, the mind is occupied with the quotidian details of a new life—locating the fruit-and-vegetable
trucks that stop in the small villages, or finding a watering
hole, or flattering a tavern owner to crank up the coffee
machine for a *café con leche* during the odd hours.

A few miles out of Espinal and shy of Mezquiriz, I discover
another pilgrim sport. I am patching up two nicks in my legs
after unsuccessfully negotiating a barbed-wire fence when a

peripheral flash catches my eye. I look down a valley, across a small stream, and over another fence and spot a figure hooded by the high rise of a pack. For only a second, I see a familiar movement. The swaying lope is distinctly pilgrimesque, and then the man disappears into a dark copse of oaks.

I know there are pilgrims just ahead of me. From time to time from a field or window a local will shout a freelance update of what they know about the road. I have heard already of two men walking together. Somebody else up the way has a mule. And this morning, en route to Pamplona, I know that there is a pilgrim just ahead. Hurry up, the locals tell me, assuming that I am anxious to make contact with another on foot. Which I am.

The dark trees on this stretch form a humid tunnel, and evidently, when pilgrims aren't around, it is a favored trail among the local holstein. The cow flops are fresh and numerous—piled one atop the other. In the funky embrace of dense oaks, the road achieves a certain primal soupiness and piquancy that the pilgrim would gladly trade for a busy interstate. But it makes tracking my immediate predecessor easy. His bootprints are longer and deeper than my own, leading me to conclude through elementary sherlockian logic that my pilgrim friend is one big guy.

Where the trees above occasionally pull back to let in a ray of sunshine, the cow plops harden into a path of sawdust pancakes that burst underfoot with a satisfying crunch. One time I hear just ahead of me the snap and crackle of brittle cow flops giving way underfoot. I rush up the road but the sound recedes Doppler-like, and I never catch the source.

After a while, I think I may have imagined this other person. But the evidence keeps arriving. On the outskirts of a wretched hamlet called Zubiri there is a magnesium factory that laminates the entire valley with a fine gray-white talc. For a mile, the road appears hosed down with yuletide Styrofoam snow, and even here I make out the familiar boot treads.

The phantom pilgrim never materializes. By the time I get close, the road dissolves among the cloverleafs, entrance ramps, and bypasses of the city of Pamplona. But the hope of his appearance has served as a perverse incentive. Instead of walking the fifteen to twenty kilometers I have budgeted as the per-diem limit of the first week of the pilgrimage, I have clocked a good forty kilometers. I have a headache, and my legs feel as if they have been filled with concrete. I check into a hostel off the Plaza del Castillo in the heart of town, lie down on my bed, and assume the curled, whimpering position of the moribund.

Ten minutes later I cannot get up. A syrupy sweat pastes my arms to my sides. Every muscle is winched tight. I have to push my feet off the bed with my hands when hunger insists I move. I cannot straighten my arms, and my fingers are curled into dry claws. Hunched over, I have stiffened into a bow-legged question mark. A two-minute trip across the town square to a restaurant takes twenty minutes of struggle. I move like a sick penguin, waddling in super-slo-mo. Teenagers are quietly laughing at me, and I am laughing, too. But mine is an unhinged hilarity. I am scaring small children.

Two days of rest later, I let out from Pamplona and walk straight down into a valley and up the other side. The sun is brutal, but a deep warm sweat lowers the voltage of the bolts of pain that fire up from my feet and explode in the femur of each thigh. By late afternoon I ascend the top of a ridge and look back to see that where I had begun this morning is perched on the other side of the sky. The entire vista of the earth, all that I can see and as far as I can see, I have covered on foot. Pilgrimage creates a paradoxical effect. Instead of short distances seeming long, it's just the opposite. The vastness of a great distance shrivels when it falls within one's grasp. This afternoon, the length of the earth has been reduced to a half-day's work. I can see each stop from Pamplona—the clutch of houses called Cizur Menor, then Guendulain, and, just below me, the shadowless village of Zariquiegui. I can trace every foot of the winding path I have followed from one horizon to another.

Turning west, I step down from the ridge into a bleached rocky slant that drops into a sparse overlit forest. Behind me the two horizons blink, and the day's view is gone.

A few kilometers into this small valley, I enter a tiny village called Uterga. An old man calls me from a window to come in, rest, and have a drink. He is the patriarch of a Basque family, all of whom are visiting. His daughter, a jolly woman of about fifty, insists on pouring a dark liquid from a decanter and crying out until I down a few. It is very good, smoky, alcoholic. I want to know if it is some local confection or an authentic Basque libation. Oh, no, they tell me, excited that they're about to impress me. From a cabinet they produce an enormous bottle of Jack Daniel's Tennessee mash.

Americans have a strange effect on Spaniards, even Basque Spaniards. I'm not sure what it is, but I think it has to do with our reputation as hardworking, successfully profiteering capitalists. Spaniards still fear that they are inferior to the more brutal capitalists one finds in parts of Italy or all of Germany. The lazy Spaniard, drunk and stretched out in siesta, is an image they seek constantly to dispel.

When the old Basque grandfather wants to show me his accomplishments—trophies for some obscure sport he mastered in the 1930s—his three grandchildren wince in anguish. In a glass case is some kind of baseball bat and beanies embroidered with dates. I am listening attentively, but the two boys and one girl—all teenagers—are in unspeakable agony, whispering hostilities in hissing Basque and slapping their heads in silent-movie displays of shame. Then the grandfather reaches for a musical instrument—a version of a fiddle.

The road has a long tradition of folk music. The writer Walter Starkie, an English fiddler, walked the road to Santiago in the middle of the century and wrote about the changing musical traditions along the way. I long for a Starkie moment, a purifying dose of old-time Basque melody. But I won't be hearing any authentic tunes this afternoon. The grandchildren are apoplectic. I can make out patches of their remarks, and they boil down, more or less, to this: Grandfather, our American guest gets to listen to Michael Jackson and REM all day long. Please don't humiliate us with your corny old queer music.

My Spanish is getting more and more fluent as the refills of the smoky brown liquid keep coming. The grandfather man-

ages to understand that I *do* want to know more about the
past and the road. When he begins an anecdote about pilgrims
from fifty years ago, he is silenced by the teenagers' daggered
looks. And my attempts at expressing heartfelt interest in what
the old man has to say *are* understood as mere courtesy for the
elderly. And somehow in the argle-bargle of my Jack Daniel's
Spanish, my questions become a request for a tour and a non
sequitur description of every item this old Basque man owns.
After examining some of the motel paintings on the walls and
hearing a story for each chair and couch, I am taken to the cellar to view a lifetime of junk.

After handling every tool on the workbench, the old man
spoons a handful of ball bearings from a box. They range in
size from golfballs to fine birdshot.

"These are Basque ball bearings," he says proudly. "They
are made in the Basque lands. See how round they are." In the
slim doorway to upstairs, the three kids cringe in horror,
haloed in the amber basement light.

"Yes," I say, "they *are* very, very round, impressively round,
really."

Not far up the way, just outside the small town of Obanos, the
road from Pamplona merges with the other major French
path. This trail slides downhill for a while, joins the highway
for a few hundred meters, and winds into the ancient town of
Puente la Reina (literally the Queen's Bridge), built to help pilgrims. It was settled by the French in the late eleventh century
during one of the early bursts of propagandistic expansion of
the road. Either Sancho the Great's wife or his granddaughter
Stephanie erected this beautiful Romanesque stone bridge in
1090, and according to my waiter at dinner later this evening,
things have been a bit slow since.

On the edge of town, I encounter my first pilgrim near a
modern cast-iron sculpture honoring those of us who walk the
road. He introduces himself as Carlos from Brazil. Sinewy and
deeply roasted by the Spanish sun, Carlos wants me to join
him in a scheme. In about three weeks Pamplona will hold its
famous running of the bulls. But, says Carlos, the parties have

already begun. So he wants to hitchhike back to Pamplona, stay drunk for about a month, and then hitchhike back to Puente la Reina and continue the walk.

"You know, Carlos," I say, "as it happens, you are talking to a profoundly flawed and corrupt pilgrim, and yet this plan stretches even my powers of rationalizing."

(Several weeks later, far down the road, I will pick up a newspaper in a small town and see a photograph of two or three drunken "foreign college students" who will have been gored to death in Pamplona during the running of the bulls. One of the wire photos will show a fallen man, skinny, long, and brown. I never did see Carlos again, and after Puente la Reina, no one on the road would ever report running across him.)

The brothers at Los Padres Reparadores, who provide shelter, welcome us with the joy of immigration officials out of Kafka. Our pilgrims' passports are stamped in jaded silence by an old man, and a grumpy novitiate escorts us to our sleeping arrangements—a sonorous room of metal bunkbeds. Inside I meet a gregarious Spanish banker named Javier, a stoic Frenchman, and two sullen Dutchmen whose willful ignorance of Spanish and English is matched by their refusal to tell anyone their names.

When they first meet, pilgrims are quiet people, and modern ones especially so because we are in an arrested state of embarrassment. We are afraid that someone might ask us to explain *why* we are doing this. So each of us feels about as comfortable as someone who has stumbled upon a stranger in a bathroom stall. The sublimities are kept to a minimum, but once we find our common tongue, we prattle on. We talk about what we know best—basic human suffering generally, blisters specifically.

Like my new friends, I have taken to mapping my suffering, quantifying it, measuring it. My feet are damp blocks of pain all day long and all night long, too. I haven't merely a blister or even a lot of blisters. I have constellations of them. They seem to have a life of their own, like cellular automata. Little blister outposts form and send inquiring tunnels to make contact with the others. Recent reconnaissance has scouted the tender flesh between my toes and cinched a few of them in blister bows.

Like hiccups, blisters attract all manner of homemade cures. One of the Dutchmen makes known his recipe of sprinkling sugar water on a Band-Aid. Carlos recommends running a fine thread through each blister before bed. In the morning, he says, they will be gone. The stoic Frenchman, Louis by name, tells us never to acknowledge blisters. Just strap on your boots, ignore them, and walk. We regard him suspiciously for the rest of the evening.

Pilgrim literature is filled with ancient remedies. Our predecessors cured their feet ailments with plasters of sarsaparilla or poultices packed with blackberry leaves. The extract of the iris bulb was said to reduce swelling. The digestion of spiderweb— rolled between one's fingers into little white beads—was reputed to prevent the vomiting of blood (an ailment I still have to look forward to). Jean Bonnecaze, a pilgrim in 1748, wrote in his journal the recipe for a remedy said to cure a host of pilgrim ailments:

> Take a cleaned chicken, some pimpernel, chicory, chervil, and lettuce—a fistful of each. Clean it well, wash it, and dice into some pieces. Add a viper flayed alive which you will cut into little pieces after removing the head, the tail, and the entrails, keeping only the body, the heart, and the liver. Boil it all in three quarts of water, until it is reduced to three half-quarts. Remove it from the fire, strain it through a colander, and ladle it out into two soups to take one on the morning of a fast. Continue its use for fifteen days, purging before and after the fortnight. . . . If you cannot find a live viper, substitute for it a fistful of dust.

Quite early the next morning, we all arise. Carlos is not offering to show us his cured blisters. And all the other remedies of the prior evening don't seem so efficacious in the dawn before a long walk. With a minimum of grumbling, we ease our swollen feet into their boots and, in our silence, salute the Frenchman for his wisdom.

At the edge of town just before we cross the Queen's Bridge to begin the day's walk, Javier invites me into a café for a morning coffee. This invitation serves several purposes. It allows us politely to extricate ourselves from the company of others, and it's Javier's way of asking that we walk together to the day's goal, the town of Estella.

Javier, my Spanish friend, is a banker with a wife and kids. He's in his forties, bald, with tufts of graying hair above the ears, and possessed of a lanky body riven with restless tics. Javier is anxious to talk. He confesses that he has longed to walk the road all his life. Then, quietly and sweetly, he describes himself as a lifelong Catholic who is earnestly shaken by the vicious history of all organized religions.

"Every year," he tells me, "I reread three books—the Bible, Plato's *Republic,* and the writings of Marcus Aurelius. That is my religion. Everything a man needs to know is in those three books."

"That's as good a canon as any I could devise," I quip, and throw my hands up in the air. But I miss the solemnity of what has just happened. For a good Catholic boy who grew up to become a respected Pamplonan banker, his words are heresy: he is denying the world of a hundred generations of his Spanish ancestors. I try to make up for my flippancy by shaking my head with grave concern, but now there is nothing but silence.

Javier has a wandering eye, and in the contemplative haze of his confession, it cuts loose, strays inward, and disappears. His other eye locks on to the view of the road out the window while he finishes his *café con leche.* Javier is a sincere man whose earnestness is so pure that it is impossible not to be moved by the gravity of his pilgrimage. He longs to convince himself of his own ideas.

He asks me why I am walking the road.

"I used to know," I tell him with a nervous guffaw, "before I started."

He understands this awkward evasion. "Let's walk," he says, and hoists his pack on his back.

Not far on the other side of town, a farmer approaches us and seeks the blessing of passing pilgrims.

"Please, when you arrive in Santiago, ask Saint James to deliver us from the socialists. They are taxing me to death. I can't run my farm. See if you can get González out of office." (Felipe González is the socialist prime minister of Spain who is universally denounced by left- and right-wing voters and then always reelected.)

Javier and the farmer trade obscene epithets for the prime minister, and then the farmer tells us that we reek like a shut barn. He says that pilgrims smell worse than any ruminant he knows. From his front yard garden he rips out two long sprigs of mint, fashions each into a loop, and hangs one around each of our necks. Then he pops the stem backward and ties it off so that the top spray of mint points back to our noses like a microphone.

"See, now you don't have to smell yourselves. It's the greatest gift I have for pilgrims. Hug the apostle, and pray for lower taxes," he says, steering us back onto the road.

According to the old tradition of the road, when a pilgrim arrives in the cathedral in Santiago, he embraces a statue of Saint James and asks for the fulfillment of the wishes of all the people who helped him on the road. Javier swears he will hug Saint James and ask for lower taxes. But neither of them seems especially confident in the apostle's power against the collusions of González and the European Economic Community.

Javier walks at twice the speed I do, and I struggle to keep pace. Of course, his backpack is considerably smaller—a sleeping bag, a change of clothes, and a small toilet kit. He hasn't any of the high-tech machinery I am lugging—tent, mess kit, inflatable air mattress, tube of Instant Fire. And he is a model of contemporary denial. At lunch in a small town, I want to sit down to a plate of lamb chops and greasy Spanish fries, maybe half a carafe of red wine. Javier, though, wins the day. We sit on a rock beneath a tree on an empty plain, throw down a fistful of shelled pistachios, gulp a quart of water, and move on.

To Javier, all unnecessary distractions violate the spirit of the road. I acquiesce in the presence of someone whose certainty of what he's doing is so thorough and convincing.

By two P.M. the sun is slaying me. I'm a redheaded, ruddy-faced six-footer of Viking stock. The unfiltered heat of midday in a freshly plowed field reacts with my skin like a barbiturate. I am groggy, unsteady, and weepy. In order to persuade Javier to rest under the occasional tree, I must nag or cry. He has the tawny skin of a Basque, and his restless energy allows him to insult me with helpful folklore, such as "The best remedy for fatigue is to keep walking in the heat."

Up over a ridge, Estella appears as winsomely as her name—the Star. Like so many on the road, this city was founded by French clerics during the Middle Ages. Several French orders benefited from the road, but first among them all was the Abbey of Cluny, which built many of the monasteries and cities along the way. The Gallic presence here was so entrenched and long-standing that until the mid-1700s the street language of Estella was French.

The yellow arrows for the last half mile into the city are all visible from a ridge. They point straight down a deep gorge in the sloped fields behind a farmhouse and then direct the pilgrim up a zagging route to the edge of town. The asphalt highway, meanwhile, winds upward gently, following the path of least sweat to the city gates. Without even thinking, I step onto the highway. Javier calls out.

"The arrows point this way," he says.

"Yeah, but this road is a bit easier, and I am beat."

"But this is the way of the yellow arrows."

"Javier, those yellow arrows are simply an attempt to keep us off the highway. Look where they go. Down into the gorge and back up. It's essentially someone's driveway."

There is no question that I am right. Most of the road suggested by the arrow painters is authentically the old cart routes between towns. But, very often, one can sense that the arrow painters are just trying to keep us away from automobile traffic. Normally I would accept this intention as well meaning and follow them without question. But not today.

"Javier this is make-work. Why climb down into a valley and back up a steep hill when we don't need to?"

"These are the yellow arrows. This is the road." He can't break away from the stern authority of the arrows.

"Do you believe that this long driveway is really the old road?" I ask. The thing is, Javier doesn't want to walk down there, either. He wants some cold water and a rest. A solid day of walking and sweating is enough. But he can't convince himself.

"This is the road," he says with a crack in his voice.

"Listen, Javier, do you really think that this is the road? Or is it more likely that the ancient route that approached Estella was widened into a merchant's road and then in the twentieth century was paved into this highway? I assert, Javier, that the true *true* road is, in fact, this highway. Medieval pilgrims wouldn't have just walked into this gorge. They'd follow the main road into town. From this point into town, the highway *is* the true old authentic actual real pilgrim road."

Javier is tortured by my logic. On the one hand he knows I am right. Yet somehow my observations are in conflict with his desire for the true road and the deeper reasons he has for being here. My logic may be clear, but it makes him feel bad. In the end, he is too tired, and he yields. Without comment he stomps off up the highway. It's almost as if he *knew* the truth of what I said but would have preferred that I had never spoken it out loud.

For a moment I feel righteous with my arguments. I have challenged the authenticity of the yellow arrows, the guidebooks, and the unseen experts. Am I not closer to a truth as it might be sung by boozy serfs? Am I not listening to the song of history rather than reading its words? Sure. But when Javier buys me a Coke at the local bar, he's sullen and quiet. I am suddenly stricken with guilt, as if I have tempted a small boy from attending mass with a raincoat full of porno pictures. Javier and I eat a terse dinner in Estella that night. When I awaken the next morning, he is gone. I search the logical places. But it's obvious. He slipped out of town before dawn.

FOUR
TORRES DEL RÍO

A good week into this walk, past Pamplona, the road winds through ragged ugly plains, broken up by a brutal hill or distant ridge. Between the tiny stone villages is the pilgrim's road, a trail of dusty clods of soil occasionally overtaken by swatches of volunteer wheat. One morning I spend hours trying to find a puddle of shade beneath a tree. The infamous Spanish sun appears twice its normal size. In these parts the old pilgrim's road overlaps the uninhabited corridor where earlier authorities strung heavy electrical lines, thick as ship's rope. The bulky cables sizzle like agitated crickets.

Relief does come occasionally, and the pilgrim is tempted to find in the slightest variation of his suffering a sign or a portent. In a fierce heat, I arrive in Los Arcos. I locate the town fountain and plunge my head up to my shoulders directly in the water. I plop down to a lunch of tepid plums when a group of old men and women signals me over. They are cooking homemade chorizo and fresh bread over a few cinders on the hot stone street.

I wouldn't mention these coincidences except that they arrive almost expectedly—as if the suffering of the day entitles me to stumble upon a cookout in town or, another time, a family who takes me in. One extraordinary coincidence takes place with comforting frequency. Outside of Azqueta, I can find no arrow at an intersection of two country roads. Out of nowhere, an old Dodge Valiant appears at the corner. A Spanish man hangs his head out the window. "Pilgrim," he advises, "continue straight ahead."

Farther down the road, a grassy path seems up to no good. Upon approach, a pleasant looking tree has a rotting dog, wearing death's sinister smile, wedged into the crotch of two limbs. Farther on, an oily bog is inhabited by huge frogs that bark like wild beasts. The landscape is otherwise deceptively barren and unwelcoming. The locals grow white asparagus. This Spanish delicacy is achieved by piling up dirt around each protruding plant so that the sun and the chlorophyll never interact, yielding thick white juicy stalks. In the bars they are delicious, but fields of them resemble rows of freshly filled mass graves. Again the path diverges, and there is no arrow. A man on a bicycle pops into existence. "Pilgrim," he says, "take the road to the right," and disappears.

By midafternoon, on a day more grueling and punishingly hot than the last, I enter the village of Sansol, which seems to mean Holy Sun. There are no open bars or shops. One man working on a truck suggests that if I'm looking for water or bread, I should press on down the next vale and up the hill to Torres del Río. The time for siesta has arrived and slowed everything, including me, to a near standstill. I can't go on, but I have no choice. At the edge of Sansol, during a momentary confusion about the road, a woman materializes on a tiny crumbling porch and directs me to the shortest route.

Torres del Río is misnamed. It means Towers on the River. There is no river, and the only toweresque thing is a stumpy church steeple. The squib in my guidebook says that this town is so often short of water that the locals store it up during the winter for summer use. I can find no fountain. It is three P.M., and the heat and sun are crippling. No one stirs. I have not seen a human being.

Everything in town is built of the same yellow stone, so that the squat yellow houses rise up from the yellow bricked streets like baked goods. The air makes a rasping noise, as if it were scratching the hot stones. I see a Spanish widow, dressed in the familiar black weeds, disappear around a corner. I dash to catch her, but with the weight of my pack I turn to stare down an empty cul-de-sac. A dog occupying the only smudge of shade beneath a stone bench snarls territorially when I pass.

I grow paranoid in these conditions. I sense that people are hiding behind their heavy wooden shades, peeping at me through the cracks. A German tour bus—strange to see—idles along one street, belching waves of heat. I gesture, but the driver motions me to move on. From behind the tinted glass windows, a bright red Teutonic face stares at me as she pulls herself into a coat. The Mercedes air-conditioning must be too chilly.

At last I come upon a group of kids, Torres del Río's version of the Wild Bunch. One boy is scarred menacingly on his cheek. The girls are dressed sluttily, an attempt at heavy metal rebellion. They sulkily direct me to the bar.

It is closed, of course. My fingers drag on the glass door because the air-conditioning within has caused lovely droplets of condensation to form on the door. I press the side of my face to the glass. I shout for the owner. But in the scorched stillness and stony acoustics of Torres del Río, my ample voice is useless.

One of the miracles chronicled in the old books speaks of five eleventh-century knights who swore to accompany each other on the road. When one named Noriberto fell ill, a testy debate ended with three of the knights walking on. Felix, the fourth knight, stayed behind to care for the sick knight. After Noriberto had rested, he got up to walk. Moments later Saint James appeared from the sky on horseback, swept up the two noble pilgrims, and flew them to Santiago.

This story may sound like harmless myth, a quaint hallucination from the collective mind of desperately tired people. But in the unforgiving sun of the road, impossibility segues easily into improbability, melts into uncanniness, and then registers as quite likely. The pilgrim goes over the details of the story just one more time. Exactly what was it Felix and Noriberto did to get a lift?

On foot, a pilgrim finds that his mind can get so blurred by the stroke-inducing sunshine that in his reverie he almost believes that he can control these coincidences. Wish hard enough, and that horse will gallop right up. On several occasions I have eaten all the food in my pack, opened it, and found that my stash has reappeared. Empty bottles of water have filled themselves. Money has appeared when I had none. On precisely those occasions when I was out of hard currency and hungry, strangers have offered me meals without prompting. I could go on.

Standing outside the cold door to the closed bar, I fish through my pockets, looking for money. I intend to wait for the bar to open. Among my coins I feel a piece of paper. On it is written, "Torres del Río. Casa Santa Bárbara." A few days ago, somebody—a pilgrim, a bartender, a monk, I honestly cannot remember—wrote down the address of this residence because the owner offers help to pilgrims. A few more days in this heat and I would be swearing that the piece of paper just appeared there. Saint James.

The Wild Bunch directs me to a street on the edge of town. Casa Santa Bárbara is a stunning mansion, a wide boxy symmetry of two-story windows. I've struck it rich. A set of hedges frames an impressive entrance of twin doors. Every inch of the yellow stone is blanketed in luxuriously green ivy. Above the doors is a colorful tile depicting Santa Bárbara, the patroness of military artillery. On the ground is a curled wrought-iron boot scrape. I use it and then knock.

The door opens swiftly to frame the extravagant figure of Ramón Sostres. "I am El Ramón," he says. His hands and arms are outstretched like Il Duce's, and his sense of drama makes his simple Spanish translate more accurately: "I am the One and Only Ramón." Which indeed he is.

He is a tall man for this part of Spain, with a head of hair that appears cut in a single slice of hedge clippers. It stands wildly on end, as if he had managed to sleep on all of it. But who can notice this man's hair after looking him in the eye? The right one caroms around the socket like a billiard ball, studying every inch of his guest. The other is parked madly in the corner near his nose, a small wedge of black. No pupil. Just one-half of a pair of crossed eyes. His laughter has the staccato rhythms of Woody Woodpecker. Droplets of saliva leap from lip to lip as he talks excitedly. He is dressed in thick hot flannel, bedroom slippers, and several shirts and sweater. I stand dripping with perspiration and look at him again. A *sweater.*

The Amazing Ramón steps into his foyer. It is a neatly tiled room, touched up by an Italian table and some thin, modern looking chairs. I drop my pack. There is no air-conditioning on anywhere. Yet, when Ramón taps open his interior door, a lovely soft breeze, as if beckoned, sweeps around him. Soon this small room is as frigid as a cave. I collapse gratefully onto a chair while Ramón buttons his sweater.

I needn't call El Ramón a miracle because he is more than happy to do that for me. This is the language that he uses, occasionally punctuating my disbelief at what he says with, "El Ramón is a miracle, is he not?" He is a former literature professor from Barcelona who moved into this house after priests left sixteen years ago. He assumed the tradition of caring for pilgrims.

"I have kept as many as fifty pilgrims in my house at one time. One pilgrim miraculously conceived here," he says, his right eye exploding in ribald ricochets. He makes an O with his left hand and runs his right forefinger in and out of it to let me know he's aware of the miracle's true source. The Amazing Ramón likes to talk a little dirty.

"The baby was born in Santiago, and his mother called him Jacobeo—James. He began his life here! Right here! Where you will stay!"

I have other things on my mind just now, so I ask Ramón where the bathroom is located.

"Ramón is a pilgrim, too. My backyard is large and welcoming," he says. His eyeball does a three sixty, and a mischievous grin unfurls across his face.

"No, no, you don't understand," I venture as tactfully as possible. "I'm not in need of a bush or a tree. My problem is more . . . serious." A wincing tightens my features, and language is unnecessary. A two-year-old would understand me.

Ramón disappears momentarily, returns, and plunges a sheaf of waxy European toilet papers into my chest. He points again to his backyard. I accept his gift and tell him that I will give the matter some thought.

Ramón escorts me through the foyer to the first door on the left, the pilgrims' quarters. As my eyes adjust to the penumbra of the extremely dim light, I find myself in a room illuminated by a single low-watt bulb dangling on a fraying cord. The paint has not been touched since this was someone's elegant drawing room a century ago. The place is empty except for a few discarded car seats, filthied with the hideous smudge of too many sweaty backs and rear ends.

Ramón is far from being a rich man. He shows me the washroom, a short walk to the rear. It is dank, with a few spigots jutting too far out of blasted holes. The air spangles with flecks of plaster floating in beams of light that radiate through cracks in the walls. There is a cracked tub covered in grime, above which hangs a brittle green garden hose. Water leaks from its crumbling mouth. Out of some residual sense of courtesy, I wash my hands.

Ramón tells me to make myself at home and disappears upstairs. I hear the crises of a soap opera blare from a distant television. Those late afternoon agonies are recognizable in any language. I hear Ramón clinking glasses and then the voice of a young woman. I feel slightly embarrassed that I have imposed on him during a tryst.

I am exhausted from the day and the heat. Back in the pilgrims' room, I unroll my bedding, read half a sentence in a book, and disappear. An hour of turbulent dreams ends when the bad guys suspend me across a slim canyon. My head and feet bridge a six-foot-wide abyss. Below me, certain death.

Tied around my hips is a rope from which dangles a great weight. I struggle to keep this heaviness from tugging me downward to my death when I awaken in a cold sweat of extreme urgency. I skittle about on all fours, searching for Ramón's gift, and bolt out the door.

In Ramón's backyard, I discover why his house could keep so cool in the cruel midday heat. Almost all of this mansion, except for the elegant facade, has collapsed into itself. As I venture farther and farther toward the rear, I stumble upon an old underground bodega, whose ground cover has crashed through. The front rooms are as cold as a cave because, in a sense, that is what they are, buried beneath stone and beams and walls. I can see the hose from the bathroom snaking out a cardboarded window and across piles of rubble to a well. The house has no plumbing. Outside one second-story window, an antenna, strangely reminiscent of Ramón, pokes ludicrously in all directions.

In a corner of the yard amid a thicket of bushes and weeds, I find a tidy private corner, somewhat hidden from view. I would guess that I am standing in what might have been a kitchen nook. The sun is blazing hot. Sweat is streaming down my face and arms. Decorum and nature battle mightily here. Decorum, needless to say, surrenders. From a window, Ramón's silhouette passes by several times. He and his friend are hooting now. And the hilarity won't end. She tells a joke and he honks with laughter. He speaks and a witch's cackle explodes. There's something disconcerting about these sounds, but I can't quite finger it. Suddenly weird howls of hysteria fill the air.

As I prepare to leave for my late afternoon walk, Ramón appears downstairs and again offers the only real thing he has: water. He would be pleased if I would let him ink my passport with his very own "Ramón" stamp. He walks me down the street and sends me on my way. Saying good-bye to the miracle of Ramón, I am suddenly awakened by a revelation that would have been obvious long ago to someone not suffering early onset of sunstroke. Ramón and his girlfriend had different voices but came from the same source. There is no friend.

The Amazing Ramón seems gently, benevolently, but, in the end, completely insane.

Most of the recorded miracles that took place on this road aren't all that different from finding Ramón's address in my pocket or feeling the magical breeze in his foyer. They are often modest stories, such as the tale of the five knights, that show good pilgrims being rewarded or evil innkeepers being punished.

The most famous miracle of the road happened at a spot three days' walk from El Ramón in the town of Santo Domingo de la Calzada. The town is named for a monk who devoted his life to building pilgrim roads and means, literally, Saint Dominick of the Highway.

The miracle of this area occurred in the fourteenth century. One day, a pilgrim family—father, mother, and son—arrived in Santo Domingo. At the inn where they stayed, the owner's daughter developed a crush on the boy or, in the words of the sixteenth-century Englishman Andrew Boorde, "for ther was a wenche the whych wolde haue had hym to medyll with her carnally." But the boy's virtue could not be compromised while he walked. (Which is a miracle itself; one of the oldest sayings of the road—*Ir romero y volver ramera*—translates "Start out a pilgrim, return a whore.") Angry at being scorned, the girl slipped a silver cup in the boy's rucksack. When the family was leaving town, she informed the local authorities of the theft. Chased down, the boy proclaimed his innocence, but he was sentenced to death and hanged from a tree at the edge of town.

The grieving parents walked on to Santiago to fulfill their pledge. On their return trip, as they approached Santo Domingo, they could still see the silhouette of their son's body dangling from a branch. (In some parts of Europe, the indignity of a death sentence was rounded out by leaving the body to rot out of the rope.) As they neared the tree, though, they could see their son moving. He spoke right up, explaining that their dutiful journey to Santiago had won James's heart. The saint had returned the boy's life and then held him up by the arms until their return. To us, perhaps, a pretty serious miracle. But in the Middle Ages, various states of unconsciousness were thought to be "death," so resurrection was actually common. The story continues.

The parents ran to the town mayor and insisted that he come and see what had happened. The mayor, always depicted in paintings as a portly, well-fed bureaucrat, was seated at his dinner table, ready to cut into two hot roasted chickens. He dismissed the parents as insane and complained that their crying was interrupting his meal. Annoyed at their persistence, he finally shouted, "Your boy can no more be alive than these chickens could get up and crow!"

Immediately, the main course stirred. The roasters kicked away the garnishes and vegetables. They stretched their plucked brown wings. They squawked and danced across the table. The boy was cut down and the miracle proclaimed. The story of resurrected chickens had a profound tug on the medieval mind. Hundreds of versions of the miracle—dead and dancing fowl—can be found throughout Europe, and paintings of Santo Domingo's chickens can be seen as far east as Uberlingen and Rothenburg ob der Tauber.

We moderns have a hard time enjoying miracles. Whenever a miracle makes a public splash nowadays, it suffers from a comical absence of gravitas. Just before I left America, crowds were gathering near an Atlanta franchise of Jiffy Lube, where a Pizza Hut billboard depicted an uplifted forkful of spaghetti and meat sauce. Some said the mouthful of spaghetti looked like the postcard image of Jesus.

The miracles of the road are simple tales in which pilgrims best those out to harm them. The meaning of the story of the dancing chickens is not difficult to figure out. Another miracle tells of a pilgrim who asks a woman if he can share her bread which was baking beneath a hot stone. She lies and says there isn't any, and after the pilgrim departs, she upends the stone to find that her loaf has disappeared. The miracles of the early history of the road and those that predated the pilgrimage throughout Europe are charming tales of what we might call coincidence, like the constant appearance of the stranger on the road who gives me directions. Miracles were those occasions when circumstances conspired to shatter one's preconceptions. They were times of joyful surprise, moments of pleasure. The word *miracle* comes from the Latin *mirari*, which means to look upon in wonder. In its etymology lies the warmer meaning of this word. *Mirari* also came into English as "smile."

The earliest understanding of miracles was quite simple. St. Augustine, writing five hundred years before the pilgrimage, said there was only one miracle—creation. Every other extraordinary occurrence we encounter is merely a ripple emanating from this original miracle. At times, Augustine's thinking sounds modern. "All natural things are filled with the miraculous," he once wrote. His commentary would make excellent poster copy for contemporary environmentalists: "For consider changes of day and night, the very constant order of heavenly bodies, the fourfold change of the seasons, the fall of leaves and their return to the trees the following spring, the infinite power in seeds, the beauty of light, and the varieties of colors, sounds, smells, and tastes; and then give me a man who sees and experiences these things for the first time, with whom we can still talk—he is amazed and overwhelmed at these miracles."

Miracles were small epiphanies that confounded our expectation of nature and creation. Augustine lists dozens of them: there is the magnet that "by some insensible power of suction attracts iron, though it will not stir a straw." Isn't that a miracle? How about fire, which burns a stone white yet blackens almost everything else? Or the chaff of grain that, when piled on something cold such as snow, keeps it cold yet also holds in warmth?

Augustine tries to convince his readers that miracles are delightful, even humorous, moments of surprise that open up a new way of looking at things. His account of the miracle healing of Innocentius, the modern reader suspects, is written as much for laughs as for awe.

Innocentius was a well-off man in Carthage, Augustine explains, who "was under treatment for fistulas [a kind of abscess], having a number of them intertwined in the rectum, and others more deep-seated." The doctors had already performed "surgery"—a word whose exact meaning in fourth-century North Africa I am not sure can even be imagined. The doctors said that they hadn't cut out all the fistulas and would have to return with the knife. Innocentius called together all the holy men of the area, including the bishop of Hippo, for a prayer meeting. In deadpan prose, St. Augustine reports the occasion:

> Then we betook ourselves to prayers; and when we knelt down, in the usual way, and bent toward the ground, Innocentius hurled himself forward, as if someone had pushed him flat on his face; and he began to pray. It is beyond the power of words to express the manner of his prayer, his passion, his agitation, his flood of tears, his groans, and the sobs which shook his whole frame and almost stifled his breath. Whether the others were praying, whether they could take their attention from him, I could not tell; for my part, I was utterly unable to utter a prayer, all I could do was to say this brief sentence in my heart, "Lord, what prayers of your people do you hear, if you do not hear these?"

When the doctors examined the patient before cutting, the fistulas had miraculously disappeared. There were celebrations all around.

Augustine's broad, even sentimental view of miracles makes sense if you *don't* think about it too much. Strict analysis of miracles leads to difficult questions. What about the miracles in the Bible? Those were not gentle surprises or moments of serendipity. They were specific actions conjured up by holy men. Augustine explained these better than average miracles by arguing that they were intended to get people's attention in the early days. When pressed on one occasion, Augustine replied, almost with irritation: "Why, you ask, do such things not occur now? Because they would not move people, unless they were miraculous, and, if they were customary, they would not be miraculous."

So Augustine identified the contradiction of imposing too

much meaning on simple coincidence. He strove to keep wonders and signs from being so burdened. He worried about those who became too enthusiastic over miracles. "They worship every bit of dust from the Holy Land," he sneered. But miracles had the power to excite the public mind. If they were meaningful actions by the divine, then they conveniently confirmed a worldview that was powerfully different from the pagan's. Life was not just a whirlwind of chaos in which the best hope was to appease the anger of the gods. Rather, the world was a harmony, with a just god at the center dispensing miracles as gifts to the good.

The public desperately believed in miracles. But once you've leapt to the belief that miracles are intentional acts meant to convey a specific meaning, it is not difficult to pass on to an assumption with more serious implications: miracles did not happen spontaneously, they could be *summoned* by those on really good terms with the divine. This belief gradually overtook everyone, even Augustine.

One day a sick man approached the bishop of Hippo and begged for a touch to heal some serious ailments. Augustine demurred with a joke. "If I had the gift you say I have," he said, "I would be the first to try it on myself." But when the man failed to laugh, Augustine could no longer refuse. He laid his hands upon the old man.

Perhaps that moment was a turning point. If better than average miracles helped found the church during the earliest days, Augustine now reasoned, then maybe miracles in his day were meant to *expand* the numbers of the faithful. What he had once tenderly described as a private joy, an intimate delight between a believer and nature, became a public affair. As it happened, this shift occurred just at the time the organized church was pondering a different problem.

Before the Roman emperor Constantine converted to Christianity in the fourth century, it was easy to identify a saint. They were martyrs—the ones who bravely proclaimed their faith when they knew it meant suicide. Obviously these were special people. After Constantine converted, though, the imposition of death on Christians was lifted. Martyrdoms declined precipitously. Without hideous suffering and death as the sign of a saint, what would become the standard? This vacuum appeared at practically the same time that miracles were becoming more public and more accepted as purposeful signs. The two trends merged perfectly, the one becoming the measure of the other. Did the potential saint have a special relationship with the divine? Well, could he perform miracles?

At first, this ad hoc solution seemed tidy. But the dynamic caused problems. Originally there were no rules. Miracles just happened—they were spontaneous events at the local level. Yet for precisely that reason, they presented a problem to a centralized organization. In Rome, the task of controlling the outbreak of miracles and streamlining their meaning became a thousand-year nightmare.

The central authorities tried several remedies. They appointed the local bishops to take responsibility for affirming the authenticity of miracles. Over time, this system grew more strict. Several papal initiatives eventually pushed the final authority all the way to the top. In 993, Pope John XV declared Ulric of Augsburg the first papal saint.

Clearly, this process was going to require a lot more work. Miracles would have to be reported in certain ways. There would need to be witnesses who would have to be interviewed by proper authorities. Depositions would have to be consistent. Paperwork and clerks were needed in Rome. Reports of miracles assumed the tone of legal briefs. The confirmation of miracles became an official proceeding. A devil's advocate was appointed to make the opposing case. Committees screened at the local level, and loftier commissions in Rome screened the committees' work, until the confirmation of miracles meant the pope had to sit down before a file of position papers. This institutionalization began to resemble any human bureaucracy, and thus the formality of adding someone to the list or canon of saints became a process, still called to this day by its bureaucratic name: canonization.

In this century, the paperwork required to consider Pope John XXIII for sainthood filled twenty-five, three-hundred-page volumes.

But problems still remained with the locals. Rome wanted miracles to serve as Sunday school lessons or examples of personal piety. But the masses longed for big, vulgar miracles. They wanted their crops to grow, their child's withered arm to heal, maybe some money. On the local level miracles exploded all over Europe, despite the best efforts of the authorities to rein them in. Many of the miracles recorded during the Middle Ages continue to echo the charming innocence first noted by Augustine. Saint Thomas Aquinas, the thirteenth-century theologian, was renowned for levitating about two cubits (three feet) off the floor. There were kings who could rub the heads of serfs and cure scrofula—the origin of "the royal touch." A group of nuns once prayed on their heads. Miraculously, their skirts clung tastefully about their ankles.

But the proliferation meant miracles became increasingly weird and grotesque. In effect, each generation of them had to be more outrageous and bizarre than the last in order to sustain attention.

Peter Martyr was confronted by a woman whose son was born without any features or limbs. He was described as a breathing piece of meat. By the touch of Peter's hand, the child assumed the shape of a human being.

St. Bernard of Clairvaux once excommunicated flies from a church.

A man named Withbert went to Conques. Both of his eyeballs had tumbled out of their sockets, and before Withbert could retrieve them, two birds swooped down and plucked them away. Several years later the birds returned and popped them into Withbert's eye sockets. His sight was restored.

Adelheid of Katharinental saw Christ appear one day, tear the palm from his hand and present it as a eucharist.

Lukardis of Oberweimar pounded his middle finger against the palm of his other hand, making a hammering noise, until he had driven through it and miraculously produced stigmata.

When Beatrice of Ornacieux did the same thing with an iron nail, the stigmata did not bleed but ran with clear water.

A nun named Angela of Foligno sipped the open wounds of lepers and found the drink "as sweet as communion."

A teenager named Christina was said to be so poor she had nothing to give up except food. She lived in the desert on nothing. Miraculously her "dry virgin breasts" filled with milk, and she fed off them.

Giovanni Colombini had a chamber pot that issued a lovely fragrance upon his death. Many locals believed that the contents would work wonders. One woman rubbed the odoriferous feces on a facial disfigurement and prayed for a cure. Strangely, the miraculous perfume was swept away and was replaced by its customary aroma. The church elders explained that this occurred because the woman's intentions were born out of vanity. Colombini's chamber pot was a miracle with dual lessons.

Some miracles were meant to reveal a divine sense of humor, perhaps a vestige of those early wonders. These miracles were called the *joca sanctorum,* jokes of the saints, which put on display the medieval virtue of *hilaritas.* Like most humor writing, it doesn't age well. One miracle concerned some children who hid a block of cheese, lost it, prayed, and found it. Guess you had to be there. Yet given the intense solemnity of most miracles, these jokes found their audiences. Odo of Cluny was the class clown of the Middle Ages whose miraculous *joca sanctorum* could make other clergy "laugh until [they] cried, and were unable to speak to one another."

Throughout the Middle Ages, the clergy knew that they had backed themselves into a corner. They realized that the expectation of miracles was so high that their absence could pose problems. In eleventh-century Fleury, a mason working on a new church fell and seriously injured himself. The monks began to pray excitedly because, as one wrote, "We were afraid that if he died, the whole building program would be interrupted as a result of a sudden fall in contributions to the building fund."

Increasingly, the contradiction of miracles was becoming apparent. Thomas of Monmouth, the author of the paperwork forwarded to Rome on behalf of St. Thomas of Canterbury, wrote, "But as each miracle follows the last and the astonishing is succeeded by the spectacular, I must take care to restrain my enthusiasm, or else the piety of my readers will be dampened by the tedium of reading so many marvels."

The proliferation of miracles had trapped medieval thinkers on an intellectual Möbius strip. What was a miracle? It became more and more difficult to say. Caesarius of Heisterbach wrote, "We speak of a miracle whenever anything is done contrary to the normal course of nature at which we marvel." But Thomas Aquinas wrote that the Creator "does nothing contrary to nature." Augustine had tried to prevent this debate by acknowledging the contradiction inherent in divine miracles. But now that the discussion was seriously engaged, only ridicule would end it.

In 1748, David Hume's essay "Of Miracles" halted the debate by stating a blunt truth: "But it is nothing strange, I hope, that men should lie in all ages." In the current Catholic encyclopedia, Hume's position is scorned as "superficial." Indeed, but it was enough.

What happened to the idea of miracles is that it got saddled with too much meaning. Augustine's small private pleasure was creation's constant reminder—often funny—that there are always new ways of imagining things. This simple idea was burdened with a lot of heavy lifting, and a complex administration was set up long ago to manage miracles and their meaning.

The functionaries of this bureaucracy, who first took their seats around the time of Charlemagne, continue at their desks. Canonization is still carried out in Rome. Today to be a saint, a man or woman needs two proven miracles. It used to be four, but the church quietly reduced the requirement in 1983. From time to time in Rome, a board called the Consulta Medica convenes. Since all miracles these days are those of healing, this commission is composed of nothing but Italian doctors. They review the files of miracles to determine authenticity. Each doctor is paid roughly $250 per miracle, rejected or affirmed. According to the Vatican, the average number of miracles authenticated annually is fifteen.

Saint Dominick of the Highway taught his craft to other monks. Two days past Santo Domingo, I enter San Juan de

Ortega. This town is named for Santo Domingo's most famous student, who also picked up his master's sensibility for epithets. San Juan de Ortega means, literally, Saint John of the Stinging Nettle.

For centuries San Juan was an oasis in the scrub forests of Burgos Province, a thriving pilgrim hub famous among my predecessors for uncommon generosity. Over time, the town boasted a beautiful church, a full monastery, and a convent. In the late seventeenth and early eighteenth centuries, the place ran out of money and respect. One of the many waves of anticlerical fury washed the last monks and nuns from the area. The abandoned cathedral, with its high ceiling and cavernous stone niches, was adopted by the local farmers as a hay barn. Today six or seven descendents of those farmers are all who live here.

A few other pilgrims—the Frenchman Louis, a young Italian fellow named Paolo, the two dull Dutchmen and a Swiss man—have converged here this afternoon. All of us have gathered out front of the old monastery and hear the story of this place, told by Father José Marie. A part-time resident, he has personally presided over San Juan's rescue and rehabilitation. José Marie is a part-time priest at five churches in this region. But he's been working on San Juan for decades, cadging a few pesetas from pilgrims, flattering tourists until they poke a bill in his offertory box, and hounding the federal government in Madrid to come forward with some historic preservation money. Coin by coin, he has saved the church. The old monastery has been partly converted into an impressive pilgrims' shelter. The rotting convent next door awaits future work—a sideshow of smashed walls, rooms exposed to the elements, and high weeds sprouting from cracks.

José Marie is an extraordinarily short man with a throw-pillow paunch. He has the face of a smoker, although he isn't one. Euclidian lines and angles are etched deep into dark skin. His face looks like a crumpled paper bag.

He's a restless man, always in motion, rearranging himself. He slides and clicks his feet, tapping the stone floors with his loafers, forever in search of a comfortable position. His introductory banter is a friendly questioning, yet he barely waits for answers.

"Where are you from? No, let me guess.

"Where did you start?

"How long have you been walking?

"Isn't San Juan the best pilgrim stop on the road?"

His hands slip in and out of his pockets. Items are extracted and forced to re-up in the continuing odyssey of objects orbiting his body. Keys appear from his pants, are fiddled, and then are secreted inside his sports jacket. A knife emerges, opens, and closes before disappearing behind his back. He checks his shirt buttons and his collar. An envelope is examined, read, and then dispatched to a new location. While talking, José Marie steps outside the building for no reason. All of us follow and rearrange our group around him, and then he moves again.

"Come, come, come, let me show you," he says, hastily waving a few of us into the church. A pilgrim gets to see a lot of churches, so by now standards are pretty high. José Marie shows us the ornate sepulcher of San Juan himself. And he tells us the story of one of San Juan's miracles, which ends with a pilgrim opening his empty rucksack and finding a loaf of bread. Knowing nods are exchanged.

Near the nave he directs our attention to a finely carved capital of the Annunciation. As amateurs in Romanesque architecture, we admire its pristine condition. Being nearly a thousand years old, it's in better condition than any I have seen on the road. José Marie explains that because the church spent a century or two stuffed with hay, a great deal of the destructive water was soaked up. The paradox of neglect, he explains, is that it bequeathed to him a church of unmatched preservation.

José Marie's smile draws open to show a big, perfectly arranged display of ivory dice. He has an overcompensating grin, the kind that tries too hard and is common among priests and TV hosts. But his schtick, this energetic gregariousness, is tempered by an amusing intelligence, and it's tough not to cotton to him. José Marie points to a window and says that for many, many years in the old days, the pilgrims walked the road and tried to time their arrivals to San Juan de Ortega on the day of the equinox in March and September.

"On those two days," José Marie says in an exaggerated hush, "when the length of the day and the night are exactly the same, at five P.M. precisely, a single ray of light spills over the bottom of that arched window there and illuminates the capital of the Annunciation perfectly from corner to corner." From a pocket he produces a postcard photograph of the capital bathed in a soft squared golden light. The postcards are for sale.

"Look at this," he cries. José Marie is handing out glow-in-the-dark rosary beads. He puts one near a lamp and then cups it inside his sports jacket. Each of us is obliged to put our head inside his coat to see the glowing beads.

"Think of what we could have done with these—in the old days." His eyes light up mischievously.

José Marie invites us to dine with him tonight and then sends us to our quarters to get washed up. They are extravagant by pilgrim standards. Huge rooms with great windows. Comfortable beds. Expansive bathrooms. Hot and cold running water. Even makeshift laundry facilities—a place to wash and, crisscrossing the cloister, drying lines on pulleys pinched by clothespins. There is even a sitting room for pilgrims to relax—comfortable chairs, side tables, clean ashtrays.

After we wash up, we return to the center of action to find José Marie chatting with tourists who have driven out of the way to see the old church and monastic buildings.

From across the way, we see José Marie at work. He greets the only woman in the group by taking her hand, bowing grandly, and madly kissing the back of his own palm.

It is difficult to maintain any cynicism in the face of such cornpone. This is Father José Marie, and he knows what works. At the end of the afternoon, he will ask these tourists for a donation, and they will give amply. The show is vaudeville, but he does well with what he can.

"How many stars do our accommodations have?" he shouts to us as we walk up.

"Four, four stars," each of us cries in our competing tongues.

"No. One star. There is only one star," says José Marie.

"No, no. Four," comes the response. Louis the Frenchman looks at me, and I look at a Paolo. The Dutchmen and the Swiss guy—all of us—exchange wide-eyed glances to underscore our sincerity. We *mean* it: San Juan is debauchery, luxury, flowers on the table, mint on the pillow.

"Four stars," we insist. "Hot and cold water. Four stars."

José Marie launches one hand straight into the air like a traffic cop. "No, no," he says, and his hand sweeps through the air with the practiced ease of a leggy model showing off a car at a trade convention. Father José Marie finally winds up pointing to the woman. "As long as there is one beautiful woman among us," he says, "all the other stars are dimmed. So there is only one." In five languages, eyes roll.

Before having us to dinner, Father José Marie would like us to attend church. We report to a small chapel off the larger Romanesque church and take our places among a few scattered chairs. Over the altar, early Renaissance paintings by no one particularly famous have been cut out of their frames with a knife sometime earlier in this century. Vandals long ago pried the goldworks from their mounts. Screws and various sconces hang empty all around. Only the relics—glass tubes filled with bones or locks of hair—remain unmolested.

José Marie steps from around the altar and begins the service in Spanish. Paolo nudges me to point out three Spanish widows who have appeared in the back of the chapel. All three are dressed in solid black widow's weeds, with thick wool stockings bunched at their calves and black blocky shoes. Wherever in Spain a church opens, these women appear as if by spontaneous generation. In this town where almost no one lives, in a small service in a side chapel for pilgrims, they have found us.

"You only see them," says Paolo, "in the churches and at the *Once* windows." *Once* is Spain's national lottery.

I nod in agreement.

"Same odds, I suppose," he says.

Dinner is a collection of plates—a plate of bread, of chorizo, of cheese, of ham, another of cheese. José Marie sets out several bottles of a good red wine (this man knows how to eat and drink) and then brings on an enormous pot of his garlic soup. This soup has been the subject of much rumormongering on the road. The Frenchman has declared it to be divine and mysterious. For the rest of the pilgrimage this soup is the source of much speculation. The ingredients are simple—garlic, water, bread. This combination may sound unappetizing or too simple, but it is delicious. José Marie does something with it that no one has cajoled from him. I give it my very best to slip the secret from him—sneaking into the kitchen, cunning conversational gambits—but I get nowhere.

José Marie is witty tonight and full of stories of pilgrims who are just ahead of us—a pilgrim with a monkey, a divorced woman, a barefoot penniless priest, a pilgrim with a fatal disease, a seventy-eight-year-old pilgrim, a pilgrim with a mule, two married pilgrims with their two pilgrim children *and* a mule, a pilgrim on horseback, *negro* pilgrims.

Before any of us knows it, José Marie is launched into the long story of his rescue of San Juan de Ortega. It is a morality play of sorts, with José Marie as the hero. He tells of the day-to-day existence of the rescuer, begging for money. He rehabilitated the church stone by stone. He has built the pilgrims' quarters shower stall by shower stall. It is ongoing and terribly expensive. His story even includes a *refran*—one of the millions of Spanish axioms that pepper all conversation. (On the wall in his kitchen appears Saint Teresa's famous *refrain:* "God can be found among the pots and pans.") José Marie tells us, *"Los palacios son despacios."* More or less: "It takes a long time and a lot of patience to build a palace." José Marie fixes a bead on me.

"The streets are paved with gold in America, no? Isn't one of your car companies Catholic?"

I assume he has read that the head of Chrysler is Lee Iacocca, and presumably he *is* Catholic. I tell José Marie that while the streets are paved with gold all over America, in my neighborhood they are simple asphalt.

"I understand, I understand. But you must go back and tell

people about San Juan and what has been done here. If every pilgrim spreads the word, then my work can continue."

I haven't a dime on me. It's Sunday, and I can't cash a traveler's check. But a few miles up the road, I mail some money back to José Marie. At each pilgrim's stop, I have donated money. It only seems fair. And José Marie seems worthy of more than the usual few pesetas.

Not according to the Dutchmen or the Swiss man, though. Back at the pilgrims' sitting room, they are furious that the sacred moment of a pilgrim's meal was defiled with fund-raising. Perhaps as an American, I don't blanch as quickly at the mention of money.

"The Catholic Church is rich," says one of the Dutchmen, sneering. "Why do they want our money?"

The evening broadens into a general bitch session about the road and eventually arrives at the subject of Ramón Sostres. All these pilgrims have experienced the miracle of the don of Torres del Río. The Swiss man thinks Ramón is a menace and scares people. He says he met half a dozen French girls on the road who stayed there one night, but at three A.M. the whoops and cries from upstairs drove them to pack up and hit the road. I try to defend Ramón. Sure, maybe he's crazy, but he offers pilgrims a cool place to rest and cold water to drink in a town that is otherwise uninviting. He even provides bathroom facilities, after a fashion. Where else but on the road to Santiago could a schizophrenic living in a collapsing mansion find such a fitting use for his fading wits? This earns a harumph from one of the Dutchmen. The Swiss man goes on, talking darkly of multiple personalities, and hints at the possibilities of rape and serial murder. This is the age we live in. He and his friends intend to draft a letter to the Santiago organization that paints the arrows to ask that Ramón no longer be suggested to future pilgrims.

The Swiss man is that kind of fellow. He makes a grand show of piety, but he is a true debunker. While we're talking about the resurrected chickens of Santo Domingo, he assures us that the miracle is a cheap carnival trick. Here's how it's done: Pour a capful of some tasteless alcohol such as vodka into your palm. Feed it to the chicken, which will consume practically anything. The effect will be anesthetic, knocking the bird out for a while. Then pluck the feathers from the bird, exposing his skin. Rub that down with some condiment—cinnamon works best—so that he appears to look cooked. Set him on a plate surrounded by garnishes so that with his limp head and dangling claws, he looks like an aristocrat's lunch. At the precise moment when the audience is listening to your patter about the bird, slowly push a small saucer of vinegar or ammonia near the chicken's beak. This will arouse the bird and awaken him to the painful fact that he is without feathers. You can count on him to dance and crow with astonishment.

When I had arrived at Santo Domingo de la Calzada, I entered the church and looked up to see the continuing hilarity of this miracle. In the transept of the church set above the door is nothing more ludicrous and inappropriate than a chicken coop, gilded with rich ornament. Inside are two scurrying fowl, clucking at passersby and pecking noisily for a kernel of food. Any local will tell you that the chickens you see inside the church today are the direct descendents of the original miraculous pair. During mass, the priest often has to shout his sacred words so the congregation can hear above the cock-a-doodle-doos screeching from this holy little barn. According to legend, only a pilgrim can feed these chickens. In the winter months, when pilgrims are scarce, it is said that one of the old folks in town has to dress in traditional pilgrim's clothes to get them to eat.

Miracles are "a reminder of the bounds imposed on the mind by habit," according to St. Augustine's biographer. In the seven hundred years since those chickens danced, this single amusing act has defined and carried away this town. Outside the church, in the public square, the local kids play. When they see a pilgrim, they sing an old song that has only two rhyming lines. *"Santo Domingo de la Calzada, donde cantó la gallina después de asada."* It means, "Saint Dominick of the Highway, where the hen sang after being roasted." Sort of loses its playfulness in translation.

FIVE
FRÓMISTA

After a month of walking, a pilgrim loses his mind—not in the psychiatric sense, but like an obsolete and forgotten appliance. Think of an eight-track tape player permanently misplaced in the cellar, but you know it's there, so that one day, should you ever need it, you can always go down there and retrieve it. When I walk, I stare at the ground sliding beneath my feet, and I am speechless, lost in a hot, pulsing haze. Long-distance athletes speak of a runner's nirvana—a euphoric state achieved in the proximity of utter exhaustion. The pilgrim has his equivalent, only it doesn't look as graceful. Runners have their knees pumping, head up, chest out, arms chugging. To look me in the eye, you'd see the milky cataracts of an aged ox strapped into his traces, lugging his burden.

I've spent entire afternoons slogging through a trench cut so deep into a wheat field that I am invisible to all except the birds flying directly overhead. Central Spain is nothing but wheat fields, vast parcels of countryside devoted to nothing but wheat, and wheat, it seems, finds me fetching. Mosquitoes inexplicably prefer some people over others. I've never had this problem with insects because apparently I am spoken for by the plant kingdom. I am beloved by wheat. Their stalks bend toward me in the wind, anxious to propel their seed my way. They mistake me for rich topsoil (not so surprising after a month of pilgrimage) or simply a large strip of ruddy Velcro. Wheat burrs assault me from all directions, hitting me in the face, once swiftly—whoa—plugging up a nostril. I frequently pull them out of my ear. They gather into harvest decorations in my hair. They bury themselves in the wrinkles of my filthy flaccid clothes. After a morning's walk, my legs and socks are dense congregations of future generations of wheat.

When the road occasionally veers out of the wheat fields and overlaps with a real highway, I seem invisible, occupying a sphere all my own. The cars zoom by so fast, I am nothing more than a blur to them, as they are to me. At the rate a car travels, I cannot make out a face. Neither of us can manage a hello or a polite tilt of the head. I have left that dimension. My only acquaintances are the poor farmers puttering on tractors or families piled onto an old hay wagon drawn by mules. These people see me and always greet me kindly. I am one of them.

One morning an old man on a moped buzzes by me. After he passes, I hear the sputtering cough of a tiny engine gearing down and turning. He pulls up alongside me and removes a handmade cigarette from the torn pocket of an old white shirt, brown at the seams. He is small and frail with a transparent face and a wheeze like a child's rattle. He smokes constantly as he speaks in the slack accents of a rural man. If the deep drawl of inland South Carolina has a counterpart in Spain, it's in the nearly indecipherable all-vowel nosespeak of this man.

"You must be careful up ahead," he advises.

"Careful?"

"There is much danger up ahead."

"Danger?"

"Yes, and great torments and evil."

In Spanish the words ring medieval. *"Hay tormentas y mal tiempos."* Great, I am thinking. At last, some action.

"Will I encounter the *tormentas* soon?"

"Yes, a day's walk from here, when you come to the plains of Castille."

"What should I do?"

"You should just be ready. I don't know what pilgrims do. Perhaps you shouldn't walk."

"Are the plains always full of torments and suffering?"

"No, but when it comes, it's bad," says my thin mystic.

"How do you know this?" I ask.

He pauses, a bit sad. "I saw it on television."

As my shaman putters off, I marvel at this surreal answer, a charming mix of folklore and technology. In the mindless fog of pilgrim's nirvana, it is a good hour before I am moved to open my dictionary and learn that these words mean "rainstorm" and "bad weather." My shaman was quoting the TV weatherman.

Every pilgrim claims a specific saint to serve as a guardian spirit. Saint Groucho of Marx, watch over me.

The only relief from the wheat field is a tiny village named Hornillos. It means "Little Stoves" and was founded in 1156 to provide pilgrims with a last meal before walking into the vast emptiness of the Castilian plains. Now there is nothing left here for the pilgrim except a tilted shed beside the church, so infested with flies that I skip my daily siesta and continue to the edge of town. Three widows, black with elaborate lace, sit on a bench in the pose of eternal silence. They call out: *"Un abrazo por Santiago."* A hug for Saint James.

I nod my head to acknowledge them and their request.

"Beware of wolves," says one.

"Wolves?"

"On the plains, there are wolves," says another.

"Wolves?"

"Sharpen your stick," she says.

"Wolves?"

"A hug for Saint James, eh?" says the last widow.

These words sound eulogistic.

The famous plains of Castille are misnamed. They should be called the plateaus. A few miles outside Hornillos, the road zigzags up a fierce incline until arriving to a level lip. Ascending those last few feet is exhilarating. The cramped acreage of the bottomland opens to an infinite vista of—wheat. Wheat and more wheat, as far as the eye can see. Dorothy's poppy fields on the outskirts of Oz hold nothing to this view. I have never seen this much of the planet in one take.

I had been warned about the plains, not only by the old man, but by others who said that they were frightening and hot. There are no towns up here. No bars. No shed. Not even shade. The farmers drive here in their tractors to tend their wheat fields, and the occasional shepherd visits his flock. Otherwise, there is no one.

No matter how far I walk, the horizon unwinds like a scroll, laying out more wheat fields. But the wheat up here is different. It is sickly thin and almost translucent up close, no more than eighteen inches high, struggling amid tough clods and rocks the size of fists. The larger rocks and boulders have been plucked out, probably centuries ago, and gathered into unintended cairns. They are blanched an unnatural white and pitted with hollows by centuries of wind blasts and hot sun, like monuments of skulls.

The afternoon moves slowly and seems ripe with portents and signs. Up ahead a dark figure appears on the horizon, clad in black from head to toe. As it approaches, I start to worry a little. I *am* out here all alone. I fondle my Swiss Army knife, always in my left hip pocket like a talisman. Maybe it's one of the highwaymen or blackguards so often mentioned in the old books.

Pilgrim testimonies frequently speak of the terror of the Castilian plains. Even by medieval standards they were considered unnaturally barren and inhabited by strange beasts. In April 1670, an Italian pilgrim named Domenico Laffi left Bologna for Santiago. He saw many odd things along the way; but here, on the plains of Castille, according to his diary, he saw a pilgrim attacked and eaten alive by a swarm of grasshoppers.

As the ebony figure gets closer, the wind picks up and blows its black skirts from side to side. But what is it carrying? An

eight-foot pole with a long crescent blade. This is not a hallucination, but definitely a tall man in a black robe carrying a
scythe of exaggerated proportions, a badly cast Mr. Death
from a high school drama.

As I get closer to him, it is clear that he is not on the road,
but far off to the right, cutting or weeding the wheat. His large
hood envelops his face. He shouts something unintelligible at
me. Maybe it was hello. Maybe it was a request for a hug of
Saint James. It sounds oddly urgent. Another warning, perhaps? I wave grandly and pass on.

The narrow channel of dust that scores these wheat fields is
so dry that the ground has cracked open in places. Why hadn't
I noticed these before? Did these fissures yawn open a few
moments ago? These are not minor cracks, the kind I would
expect on a dry road burned by the sun. No, these are crevices.
I could trip on one. My gaze goes downward, oxen-eyed and
cautious.

Now, I am a little scared, I will admit. In South Carolina,
they call it getting snakes on the brain: You're walking in the
woods, having a dandy time, and suddenly you hear something rustle in the bushes. For the rest of the day, any slight
movement and you jerk back in panic. That's having snakes on
the brain. I got them on a wide-open plain, and suddenly it's
crowded up here—wolves, carnivorous grasshoppers, serial-
murdering scythe-toting shepherds, poltergeists, and cracks
open to hell.

I also don't want to look up because I have seen the clouds
rolling in. Big, glorious, Hollywood clouds. These are Steven
Spielberg props—cottony bales that hang so low over these
plains, I imagine I could reach up on tiptoe and finger their
dark, feathery bottoms. Some remnant of childhood supersti-
tion keeps my eyes on the ground. To look up would encour-
age them to break open and soak me with rain.

About ten feet in front of me, a small brown bird wings its
way out of the clouds and falls lifelessly on the road in front of
me.

Oh, come on.

I am jabbering aimlessly to myself. I have sung every song

and recited every poem I know. Movies that I have visually memorized, *Diner* for example, have played from beginning to end out here in the whistling expanse of the spacious Castilian Gigantoplex. A few weeks ago the wind bore only the squeal of a phantom car. That was then; today it's a hallucinatory open house. I hear singing in the wind: four-part harmonies of Renaissance madrigals, shopping mall renditions of Christmas carols, all the top-forty hits fried onto my synapses before I left (the opening mandolin riff of REM's "Losing My Religion" perversely floats up every ten minutes like a human-rights violation). I hear arguments and conversations—my mother frets again about my quitting my job, Madame Debril offers her apologies, an old girlfriend confesses she can't live without me. It's an auditory Rorschach out here.

The distant clouds have grumbled a few times. I try not to listen to what they have to say. The horizon never changes—a thin black line drawn between the brown wheat and darkening clouds ahead. From time to time the fields betray a slight upward incline. As I make my way up, I hope to see a gorge or valley appear on the other side, maybe even take in the warm sight of buildings. But one mild hump leads only to another, more wheat, more stones. In the middle of this new field, three dogs scour and sniff in the distance. I open my pocket knife and sharpen the point of my stick.

Pilgrims don't like dogs. At the museum of Roncesvalles, the one icon I remember most vividly was a wooden bas-relief of a pilgrim being devoured by five or six dogs. One greyhound was stretched the entire length of the pilgrim's height, his paws set on the poor man's shoulders and his maw ready to sink its teeth into his face. The pilgrim's expression of primal horror was finely carved and particularly memorable.

A pilgrim gets to know dogs pretty well after a while. Dogs are everywhere in Spain. Trained ones work with the shepherds to control flocks of sheep. Each yard has a savage dog chained to a stake. Every small town is overrun with skinny strays. They snake around the corners of buildings and nose up the alleys, prowling for scraps. Tailless cats with slack bellies scramble in their wake.

In America, dogs are domesticated. In Spain, even yard dogs are wild to some degree. Animal training is not how a Spanish pet owner spends his time. People are expected to learn how to deal with dogs, not the other way around. Pilgrims learn this in a jiffy.

Dogs generally keep their distance. They are pack animals and aren't particularly brave. I know the timbre of their bark and what it means. A pilgrim learns to speak the idiom of a dog's bark as fluently as a parent comes to know the meaning of a child's cry—the squall of wounded pride, the chugging yelp of a skinned knee, and the sickening tocsin of bloody pain.

Dogs' barks are similar, and one can understand this language. A healthy throated sound, deep in the bass register, is a statement of territory. It is a declarative sentence and nothing more. As long as the pilgrim maintains his pace on the road, he hasn't much to fear. But there are other grammars. Skinny dogs, desperate from hunger, can let rip with a fierce scraping sound. In the syntax of the wild, these are the irregular conjugations. Be very afraid.

Direct eye contact is not good in such circumstances. Wild dogs, like thugs in New York City, don't like being stared at. It implies some kind of judgment. Peripheral vision is key. These three dogs are deep inside this field but well within my scope. As I approach their parallel, they send up a few introductory barks. I have no fear because I read them perfectly. They won't be bothering this passing pilgrim. These are territorial claims, pure and simple, nothing more than warnings to stay on the road.

Suddenly all three break into a furious sprint, tearing at the air with their howls. They are coming straight for me.

I can see that they bear the marks of wild Spanish dogs. They are plagued by mange. One is large; the other two are medium-size. One has a dead ear, permanently bent over. Another runs a little crabwise sideways; his backside is rubbed raw, absolutely hairless in bleeding patches. These are seriously ugly dogs.

The leader is the one with the bleeding rump. They pull up short some twenty feet from me. I walk very slowly but deliberately. I don't want them behind me. The three stand side by side, moving as one. They begin to circle. They stop in front of me and I inch closer. The lead dog rips with a frightening bark, fierce shredded blasts. He knows what he means, and I read him clearly.

A strange fear overtakes me, and it's one I have never felt. Of course I'm scared of them attacking me, alone, on this empty plateau. But that's not it. I am scared because I know that I am prepared to kill them. I have my knife in my left hand and my stick in my right. My breathing is rapid. My pupils must be pinholes. We are locked in direct eye contact. My frontal lobes have closed down and handed off total control to that reptilian stub in the base of the brain. Nerve bundles that haven't been tickled since the Pleistocene epoch have taken over my main features. I am instinctively making faces. My mouth is pried open and my teeth bared. Sounds gurgle in the back of my throat. There are no choices left. I am almost standing on the outside, watching, when it happens.

On the plains of Castille, I bark. I didn't know humans made noises the way birds of prey caw, cats caterwaul, or coyotes bay. But we do. And you can't really appreciate the human ululation signifying the will to kill until you've felt it pour out of your very own face. It's a ragged, oscillating sound (Tarzan isn't that far off). Strange, it's rather high up in the register, pubescent, and not all that dignified, even comical in its bestial ineptness.

With my pack still on my back (to drop it would signal cowardice), a force that says it is better to charge than to be charged sweeps through me, and I bolt directly at my enemies. My knife is gripped underhanded, and my spear waggles in the air. And then I bark—again and again. It originates somewhere in a sleeping pocket of my solar plexus and screeches through my vocal cords with the force of a childhood vomit. My entire body convulses with explosions: *"Lalulalulaluaaaaaaa."* More or less.

The dogs jerk forward, but the force propelling me toward them won't let me flinch. Like any good bluff, you can't let up on your pose and you have to suffer the consequences if you get called on it. My face is squeezed into a Nordic mask of blood-red fury. I lunge and bark. The effect is a threat that translates roughly "I will slice open your bellies, smear your entrails in this dust, and perform grand pliés in the viscera."

This is a simple, straightforward message, and one that on some primal level they comprehend. And without further linguistic exchange, they signal their comprehension by suddenly sprinting into the wheat field and leaving me be.

They continue barking. But I know this sound well. This is the cry of losers; they are trying to save face. This is the canine equivalent of shouting insults—from a distance—at the big guy who has just laced you in the playground. I storm up the road, unafraid that they are at my back. (I glance once or twice to make sure.) But they haven't moved. The two pack dogs bark the loudest—a kind of toadying sound. Maybe they are kissing up to the lead dog, who snarls.

My hands are shaking. My pulse, which is usually high with all the work of walking, is racing. The succubi who have haunted me all day redescend, and a new spookiness consumes me. I am carrying on a delightfully stupid but vaguely reassuring conversation with myself when a grand blast of thunder rolls across the plains. The clouds are now in full costume dress, big black tumblers wheeling from left to right across the stage before me. They have dropped a little more in altitude, brushing my hair with static. A sweet metallic aroma fills the air, and I see a few drops of water darken the blond earth.

Vast sheets of rain explode from the clouds as I frantically pull out my poncho, logically located at the bottom of my pack. The wet plastic sticks to my skin, and the dripping cowl obstructs my view. On the horizon a broad streak of light flares, as if someone turned a spotlight on and off. It's sheet lightning, well known to be harmless. But I count the seconds—thousand one, thousand two, thousand three, thousand four, thousand five, thousand six. A peal of thunder sounds. I remember my father teaching me this trick when I was a little boy. Each second between the blast of light and the sound of thunder represents a mile. This is part of the lore of storms we learn as children. I am dredging up a good deal of that lore just now.

The lightning is six miles away. How much farther do I have to go, and will I walk into this lightning storm? I have been walking for nearly five hours. A kilometer is roughly twelve minutes' walk. And how many kilometers is it to the next town? And how many kilometers equals a mile? Two point two, or is that kilograms? It's metric, so isn't it the same? But how could it be? Gallons and miles don't share the same ratio as kilos to kilometers. But maybe—

A jagged white line tickles the horizon. This is not sheet lightning anymore. Thousand one, thousand two, thou—

Not a good sign.

Another flash of light momentarily drains all the color from the landscape. I saw this one *hit* the ground—far up the road, but still within the field before me. I walk to the left side of the road since the clouds are tumbling to my right. I pick up my step. What was that other bit of lore? Lightning strikes the tallest object. My eyes sweep the panorama of endless wheat fields—midget stalks stretching to two feet at best.

I am six feet one. Lore is surfacing freely.

Never stand beneath an electric line.

Never stand beneath a tree.

Lightning is just a gathering of static electricity.

Lightning doesn't come down to earth but actually moves up to the sky.

In a car you are safe because the wheels are made of rubber.

My shoes are made of rubber.

Lightning never strikes in the same place twice.

A bolt blasts the earth directly in front of me, maybe fifty yards away. This is a network of bolts, like a grid. A tic-tac-toe board of light and heat. The thunder booms at once. Should I turn around and back away from the storm? Can I outhike a storm? Should I curl in a little ball and try to hide among the wheat? Should I stand still?

I decide to run in a forward direction and augment it with a bit of heartfelt shrieking and babbling. With a pack on my back, this job is neither graceful nor particularly effective. I can't scare away lightning like dogs. This really is some kind of message. The dogs failed, so they wheeled out Zeus' old-standard deus ex machina.

I can't believe that I am going to die out here, struck by lightning. Bolts are now exploding on both sides of me like bombs. I can see them clearly. I can *smell* them. In my mind, each spot is marked by charred wheat stalks and a modest puff of smoke. I run for fifteen minutes. Run and scream, to be accurate. Run and scream and hoot and howl and hoo-wee, to be even more accurate.

I am surrounded by illusions. Lightning is blasting at my side. Voices scream in the wet wind. I hear footsteps pursuing me. Up ahead, another hallucination makes the horizon suddenly telescope and shrink, drawing itself toward me. It gets nearer, and as it does so, the earth cracks open at the edge and a small black cross pops up out of the ground before me. Following behind it, a small stone pyramid forces the cross higher until it is clear and visible and lovely—an optical illusion that undoubtedly has comforted pilgrims for a millennium. And, shortly, an entire church pushes its way up out of the muddy earth and into view. Other buildings crowd around its side and rear up. A town in a valley.

The pilgrim's path suddenly drops off into an alley of stone. I can hear the rumble of cattle and the cackle of fowl. The rain gathers and sluices through this street, softening the manure into a sludge and freeing pent-up odors. At the church I run to its wall to try to get out of the downpour. This is the town of Hontanas. In old Spanish the name was Fontanas, literally "Fountains"—so named since it was the first watering hole after the hot blistering plains. An open doorway across the street reveals four old women playing cards.

"Pilgrim, would you like a sandwich?" one of them says to me in Spanish.

"Yes, yes, please, please, yes."

"I will bring you one."

I call out a thank-you from under the slight eave of the church.

"You were caught in the rain," another says.

"Rain!"

I can't even think of what to tell them.

"It was raining very hard, wasn't it?" another adds.

"Rain!" I say in my simple, awkward Spanish. "Beautiful ladies. Rain! Dogs death birds hell fear"—I am capable only of uttering nouns for the moment—"Rain! Yes, rain, but there were, there were"—I can't call forth the word for lightning. "How do you say in Spanish when light comes down from the sky?"

"*Tormentas?*" one of the ladies answers.

"*Tormentas.* Yes, yes, that is the word, isn't it?" I am laughing crazily, at myself a bit, but mostly from relief. "*Tormentas, sí, sí, tormentas. Muchas tormentas. Tormentas grandes.* Muchissimas *tormentas.*" I am laughing the laughter of an idiot. I am hysterical. I can't stop until the woman appears with a sandwich. She hands it to me cautiously. The sandwich is huge—ham and a Spanish omelet on a baguette the size of my arm. I tear into it like a jackal.

By about the halfway point of the Spanish leg of the road, which is where I am here on the Castilian plains, the pilgrim becomes something of an amateur of the church. Not the abstraction of "the Church," but of the building itself.

The road to Santiago is absolutely littered with churches. They anchor every village, town, and city. Often, they are seen situated alone in a field or tucked into the corner of a glade, taking in the country air—all that is left of a village or monastery that went belly up a few hundred years ago. The road is a walking tour of the entire history of western architecture up to and including some of the most embarrassing contemporary monstrosities: new churches that look like bloated cafeterias with chainlink fencing twisted into the shape of a cross, a fish, or something unidentifiable.

The pilgrim takes up church watching for many reasons. They are always the first view of any town. In Hontanas, the church burst from the ground and swept me into her embrace. On any normal day's walk, a church always appears in the distance like a waiting behemoth, the buttresses of her haunches tucked at her sides, with her head up, always vigilant and alert for the call to stretch and slouch toward Jerusalem. In time, the little houses come into view, like pups gathered around her for safety.

It is said that Gibbon received his vision of the decline and fall of the Roman Empire after witnessing a group of monks ambling and praying among Latin ruins: the rise of Christianity had necessitated another bureaucracy's collapse. One would like to know what Gibbon would make of the image of the church on the pilgrim's trail today. Most are unoccupied, unused, and unwanted. I have yet to meet a priest who manages fewer than four of these village churches, and none is too happy about it. On any given day at any hour, even in the smallest towns, the churches are always bolted and locked. The few silver chalices that haven't been filched, or the paintings that haven't been cut from their frames, or the silk robes with gold embroidery that haven't been lifted at night, or the few elephantine folios of five-hundred-year-old illuminated liturgies that haven't been fenced in Barcelona are hawkishly guarded by the ubiquitous Spanish widows, each of whom seems to carry a heavy ancient key to the nearest church.

Most of the churches are in poor condition because of neglect; their exterior sculpture has been worn by wind and rain to featureless fetal shapes. The interiors are eaten by mildew; the stone flakes into powder at the touch. But a pilgrim who says a kind word to any weathered old woman in black can watch her produce the rusty key. And then he may enter.

Pilgrims admire churches because they are always cool on a hot day and because pilgrims are, in almost every church, the star of the show. No church on the road neglects to honor the pilgrim in the presumed eternity of stone. We are cut into the walls, carved atop the capitals, painted onto panels, and sculpted in wood. Our image is everywhere; and our patron Santiago, in one guise or another, looks out from nearly every wall. After a brutal day's walk, sitting in the cool of thick stone, it's hard not to feel a little flattered.

Despite the grandeur of the Gothic, Baroque, and other

styles, I find myself drawn to the secure comfort of the Romanesque—the heavy walls, dark interior, thick columns, and simple sculpture. If I could conduct a poll among pilgrims, I'm certain the Romanesque would win. The style flourished in the 1000s and 1100s, and the churches were built largely because of pilgrim traffic. Some critics even call this style of building "pilgrim architecture."

Romanesque appeals to pilgrims because it is built to a scale that is especially fitting for someone on foot. These churches are small and cozy; even the Romanesque cathedrals are manageable spaces. They are humble, comprehensible buildings. The columns are low. The sculptures are visible at eye level or just above. From town to town they play out the same themes and tell the same story. The repetition is soothing. After a while, they feel like home.

A pilgrim can't say this about the Gothic cathedrals. They are spacious, overwhelming, and impressive, and they mean to be. I came to Europe fully schooled in the architectural propaganda in favor of Gothic and expected to be transported by the sights. The critic Ernest Short writes that Gothic is the "master synthesis of religious architecture." Sartell Prentice alleges that "the rôle of the Romanesque church was that of a prophet and forerunner, a John the Baptist in stone, preparing the way for one still mightier that was to come."

The pilgrim gets a bit defensive about Romanesque after reading such remarks. We even resent the name, a nineteenth-century coinage. That "esque" makes the style sound derivative and second-rate, a rip-off of the Romans. It may be (some of the early Romanesque churches did plunder Roman ruins for their stonework). But, in defense, we pilgrims remind ourselves that the word *Gothic* comes from the Goths, famous for bullying, overbearing, loud behavior.

Romanesque is denigrated for its heavy walls, thick columns, and simple round arches. It is described as leaden and earthbound, crude and dense. The essential building block of Romanesque is called the "arch that never sleeps," as if it were some squat, dim-witted peasant, always at work, with no time for appreciation of beauty. The Gothic can claim the elegant pointed arch that relieved the stresses and pressures of the building and opened up the space until the flying buttress thinned the walls to the point that they could be fitted with mere stained glass. These inventions literally blew the roof off the Romanesque church, creating an enclosed canyon.

A Romanesque church asks a visitor to step back and make sense of what can be seen, which is everything. Gothic can only be seen in part. It is literally and figuratively beyond comprehension. Gothic doesn't serve the grandeur of creation; it competes with it. Gothic is architectural braggadocio—bullying, overbearing, loud. The stones of the Romanesque don't threaten, they whisper. They want to tell you something. Romanesque has been called the "church that speaks." The Gothic cathedral was nicknamed "an encyclopedia in stone." One has a simple story to tell; the other one can't shut up.

But there's something else about the Romanesque style. It radiates an optimism amid chaos, continually upbeat against all odds. Romanesque flourished not long after the passing of the last millennium. The year 1000 was widely perceived to be Judgment Day, the end of time. Sometime soon, the people thought, the dead would shake the dirt from their bones and literally rise up from their graves. In the meantime, the sun would go black and the moon would dissolve into a pool of blood. A common statement in the wills of that period began, "Seeing that the end of the world is at hand . . ." The gloom hung in the back of everyone's mind the way the threat of atomic destruction has more recently tortured us.

When the moment passed by and nothing happened, there was an intense sense of liberation, of pardon, of new hope. This wave of medieval glasnost was boosted by the sense that the barbarian invasions of centuries past were in fact over. As a result, building exploded. Suddenly the enclosed security of the medieval monastery could be turned inside out. Instead of having populations of laymen living within the walls, one could build a kind of embassy in the middle of town, right out in the open—a church.

There had been churches, of course. The early ones, called basilicas, were modeled on old Roman meeting halls, which the first Christians rented to hold their services. Basilicas were built of wood with flat timbered roofs. When the Goths or Longobards arrived in the old days, these buildings were the first to get the torch.

The idea was to replace them with buildings that were not only fireproof, but worthy of the new mood that inspired them. Instead of dark wooden beams, they would be built of rich blond stone. They would raise high those roof beams by adapting the Roman arch. The rebuilding of medieval infrastructure was so widespread and fast that one contemporary observer, Rodulphus Glaber, wrote in 1003 that "the world seemed to be doffing its old attire and putting on a new white robe of churches."

The church was to become a way of disseminating the essential idea of Christianity: although the chaos of the world was frightening, the scriptural word granted access to the harmony and transcendence of the divine. But how does one educate a continent of peasants about the power of the word when none of them can read? There were ideas. In 1025, the Council of Arras concluded: "Certainly there are simpletons and illiterates in the church who cannot contemplate the scriptures. . . . And although one does not worship a chunk of wood, the interior mind of man is excited by the visible image . . . which can be written on the tissue of one's heart." Even then, the seductive power of the image over the word was apparent. A narrative carved in stone—this was the Romanesque church.

Tens of thousands of Romanesque churches with the same basic story to tell were built in the century and a half after the year 1000. Even today, after another millennium, there survive more than ten thousand Romanesque churches—from Bohemia and Poland in the east, to the Italian islands in the south, to Ireland and Scandinavia in the north, to Spain and Portugal in the west. The Romanesque church repeated these same coherent images to widespread audiences—a single story rerun over and over again. It was a form of mass communication, of broadcasting. Crude though it was, the Romanesque church was the first successful attempt at a medium we would later call television.

The most famous Romanesque church on the road, except for the church in Santiago, is San Martín in Frómista. The first stone was laid in 1066, when William the Conqueror was setting sail for England. Frómista is merely thirty kilometers beyond Hontanas, and for two days I slog through heavily worked wheat fields to get there. That figure in the black hooded robe swinging an outsize scythe has gathered into gangs. At times the plains of Castille seem host to a Mr. Death convention. At last, from the tedious wheat fields that surround everything, the amber hulk of San Martín of Frómista appears. It is bolted and locked when I arrive.

On the outside of a Romanesque church, the eaves of the roof are held up by small sculptures called corbels, triangles of stone fitted against the wall and beneath the roof with elaborate carvings along the hypotenuse. Here at Frómista's San Martín, they are surprising—no biblical imagery or faces of Apostles, but pagan depictions of animals and people and vegetation.

Walking around the outside of the church is a tour of the surreal. Here is a laughing wolf, a hysterical dog, a bird of prey, a man with his head in the mouth of a lion, a toothsome maniacally grinning beast, a pineapple, a naked seated child, a hideously contorted man with a child, another animal head flashing his molars, a man with a finger in his ear, a monster inserting his hands in his mouth, a woman with the floppy ear of a ruminant whose hands point to her distinctive feature, a human head with a long neck, an animal holding the head of a naked man between his knees, an animal with human hands stuffed in its mouth.

Perhaps they are images drawn from the common bestiary, the second biggest seller in the Middle Ages after the Bible. Elsewhere on the road, I have seen corbels carved with panthers, dragons, wolves, elephants, and hyenas; mythological beasts—griffins, sirens, basilisks, centaurs, chimeras; and others whose names are still mysterious after translation—manticores, skiapods, hippopods, cenephali.

A local woman instructs me to walk a few blocks to the town's information booth to find out when the church will open. At the booth, a young man who speaks educated Spanish tells me the church is open.

"I have just been there," I tell him. "It is closed."

"No, it is Wednesday. It is open. If you go there, it will be open."

So I naively return, and it is closed. Another local advises that I visit the town mayor.

The mayor is not in, but his wife is. She stamps my passport with the insignia of Frómista.

"Do you know if the church of San Martín will open today?"

"Oh, no," she explains. "It is Wednesday. It is closed."

"Yes, but—"

"It will open tomorrow."

"The man in the information booth says it is open today."

"Yes," she says. It is not a question or a confirmation or a statement. This is Spain, in a nutshell. But I believe her because—the church *is* closed—at least she and I inhabit the same time-space continuum. I return to the information booth because there were some books and pamphlets about San Martín for sale. The young man and I chat about San Martín, and I ask him why the outside is in such better condition than all the other Romanesque churches.

"It was restored a hundred years ago."

"Really?"

"A big controversy."

"Controversy?"

"Yes. Some say they changed some of the carvings."

"Really, why?"

"They were obscene."

"Really, so where are the obscene carvings?"

"I believe they are in the Regional Museum in Palencia."

"How far is that?"

"About a half hour on the bus. There will be one here soon. But if you go to Palencia today, you won't be able to see the church."

"Why not?"

"Tomorrow is Thursday. The church is closed."

I decide to take a day off and go to Palencia. As I wait for the bus, I flip through some of the brochures on Frómista. The town's name is the linguistic collapsing of the Latin word *frumentum*. It means "wheat."

Palencia is a large town, and by the time I get there in the late afternoon, the place is beginning to reawaken from the siesta nap. My search for the Regional Museum gets me nowhere because it doesn't exist. Never has, the lady in the tourist office says. I ask after the corbels of Frómista, and I am sent to City Hall, which sends me to the Sacred Arts Museum, which wants to direct me to the Archaeological Museum, but, I'm told, it closed forever. Happened a few weeks ago. The administrators lost their funding.

I walk to the Archaeological Museum anyway, maybe to mortify the spirit a bit more than I have. The front door is a squat wooden square with thick beat-iron hinges and one of those colossal locks from centuries ago. Who's to say who possessed me? Saint James, perhaps.

I pound on the door.

A Spanish cliché drags open the heavy scraping door. He is a short man bent over with an enormous hump in his back. His head seems to nestle in the center of his chest. He explains that the museum is closed forever. I point to my shell. I pout. I let my eyes water. I wipe my brow. Pilgrims have their ways.

Presently, a handsome middle-aged man named Don Mauricio del Amo appears and introduces himself.

We ride up the elevator to his office and he fixes me a coffee. According to Don Mauricio, whatever corbels were taken down have been lost or stolen. He doesn't have any and doesn't know where any are. In the Spanish art world, he explains, there is a touch of scandal regarding Frómista because the restoration was done during the last century, which Don Mauricio assures me was as Victorian in Spain as it was in England.

Many of the corbels of the Romanesque period, he explains, were quite obscene, at least by modern standards. They can still be seen here and there in Spain and in other countries. But most of them have been removed. Don Mauricio pulls from his library some books and photographs. We slowly leaf through the surviving corbels of the Romanesque. Each photograph is labeled with its location.

At the Colegiata de Santillana del Mar is a man and woman splayed crotch to face, a primitive 69 position.

At San Martín de Elines is a man exhibiting his penis while tightening a garrote painfully around his neck. When I left America, I had read press accounts of teenagers strangling themselves during masturbation—autoerotic asphyxia—as a novel way to heighten the pleasures of self-abuse. Yet it wouldn't be so new to neighbors of Santos Cosme y Damián de Bárcena de Pie de Concha, where a corbel shows a man onanistically exercising while squeezing his neck.

At Santa María de Piasca is a beautiful corbel of a man holding a woman's chin, in cinematic fashion, kissing her lips lightly.

At San Vicente de la Barquera, a man is taking a woman from behind. They appear almost to be flying. Around the corner is a priest in robes, hiking his skirts to show his erect penis.

At San Pedro de Cervatos, it is a pornographer's dream. One corbel shows a woman with her legs pinned behind her ears, offering for public view a finely detailed, naturally proportioned vulva. Beside her is another corbel of a man with a hand on his chest and another fiddling with his visible scrotum and penis. A few corbels down is a man performing cunnilingus on a woman. Farther on is a woman with an infant dangling halfway out her vagina. Another, stunning to see, is a couple copulating upside down. Protruding generously toward heaven are their two buttocks, with a pair of testicles visible and an erect penis tightly sheathed in her vagina. Yet another shows a woman in the classical position of the *Playboy* foldout—on her stomach, her feet in the air, flashing her vulva at the viewer. Farther on, a woman is showing hers and looking flirtatiously across the space of a corner to a man who is showing his. Finally, there is a man, seated, with his enormously erect penis in his own mouth.

When language is something of an impediment, as it is with Don Mauricio and me, we can only laugh. He speaks a thicket of architectural jargon, which is straining my conversational Spanish. But he makes his explanation plain. The medieval world understood human nature in ways very different from us. Clearly, he says, they were a bit more frank. These images weren't meant to tantalize, although they may have. Rather, the outdoor corbels were meant to summarize the life that man and woman suffered outside the church. Taken as a whole, the exterior of the Romanesque was an imagistic retrospective on the human condition: the mad calling of sex, the dangers of crazed beasts, the certainty of death, the pains of daily life, and the hardship of labor. The opening chapter of the Romanesque story was a documentary: This is the world you inhabit. It is chaotic and strange, swayed and tormented by appetites and yearnings no one can understand.

"The beauty of Romanesque," Don Mauricio says, "after you have looked at the outside, is to step inside the church."

The following morning the ride back to Frómista is slow, and of course San Martín is closed. The mayor's wife remembers me and advises that I walk to a bar called Tanín and shout the name "Salva." This will open the church.

Tanín is a bar like all others in Spain. The television, fat and 1950s looking, occupies a corner and is so loud that neither Salva nor anyone else can hear me. Television in Spain is no longer cultural white noise. Here television has utterly vanquished every public room. The irritating crackle you hear in the interstices of television's humming silences is your own voice.

I locate Salva, a rheumy-eyed gentleman nursing a late-morning drink. He doesn't want to be disturbed by a tourist or a pilgrim or anyone else. He is watching a television game show celebrating the economic union of the nations of Europe. Salva agrees to take me to the church, but then orders another drink. I get a coffee and settle down with the guys to watch some television. A group of continental beauties in bikinis from Portugal, Spain, England, France, Italy, Germany, and a Benelux country—all well oiled—struggle to climb a giant greased cone to snatch their national flag from the top. This effort entails a lot of comical sliding. I think of the images I saw in Don Mauricio's office, and I conclude that some comparisons are better left unexplored.

At the commercial break, Salva produces an ancient key and pries himself from his chair.

Don Mauricio had told me to enter the church. After spending some time outside, the temptation is irresistible. Frómista is a tidy box of a church, as big as a large A-frame house. Its exterior sculpture calls a visitor to the front door. The tour of life's madness on the exterior changes abruptly. At the main entrance is a semicircle of sculpture called the tympanum, a space of carving that challenges everything else you've seen. On all Romanesque churches, it is orderly and serene. Most often Christ sits up vertically in defiance of the horizontal chaos and invites the visitor to step from this world of suffering and madness into one of perfection and order.

Within, the gracious curves of those simple arches are sustained by columns, each carved with a scene at the top. Altogether they form three forward-moving aisles. But Romanesque does not hasten the visitor. The invitation is to linger. It is not merely a mise-en-scène, but a story—distinct from the chaotic images outside.

At the beginning are depictions of what gives our world a sense of order and meaning, images of labor and daily routine. Here are men carrying a barrel of wine. Another shows a group of marching soldiers. Farther up the aisle the pillars advertise familiar stories. Here are Adam and Eve kneeling before a tree wrapped with a serpent. Or, the capitals are pure geometry—carvings of vegetation or the stone lace of chevrons, dog-tooth, twisted cable—said to be inspired by the medieval art of illuminated manuscripts, making them literally the translation of the word into image.

The sculptures visible on these capitals are cramped and flat and seem primitive. This apparent crudeness is evidence not of ignorance, but of restraint.

"Even in its most passionate moods," writes the French critic Henri Focillon, Romanesque "is held in check by a discipline which forbids it to flourish and posture about the church or to launch itself turbulently into space." Gothic architecture would end all that and pirouette up the aisles. For Romanesque, the stone was subordinate to the story, translating the message that the unpredictability of the world could be contained by the word. Order could be imposed on chaos. Meaning could be heard in the cacophony of Babel.

The Romanesque church is a balance of righteousness and humility. It doesn't think too highly of itself. Like a pilgrim, Romanesque is not really in a position to. Humility comes with the territory—flat arches all around. After reveling in the place of San Martín, I am joined by a German choir. For an hour they sing early chants and madrigals. The director tells me afterward that he and his choir are touring Europe and singing in every Romanesque church they can find. I ask him why he doesn't visit the grand cathedrals in Burgos or León.

"It is the difference between rock 'n' roll and chamber music," he says. "The Gothic and the Baroque were built for amplification. The Romanesque was built for harmony."

SIX
LEÓN

Entering a big city is like waking from a dream. My solitary days of amiable walks in the countryside, chatting and lunching with locals and winning praise from farmers and shepherds for my effort, comes to a crashing end. León is my next stop, a city of kings and cathedrals, court intrigue and tradition. The city's name is a contraction of a powerful Roman army unit, Legio VII Gemina, once stationed here. Spain's famous medieval knight el Cid was married downtown in the Romanesque church San Isidoro. A notorious Moorish general named Almanzor made several punitive raids on León. He was a tenth-century man with a twentieth-century sense of public relations. After each victory, and there were many, Almanzor returned to his tent and brushed the dirt and filth of battle into a box. When he died, his coffin was lined with this exquisite dust, and he was laid in it. Even the Spaniards begrudgingly admire him.

But a pilgrim walking into a city this size does not encounter history. If I were in a car, I could zoom straight to the old center of town. But I am on foot, entering a modern urban thicket. So my introductions are aging factories, fenced-in toxic dumps, and abandoned vistas of distressed commercial real estate. Gradually the outer industrial rim gives way to contemporary poverty. The wealth of the inner city seems distant. High-rises filled with the modern poor forge bleak canyons. The unemployed men, who gather in packs to smoke or drink, stare at me. No noble pilgrim now, I am a weirdo, a suspicion. I feel the old wariness of the New Yorker ebbing back. Just a few miles ago, the laborers in the fields fixed me with a look, too, but it was one of true curiosity and then admiration. Not here. My peripheral vision at León tunes out dogs and wolves and weather and begins to pick up familiar blips—gangs of kids in a side alley, slow-moving cars, the odd pacings of feet behind me.

The dangers of the Castilian plains summoned childhood fears. These streets call up adults-only terrors—mugging, stabbing, robbery, beating. A car full of teenagers drives past, and two faces lunge hooting from the windows. I hear the car turn around behind me and pull alongside me. Then, colorful Spanish invective.

"Eh, German! Asshole. Fuck you. Fuck your mother."

I am not German, I want to say, but instead I smile that stupid smile that says Oh, you kids, so young and foolish, now go and play somewhere else.

"Suck my chicken!" Or a metaphor to that effect. The car speeds up, spins around, and creeps back toward me. Great. I remember that someone told me not to yell "Help!" in Spain, but "Fire!" which will at least attract attention. I consider yelling curses back at them and prove that I can give as good as I get. I have already learned the ultimate Spanish insult (actually of Cuban origin): *Me cago en el coño de tu madre muerta.* I shit in the cunt of your dead mother. It is marvelous; all the vitals—scatology, genitals, death, mothers—packed so economically. This phrase is, however, an invitation to a fight unto death. So I keep my wry grin fixed firmly on my lips.

The car slips by once again, and two behinds, unclad, fit themselves quickly and snugly into the windows.

"German asshole! Kiss this blossoming flower!" Or a meta-phor to that effect. Keep smiling. Keep walking.

The pilgrim is soothed only by the yellow arrows, constant friends, even here in the ghettos. They sneak out from behind bullfight posters or leap off litter-filled gutters. They do look dashed off, sloppy gashes of yellow. A subliminal message from the painters: Hurry.

Downtown, the arrows direct the pilgrim just past San Isidoro to a rear entrance, possibly where the Cid held his nup-tial reception. A pair of wrought-iron gates are open, and a bent arrow nods inward.

Lights! Camera! Action! The receiving courtyard is filled with filmmakers and crew. A director's recreational vehicle is parked to the side. A camera turns my way, and voices cry, "*Peregrino, peregrino.*" I am being filmed. I nod, I wave. No, wait. I am a pilgrim. A dour expression of suffering blooms on my face. How embarrassing. I am not ready for my close-up.

Laughter erupts from all sides. A priest, in a stagy long black robe and gold belt cinched tight with dangling tassels, waves me off with a "just kidding" flap of the hand. The group turns into itself and resumes a discussion of the next shot, I presume.

To my left is an open doorway to the pilgrim's shelter, and outside, sitting in the sun, is a small man.

"My name is Jack," I say in Spanish.

"From the accent," he says in English, "I would guess you are an American."

"Very good."

"I rarely misjudge an accent," he says. He stands erect and introduces himself as Willem. After reclaiming his seat, he carefully cuts up a peach.

"Would you like a wedge?"

Willem is Belgian, a slim man with a sunken chest and the jerky silent-film body language of Charlie Chaplin. He started walking from his house in Belgium several months ago. His English is grammatically perfect, no slang, no contractions. His accent is Oxbridgean, erudite and musical. He speaks

Spanish, I soon learn, with a Castilian's aristocratic lisp and German with the authoritarian tones of the kaiser. A retired air force captain, Willem exudes a military precision with every action and phrase. Each afternoon he spends his siesta writing his wife a five- to ten-page letter. Every night he calls her for fifteen minutes. His knowledge of the road is exhaustive. He takes notes at every stop and has already argued with the priest about the history of San Isidoro. A heart attack several years ago served as a "memento mori" (his words) and put him in mind to walk the road, a lifelong desire. To prepare for his fifteen-hundred-kilometer journey, he *practiced* the entire trek, walking twenty-five kilometers around town every day for three straight months. "I just wanted to be certain I could do it," he acknowledges. Makes sense, sort of. But Willem knows what he knows.

"Stay away from the Flemish, at least some of them," he advises in a coy whisper.

"Which Flemish?" I ask.

"The filmmaker, Willie, and the others. They are foolish. They are pranksters. I cannot quite guess why they are walking the road."

He leans over conspiratorially and talks in a slight whisper to tell me their story, introducing each character replete with prudish commentary. The short wiry Flemish man is Rick. He is a pilgrim cliché: bald pate, long stringy white hair, and salt-and-pepper beard to his navel. He drinks a bit too much and cannot be taken seriously. His friend is Karl, the only one among them of any worth. Karl is bearish and quiet and handsome with a trim gray beard, a Flemish Sean Connery. The two of them are local aldermen in the town of Keerbergen. Several months ago the issue of repairing a priceless ancient organ came up, but no one could find the money. The town's poor insisted the rich pay, and the rich resented the demand. At a nasty village meeting, where old friends cursed one another, Rick shouted down the room and announced with appropriate drama, "I will walk to Santiago de Compostela!" Karl jumped up and said, "If that old man can walk to Spain, I can, too." Each citizen pledged a certain amount per kilometer, and the bet was on. If the two old men could make it to Santiago, the town would have enough to repair the organ.

Willem doesn't seem as impressed by their story as I am. What a fine beginning (and so uncomplicated; I'm jealous). Pilgrims walked the road for many reasons in the old days. Many simply announced their intention. Others begged for some favor—sparing the life of a relative was fairly common. Several centuries ago, a pilgrim named Jacques Lemesre of Dunkirk begged that his mother survive a painful illness. En route to Santiago, he was kidnapped by pirates, pressed into slavery, and eventually presumed dead. When he did return three years later, his mother, who was cured, was so astonished to see him that she died of shock.

After the road to Santiago was established, the reasons for walking became as numerous as pilgrims. Over time, the walk to Santiago, Rome, or Jerusalem even became a civil penalty. Countries frequently sentenced their worst criminals to one or two pilgrimages. In one case, a murderer was condemned to a pilgrimage with the corpse of his victim strapped to his back. Typically, though, the sentences were more humane, at least by medieval standards. A murderer would be welded into shackles made from the murder weapon and sent on a forced march, often naked. The irons could come off only after they were rusted through by sweat and urine.

But the most respectable of the pilgrimage traditions was simply to make a vow. Knights often did this and then headed off to Santiago for a blessing. These Flemish seemed to me to be true pilgrims indeed. But Willem is not interested in my historical digression.

"The worst of them is the man with the mustache. He is lazy. He drinks all the time and involves himself in trouble." Claudy is his name, pronounced "Cloudy." He is a sinewy, bent-legged man with a face straight off the canvas of a Dutch master. His mustache is grand and ostentatious. Below his bottom lip is a little tuft of jazz beard. His hatchet face, almond eyes, and thin crescent smile give him a foxy look of unspeakable cunning.

The filmmaker is a man named Willie. "He is an odd duck,"

says Willem, nodding at him by way of saying, Just take a look. The filmmaker has a puffed-up pompadour, hooded Salman Rushdie eyes, and a greasy smile. He looks like a game-show host. What Willem wants me to notice, and I can't help but do so, is the filmmaker's short short pants. He seems to prefer to carry his valuables—wallet, keys, cards—in the well of his crotch. Where one might expect to see the graceful curves of human flesh framed by such tight pants, one sees instead geometric shapes protruding unnaturally. Willem's nod is his way of saying, Nuf said. And indeed, it is.

"There are others you should meet. I will introduce you," he says. He carves another slice of peach with the precision of a surgeon. He pulls the flesh free from the crenulated stone with a raw rip.

"Another wedge?" Willem obviously wants to be my Virgil, conducting me into the little inferno of pilgrim relationships at this shelter. I accept the gift, but not without the odd feeling that I've made a trade.

He touches me gently on the leg. "You are a good man," he says.

When Willem and I enter the shelter, I see a number of people ambling about. On my left are five double bunks, ten beds. At a dinner table are two elderly folks, eating out of tins. My new face causes ripples of concern. At Willem's introduction, a German man says hello but immediately informs me in broken English that this—and he points—is his bunk. Just in case I wanted to know.

The elderly couple, Belgian like Willem, kindly offer me a place at the table, but they pull their food closer to them as they do. Their generosity has limits. A man exits the bathroom. Upon seeing my new face, he introduces himself, but while he talks, he casually gravitates toward his gear and bunk. Mine, this is mine, he wants to tell me.

There are a lot of people here. Many pilgrims start around this part of the road, and the Flemish and their crew have been resting here a few days. So it's quite a scene. This is the first crowded shelter I have visited, and there is a strange discomfort. I haven't felt this way in a long time. I would date it to the first grade—that elementary Hobbesian jungle of personal jostling and wrangling. In a pilgrim's shelter, where people are separated by language and culture and class, and united only by common suspicion, the maneuvering is clumsy and obvious. We speak first in gestures and motions, actions and movement.

In society, relationships are forged with a bit more delicacy and nuance. When we meet people, we share a language and possibly a profession or a hometown or a college or a taste in movies. Pilgrims share nothing but the desire to craft a simulacrum of civilized comfort out of few elements—a bedroll, some food, a flashlight. Personal space becomes a means to form relationships but also serves as a dividing line, a boundary. Everyone is struggling to find a place. We are, as adults long out of practice, trying to create a system of trust. We are trying to make friends.

"All the bunks are taken," says the German. "You will have to sleep on the floor." His statement is not meant to be threatening, just informative, just so I will know where things stand. I say that I will be happy to sleep on the floor. The whole room seems to be put at ease by this statement.

The German stretches out on his bed and swishes his legs back and forth. Mine, this is mine.

Amid these group politics, I am being vetted, so I try to put forth my most gregarious self. But it is clear that a lot of vetting has preceded my arrival. Most of the people here already know their place and the place of others. As in the first grade, the group has already determined, with the same brutish nastiness common among children, that one among them is universally despised and openly mocked.

His name is Giuseppe, but he is known as the Italian Man. When he enters the shelter he says nothing but sits on his bunk, removes his shoes, and puts a tennis shoe on his left foot and a climber's boot on his right. He gets up and leaves. Willem says out loud, "That is the Italian Man. He is most strange."

I wince at his loud candor.

"Do not worry. He cannot speak a word of English, or any other language." A few people snicker.

The Italian Man looks like a CIA agent on vacation. He dresses in green shorts and a flak jacket lined with numerous pockets of varying sizes. His teeth are black, and he smokes incessantly, although he never inhales. He clamps down hard on each filter of his Marlboros, soaking the end, and sucks noisily until a cloud of fresh gray smoke flows from his lips into the air. Perhaps what marks him as the class wanker is his pack. It is a cloth box fastened to a steel frame with big wheels. He pulls it behind him. He looks like an old lady on a shopping spree. The pack is covered with decals from cities all over Europe, the kind one can see plastered all over the rear bumper of Airstream Trailers. His flak jacket is covered with pins proclaiming the European unity of 1992, buttons with photos of Pope John Paul II, and souvenir pins from the countries that once made up the Soviet Union.

When he returns, he goes into the bathroom, closes the door, quickly flushes the toilet, and immediately steps out again. Everyone looks at one another, and childlike grins flash from some of the bunks. What the hell was that about?

The Italian Man sits on his bed, removes his shoes, and then puts on bedroom slippers and shuffles about the hostel. He enters the bathroom, repeats his flushing ritual, and finally sits at the table.

"*Aufiedsein,*" he says to me.

"I am not German, I am an American," I say in English.

"*Buona ventura, ist ein Americanishe.*"

"I am American." This time I try Spanish.

"*Buena fortuna, pelegrino. Comme si, comme ça. La peregrinación es muy difícil,* yes?"

After the Italian Man leaves, Willem explains, "Giuseppe imagines he can speak every European language. I am not even certain how good his Italian is." Willem, for all his London erudition, is something of a bitch.

When the Italian Man returns a short while later, I listen carefully. He mangles his native Italian into a Spanish-sounding accent and throws in a few words of the language he is trying to speak, French, German, English—a pilgrim's Mr. Malaprop. What I might find charming, though, the others loathe. The Italian Man can't advance any conversation past the weather or merry howdy-dos. Like the social misfits I remember from my youth, he is despised by others not for his iconoclastic clothes or peculiar behavior, but for his stunning lack of self-awareness. On some level he is wholly innocent of just how much fun is being made of him, the classic butthead.

> See the tree how big it's grown,
> But friend it hasn't been too long.
> It wah—zint big.

The Flemish troublemaker Claudy storms into the shelter, singing in the unctuous baritone vibrato of a lounge lizard.

"You are an American."

"Yes, I am."

"Word gets around. I know all the American hits."

A pilgrim with a taste for Bobby Goldsboro. I am speechless.

"Moon river, you heart shaker, wherever you're knowing, I'm blowing your way."

"The words are 'heart breaker, wherever you're going, I'm going your way.'"

"Oh, I know all the words. I am just testing you, American. What's your name?"

"Jack."

"Claudy." He shakes my hand vigorously. I can see in Willem's face a look of disdain. "I am Flemish."

"I know. Word gets around."

"All the pilgrims will be eating dinner tonight at the finest restaurant. You must come eat with us."

Willem makes one of his faces. I see it. Willem sees that I see it. Claudy sees it, and sees that Willem sees me seeing it.

"Oh, everybody but Willem. He has to call his wife! He does not eat in restaurants! He goes to bed so early! You must come. . . . Great. Then you will come. We will all be eating at eight."

Dinner is a mad debauchery, emceed by our own Claudy. Like Willem, he is fluent in several languages, but his vocabularies are vulgar and colloquial. His English has the singsong quality of an American doing a bad imitation of a Liverpudlian accent. He opens the evening with several horrible jokes that provoke nothing but groans of pain.

But it is impossible to condemn Claudy if only because no one can get a word in. His performance is improvisational and takes its source material at random—someone's shirt, the food, a picture on the wall—but always winds back around to his own biography, which he serves up in comic dollops. He has sung in major nightclubs throughout the United States and England. He is a genius computer programmer and knows the president of Hewlett-Packard on a first-name basis. "I could call him right now, and he would beg me to work for him."

The subject of gambling comes up. Claudy brags that he holds the Las Vegas record for playing blackjack continuously—ninety-six hours—and is listed in *The Guinness Book of World Records*. The secret: cold showers during the fifteen-minute breaks. He has slept with women on all continents. The best are American. He winks at me for confirmation. But nothing beats the seduction of a good Spanish Catholic girl.

Claudy speaks the worst Spanish, the only continental language he has yet to master. But somehow he has the waiter so tangled in laughter that free wine and brandy flow all night long.

When the Italian Man (who was not invited) becomes the topic of conversation, a married British couple named Roderick and Jerri attempt an explanation but are cut off by Claudy.

"Oh, he's a bloody weird one. He smokes all day. And he takes a one-second leak in the bathroom like a dog and then flushes. At night he falls asleep in two seconds. Rick, do your imitation."

Rick makes loud snorting noises. Everyone at the table seems to know what these unpleasant sounds refer to, and they all participate. DRDRDRDR. AGAGAGAG. BTHBTHBTHBTH.

"He snores like a fart," Rick ventures in his first bit of English. The table erupts with laughter, and the waiter pours another round of Spanish brandy.

The pilgrim shelter locks its gate at eleven P.M. Just before then, we pay up and decamp. Our little room is full. Other latecomers are laying out rolls on the floor. Willem is in his bed, reading by flashlight. I avoid his look. As I prepare to unroll my pack on the floor, Claudy whispers from a bunk to come over. He removes his walking stick and boots from one claimed bed.

"You can have this one," he says conspiratorially. I demur, insisting that I don't want him to sleep on the floor.

"I won't," he says. "I always claim two bunks so I can give one to a friend."

Willem is looking up from his pool of light, and his face speaks of betrayal. I am casting my lot here. Willem or Claudy, the follower of rules or the breaker of rules. Retired air force captain or Dionysus. Hobbes never said it would be easy.

I unroll my bag on the mattress. Willem returns to his book unhappily. Claudy is already on the other side of the room, alternately cracking jokes in Flemish with Rick and Karl and cutting some kind of deal with the elderly Dutch couple. Bedrolls are shifted, and now Claudy is sleeping in the top bunk next to mine. I cringe at what Willem is making of all this sudden intimacy.

Lights are out and the room is dark. I hear the rattling of the gate, and at last the Italian Man enters through a doorway of moonlight. He undresses by flashlight. His unzippings and zippings are loud and interminable. At last he flops on the bunk with an odd grunt.

DRDRDRDR, the Italian Man says. I hear Claudy holding back a cackle. In the distance I can make out the muffled giggles of Rick and then Karl.

AGAGAGAG. The old Dutch couple make suffocating noises. I am holding back a big one myself.

BTHBTHBTHBTH. The ticklish Rick isn't holding up well; some puffs of authentic hilarity are popping out. The room is quivering with contained laughter. The contagion builds and approaches instability. Rick explodes. Claudy's out of the bag. I lose it. Oblivious, the Italian Man falls into a loud, ragged snore uncommonly like flatulence. Right on cue. The room vibrates with the laughter of an unmonitored homeroom. In the cacophony, I can pick out each of them. I know these people now. I can hear them all, except Willem, silent in the dark.

The life of the pilgrim is always advertised in the grandest terms. There is talk of stripping life to its barest essentials, paring away to the tabula rasa of one's soul. The rigors of the road scale life down to this level almost immediately. But when one is walking in a group, what gets built up again, almost before one knows it's happening, are these crude alliances, borne on puerile jokes, mean pranks, and small favors. Acquaintances are made and destroyed in juvenile terms, employing tactics I vaguely remember from the playground at recess. All our actions—the gift of a peach, the indulgence of a bed—mean to say what was said so frankly as children: Be my friend. And if these offerings fail, then: You are not my friend. I hate you.

The next morning, I lose Willem. Around six A.M. everyone gets up at the same time. It's unavoidable with that many people in a room. Willem wants me to leave with him at once. He flatters me. I am a serious pilgrim, not like them, he tells me. But I linger at the table and drink my coffee with the others. When I look around again, he's gone. Later that day, on the road, I walk with the Flemish. At a bar where we take a break, I have a beer. Willem, by perverse coincidence, walks in for a glass of water. I invite him to join us. "I do not drink alcohol before sundown," he announces. Hoots of grade school disdain from the Flemish. I have my first enemy.

And by early afternoon I have a second one. Willie, the filmmaker, has made it clear to Rick and Karl that my presence is fouling his movie. Willie pulls up alongside us in his caravan from time to time to shoot some pictures and to entice Rick and Karl with drinks and food. On the one hand, Willie is simply bribing them. They are old men and can't resist the occasional cold drink and sandwich, especially when we are walking in the heat. But this particular entanglement, I quickly learn, is perverse and political. When the two Flemish aldermen left Belgium, Willie was an unemployed teacher who showed up to videotape their departure on his home camera.

A local television station bought a piece of it for the news. And since then, Willie has assumed the tyrannical impatience of a studio director. "He thinks he's fucking Ingmar Bergman," Claudy tells me.

Moreover, Rick and Karl are boxed in. Willie's film will chronicle their trip. They can't insult him or even question him. They are politicians, and Willie is, strangely, the media. So they treat him as gingerly as the White House coddles the Washington press corps. Willie despises Claudy, who tagged along after meeting them in France, but on this account, Willie is also boxed in. Claudy doesn't take guff from anyone; he is simply too loud, overbearing, and rude to be humiliated into going away. Besides, Rick likes Claudy's bacchanal performances at every watering hole. So whatever keeps Rick happy, Willie must endure.

But the image of a red-haired American who speaks no Flemish is bollixing his film. Like so many of us, Willie has come to the road with a load of preconceptions and resists adjusting them. He wants images of intense suffering and a crew of pilgrims who look the part. Both Rick and Karl are Central Casting pictures of the traditional pilgrim: beards, long hair, leather faces. My presence confuses Willie's outline. Claudy confides to me that this morning the discussion inside the van, where I am not allowed, has turned on the delicate matter of getting rid of me. Claudy warns me that Willie is going to try to talk to me.

In the small town of La Virgen del Camino (the Virgin of the Road) outside of León, the van parks alongside a large empty field fenced in by wrought iron. Willie steps outside to offer me a cup of coffee, which I accept, and then cozies up for a little chat. He can understand English if it is spoken very slowly.

"Willie," I say before he can begin, "do you see this empty field?" He nods, and I tell him this is one of the most important places on the road. In the early 1500s this area was barren, inhabited only by poor, desperate shepherds. One of them was named Alvar Simón Gómez Fernández. One day he saw the Virgin Mary, who asked him to throw a stone as far as he could and to build a church there. The locals grew very excited at this news, and funds poured in from all over the region. Apparitions so often preceded a church raising in those times, they effectively constituted a free building program. Here, this burst of enthusiasm created an entire town, appropriately named the Virgin of the Road. The shepherd Simón was among the attractions for a while, but eventually he was edged out. This pilgrim's stop was so profitable that lawsuits between the clerical and secular powers were filed and counterfiled for centuries. When Napoleon's armies passed through here in the nineteenth century, the situation was resolved when soldiers razed the pilgrim complex, reducing it once again to this empty field in the heart of town.

Willie is very excited by this story. He has forgotten the reason he wanted to talk to me. He charges back into the van and reappears with his tripod and videocamera. He sets up at the fence, poking his lens through the wrought-iron slots. He revs up his camera and slowly pans from left to right, recording the static image of an empty field. The wind is so slight this morning that even the brown weeds do not stir.

Down the way, the weary Claudy, Rick, and Karl are hanging on to the fence, their faces pressed into the slots like children. I step over beside them. We all stare at the empty field.

"See, I told you, Willie's a fucking idiot," Claudy informs me.

"Claudy, in my country, one of the first great philosophers any child encounters is named Bugs Bunny. In such moments, he would customarily reflect, 'What an Eskimo Pie-head.'"

By the end of the day, a crowd of pilgrims pulls into Villadangos del Páramo, a place whose name dates to a time of uncommon frankness. It literally means "Little Village on a Bleak Plateau." The modern economy has slightly redeemed Villadangos. The European Economic Community wants to reclaim the road's old meaning of European unity and has spent money making the road attractive in places. Here, a freshly built EEC hostel has separate rooms with stiff bunks, a complete kitchen, clean bathrooms, hot and cold running water, and an enormous dining area with tables and chairs. The place is cleaned every morning by a hired staff member.

The facilities are more luxurious than any of the houses surrounding it.

It is clear that lots of pilgrims have decided to stay here
because of the accommodations. I meet two beautiful Spanish
girls in their twenties. There are several young men from
France and Spain on bicycles (some of whom are traveling to
Santiago to avoid the compulsory draft; the road calls for
many reasons). There is a Welsh family—an out-of-work veterinarian named Wyn, his wife, Val, and their two boys, Adam
and Gregg, ages ten and eleven. They are a popular sight since
Wyn bought a mule after crossing the Pyrenees. The mule's
name is Peregrino, Spanish for "Pilgrim." He bears a huge
straw sack with wide berths on either side of his ample belly in
which the Welsh carry their goods.

The good feelings of the place provoke Claudy to suggest
that the pilgrims all cook a meal together. A chain of language
is used to dispense the duties. Claudy speaks Flemish so he can
talk to his people. I can speak Spanish, so I communicate with
the Spaniards, whose knowledge of French brings the crowd
full circle. A menu is drawn up. Claudy will cook a stew. I am
contributing a zucchini casserole. Val will cook a corn dish.
The French boys are dispatched to buy wine. Claudy and I are
left to scrounge up cooking pots and knives.

I suggest we buy some, which Claudy dismisses as "typical
fucking American." He has other ideas. He asks Val if he can
borrow the boys, and the four of us depart the hostel. Claudy
approaches a decent house and rings the doorbell. A middle-
aged mother appears. Claudy asks me to tell her in Spanish
that we are poor pilgrims walking to Santiago without any
money. This con is beyond me, and while the lady stands in
her doorway, smiling, Claudy is shouting at me to speak. I
introduce ourselves as pilgrims, merely pilgrims. But I can see
that Claudy has no patience with my refined sense of honesty.
He jumps into the conversation with his fractured Spanish, but
it is enough. He says we are traveling with these young boys
who haven't eaten all day. We are tired, but we don't come to
beg. We have bought the food with the few remaining pesetas
we have. But we lack the pots and pans, forks and knives, with

which to eat. Santiago directed us to this house, he says, because he knew that a good person lives here. All we ask, Claudy adds, is that you trust us to borrow some equipment until tomorrow morning. We are pilgrims, honest and true. You can count on us.

It's an enviable performance—and to back it up is the sight of us standing there. A day of walking and sweating has reduced each of us to the image of pilgrim poster boys. There are smears of dirt on our heads and arms. Our legs are covered in scratches. We stink, and each of us has a rat's nest for hair.

Claudy's eyes well up with tears. The boys, cunning pilgrims themselves, put on the faces of quiet cherubic suffering. I'm no fool. I complete the tableau and allow my features to sag into a Viking's pietà. The woman clutches her hands over her chest and cries out Saint James's name. A few minutes later she returns with a bag of her best gear: pots, pans, forks and knives, plates and glasses, napkins.

Claudy says thank you in the charming superlative Spanish offers. *Muchíssimas gracias.* He says it a dozen times with the unctuous humility of a beggar. The mother encourages us to have a good night and closes the door. Back at the hostel, the boys tell this story repeatedly to anyone who will listen. Claudy, everyone says proudly, is a true pilgrim.

The hostel is buzzing with good feelings. A potluck dinner brings out the best in everyone. Food and wine abound. People are moving in and out, cooking meals, getting cleaned up for the big dinner. Everyone, of course, except Willie. He has parked his camper on a planted field behind the hostel, which we can see through a plate-glass window. Claudy volunteers to observe, as we all have, that a planted field probably indicates that someone has tilled and planted it. No doubt the owner is not too happy about having a multiton mobile home parked on his future lettuce. Willie dismisses Claudy's advice as ignorant and unnecessary.

The little tension of this moment produces one of the more bizarre events of the night. Willie and his wife sense the hostility over the parking space, and they resent Rick and Karl's chumminess with everyone in the room. So they hook up their camper to the hostel's electricity and prepare a separate meal a good bit more aromatic than the peasant fare we cook. While we have shoved together three long cafeteria tables to form a banquet table, Willie has dragged a small table off to the side, set with five places.

"You see?" Claudy says. "This is how he operates. He won't let Rick and Karl eat with us. The fifth place is for me. Willie knows he can't insult me, or he will hurt his relationship with Rick. This table is a challenge to Rick and Karl. I say, 'Fuck him.'"

When the dinners are ready, Rick and Karl actually sit on two chairs angled perfectly between the two tables. They have places at both. And plates at both. And meals at both. When I catch Rick's eye, I tell him King Solomon would be proud. "I am a politician," he confesses. "What can I do?"

During dinner the door slams open, and the owner of the lettuce patch storms into the main room in a rage. He instinctively homes in on the Spanish speakers, the two girls. They are baffled. I hasten to intervene, explaining to the girls and the lettuce man that all of us complained to the owner of the caravan about his choice of parking space, but he ignored us. I (back in first grade again) point to Willie: He did it, sir.

Willie is furious that I have fingered him. (What else could I do?) He wants to yell at me, but fury, like humor, is among the last things learned in a foreign language. His English is just not up to the job. So he yells at Claudy in Flemish. He shrieks that Claudy is somehow responsible for ratting to the lettuce man. Willie shoves Claudy against the wall. So I jump up and run over. I'm ready to pound this guy into the ground, and I *want* to slug him. I never beat up anybody in first grade, quite the opposite. But now I'm big, and I've been carrying a pack for a month.

But Claudy waves me off. He stands rigid, insulting the filmmaker with what sounds like really delicious Flemish obscenities. Rick and Karl freeze, as does the whole room. The two men bump chests and shout. It is a splendid pas de deux, the one perfected by baseball umpires and team managers. Some-

how we all know that no fight will break out. From the side-
lines, suddenly, it strikes all of us as funny. So we laugh, which
pitches Willie into a profound sense of humiliation. He
plunges his hand into his crotch, retrieves his keys, and leaves
the building at once.

We quietly listen to the sound of the caravan pulling away
from the building. "It's Saint James," Rick crows. After a
while, Willie returns and takes his seat with his wife at the
other table. They eat in fierce silence for the rest of the
evening. Rick and Karl maintain their spot in the DMZ, but
everyone knows where their hearts are.

Our table, meanwhile, is a United Nations gabfest. Jokes
and stories are told, translated, retold, and translated once
again. Probably the entire night's conversation could be tran-
scribed on two sheets of note paper. But the joy of talking and
screaming, conquering the language barrier, all aided by magnums of wine, has put us in a fine spirit. We are pilgrims. And
Willie's presence, the crass filmmaker lacking in the natural
humility that we learn on foot, only encourages our bonhomie
and spices it with a tasty dash of schadenfreude.

As we get more acquainted, I notice that we have developed
new names. They distinguish us as pilgrims rather than as people. I am known as the Red American Who Speaks Spanish.
The movie stars break down into the Funny Flemish One
(Claudy), the Pilgrim with the Long Gray Beard (Rick), and
the Quiet Flemish Man (Karl). The Welsh are known as the
English Family with the Mule. And the two Spanish girls are
simply the Beautiful Spanish Girls. We all sense that tomorrow
we will probably split up again, and what good will our other
names do? "Jack" means nothing here. "The Red American
Who Speaks Spanish" defines me as a pilgrim, a name that
other pilgrims will recognize.

Not long afterward we hear the door at the far end of the
hostel open. Unoiled wheels squeak up the hall. From the
darkened corridor appears the Italian Man. He approaches the
table as all of us fall into a knowing silence. It seems everyone
except the Beautiful Spanish Girls has had an encounter with
the Italian Man.

"*Bueno nochesa, pelerin. Un día del ambulatore termina with the food de la mesa. Que buenos peregrinas.*"

No one says a word. Everyone willfully ignores him. And of course the Italian Man is as innocent as an infant of the cold shoulder from this crowd. This is how *everyone* treats him. He's the kid with the "Kick Me" sign pinned to his backside who never figures it out.

"*Cuanta peregrinas are here?*" He counts us all out loud. "*Eins, zwei, tres, quatro, cinq, siete, eight.*"

The Beautiful Spanish Girls look to me in confusion. I give them a quick explanation of his peculiar speaking habits, and they laugh. They haven't known him long enough to sense the cruelty.

The entire day has been a series of flashbacks to childhood. I think of Scott Dorran and Sidney Carpenter, two kids who were brutalized in my grade school. I believe I joined the mob in ridicule. Perhaps I led it. And what about the time Tim Trouche, my best friend, got the crap beat out of him by Herb Butler? The crowd cried for blood in the recess yard just before homeroom. I stood silently, and the crowd got what it wanted.

The road invites its pilgrims to begin again—lifting the traveler from numbing familiarity and dropping him into new circumstances. Being a pilgrim allows all that, yet how strange and thrilling it feels.

"*Peregrino italiano.*" I stand up to speak his language. "*Wilkommen, bien venue, welcome.*" The words come easy and tug mightily at the heart of our resident lounge lizard. Claudy catches the hint. He perks up and begins to sing—Liza Minnelli blown through the pipes of Steve Lawrence. A French boy fetches another wineglass, and the others clear a place at the table for the Italian Man.

SEVEN
PONFERRADA

They overturn and desecrate our altars," said Pope Urban II about the Moslem problem in the Holy Land. "They will take a Christian, cut open his stomach, and tie his intestine to a stake; then, stabbing at him with a spear, they will make him run until he pulls out his own entrails and falls dead to the ground." The day was November 28, 1095. A few years later the People's Crusade set off for Jerusalem.

The battles did not go well for the Christians at first. One siege of a Moslem castle left the warriors stranded far from a water supply. After a week, wrote one chronicler, the men "were so terribly afflicted by thirst that they bled their horses and asses and drank the blood; others let down belts and cloths into a sewer and squeezed the liquid into their mouths; others passed water into one another's cupped hands and drank; others dug up damp earth and lay down on their backs, piling the earth upon their chests." They surrendered. The healthy were sold into slavery; the rest were executed.

The Christians learned from their new enemies. In a subsequent battle, an army of infidels rushed from their fortress into a field of Christians. The decapitations were numerous, and the Christians tested an innovative way to dampen enemy morale. They placed each head in a sling and flung it over the fortress wall.

A year later the breaching of the walls of Jerusalem ended in the slaughter of seventy thousand Moslems. "If you would hear how we treated our enemies at Jerusalem," wrote one jubilant Christian, "know that in the portico of Solomon and in the Temple our men rode through the unclean blood of the Saracens, which came up to the knees of their horses." But Urban never heard the good news. Two weeks after his original speech, he died, uncertain that his words would come to anything.

Nine of the knights who had distinguished themselves in the fighting banded together in Jerusalem. They took as their headquarters a building near the Dome of the Rock, the very location, it is said, of the temple of Solomon. They assumed the holy duty of protecting pilgrims who would certainly come to Jerusalem now that it was safe. Because they saw their job as an essentially religious exercise, these knights did something unheard of. They took vows of poverty, chastity, and obedience, assuming the attitude of monks. At this time, knights were not romantic warriors but vulgar mercenaries, mistrusted by all, especially Rome. The nine monks of Jerusalem were different and the church seized the opportunity to marry the righteousness of the clergy with the brutal force of an army. The earliest emblem of these knights is a seal showing two men on a single horse, a symbol of their poverty and humiliation. They took a name, the Poor Fellow-Soldiers of Jesus Christ, or the Knights of the Temple of Solomon, shortened to the Knights Templar.

Within seventy years their numbers swelled and the Templars became the most powerful force in the Mediterranean. Their reputation slowly assumed an esoteric character, protectors of the Holy Land and possessors of great mysteries. Money and land grants flowed generously into their coffers.

Their fortresses were flung from the Holy Land to Scotland in the north and from Hungary in the east to Portugal on the Atlantic coast. The Knights Templar built one of their most impressive and enigmatic constructions in Ponferrada, Spain, on the road to Santiago.

León is a common place for pilgrims to begin the road, and it's been three days since my new acquaintances and I left there. Where I had once walked for weeks without seeing a pilgrim, I now cannot pass an hour. Ahead, on a rising hill, a creeping fleck of yellow is, I know, a pilgrim in a rain slicker. Behind me are dozens of pilgrims. We try to walk together at times, but it never works out. The pace and timbre of one's step on a long haul has a unique quality, like a fingerprint. Each of us moves at our own speed and in our own style. For a short distance we can walk in sync, but after a while the nuances cause problems. And when the conversation runs dry, companion pilgrims find themselves disengaging like slow boxcars, one pulling away from the other. This morning the chilly mists of the hilly pastures of León province have stretched us across the landscape, an inept dragging conga line. I have come to know so many of them, many more than I met in León or Villadangos. We try to stay in touch. In each shelter are notebooks. We send messages to each other via these books or send inquiries through other pilgrims. The word on the road this week is to hold up late this afternoon at a little town called Rabanal, reputed to have a fine hostel.

The pilgrims in their ponchos and bright shirts provide the only primary tones in this land, where everything is a variation on the color of manure. The sepia buildings, the muddy street, the swarthy locals, all seem to have risen chthonically from the hills of soil and dung.

At Santa Catalina de Samoza, a squat man steps from a chatting knot of three friends into the sodden street. Half his face is an enormous purple swag the size of a handbag. The dewlap, a monstrous sagging deformity, pulls at his eyes and nose. His upper lip is a blooded fist. No pulling or tugging can rearrange this man's face into any expression other than constant sorrow. One of his friends has a dead left arm, the hand unnaturally flat. His fingers are thin and delicate in their callouslessness. He takes up a second position in the street with a light, sensual squish in the mud. His left arm is swaying, perhaps with the breeze. They assume the hip-lock position of toughs, and at first I am afraid. But this is not New York, or even the outskirts of León. The handbag snaps open; a crazy curvaceous hollow sounds the thick grunt of rural Spanish.

"Good day, pilgrim," he says.

I was always taught never to stare at a deformity. I try to look this man in the eye. But he effectively has only one; the other is sheathed in wattle. I can't help myself. His face is unbelievable. I have to study it. Rogue teeth sprout from huge exposed formations of gum and frame a jagged cavern with a tiny black tongue, a pelican's gullet. Yet I recognize the semblance of a smile.

The tradition of welcoming pilgrims is a thousand years old in these parts of Spain. The legendary southern hospitality of my home region in America is in its infancy by comparison. My new acquaintance and his friends must greet a pilgrim each hour at this time of the year.

"Have you tried our chorizo?" says the man with the dead arm.

Every region of Spain boasts homemade chorizo, the Spanish sausage, and of course every region's is the best. One of the men points to an arrow painted on a stone, indicating the direction of the town restaurant and the local sausage.

"And how about your own chorizo?" shouts the man of constant sorrow. His mouth opens tremendously and exudes a temblor of a laugh. He grabs the cloth of his crotch and bunches it up in his fist. He pulls manfully at himself.

"The pilgrim girls!" says one of the men in the doorway.

"We have seen them."

"We have talked to them!"

"Girls, girls, the most precious girls! Pilgrim girls!"

I recite the old Spanish proverb about the road—Go a pilgrim, return a whore—because, I don't know, to keep the conversation going.

"Whores!" they all shout at once. Like grotesques from the canvases of Goya, the men stump and strut. One man bends over, his hands on his knees, and pries open his mouth to hiss.

Pilgrims may be sacred folk, walking reminders of a great journey, to *some*. But we are many things, depending on where we are. In León we might be potential mugging victims. Each town seems to have its own attitude. Here, as in many small towns, we are the stuff of prurient daydreams—itinerant men and women, unbound from centuries of strict Catholic rule. Footloose and liberal. Far from the stern eye of mother and father. Young men and women in shorts, loosely fitted blouses, hair unkempt. Careless. Washing in common restrooms. Sleeping in gangs on the floors. Alone in the pastures. Our raspy breathing may be not the result of our labor, but a hint of our desire. Ignominious. Wanton. Ah, the mystery of pilgrims. Whores.

Rabanal is another town like the last, except that the Confraternity of Saint James, a British group of loyal Santiago alumni, has recently renovated a luxurious and gleaming hostel. The bedroom has forty bunks, all of which will be filled tonight. Throughout the afternoon, pilgrims arrive in a continual parade of activity. Little Rabanal, as somnolent as every hamlet on this stretch of the road, suddenly resembles the busy chaos of a frontier town. Bikers brake at the gate. The Welsh family arrive with their mule. Inside, the bathroom is crowded with men and women bent over sinks of gray water, grinding their socks. The clotheslines and banisters display shorts and shirts and, unabashedly, bras and underpants of every description. The entire village is bustling with pilgrims, most of whom I recognize. By late sunset Rabanal's two restaurants are jammed with tables burdened by wine, huge plates of lamb and steak, potatoes and eggs, and lively talk.

Allegiances and acquaintances come and go. Friendships are made and broken, all in the course of a day or a casual remark. Very few of our discussions concern the touchy subject of why each of us is walking the road. It almost seems too private.

In the bedroom, later that evening, I unroll my bag on a bunk. The Flemish are here, and there is Willem, and the old

Dutch couple from León. The Beautiful Spanish Girls are just next to me. The friendly hellos are interrupted by the old Dutch man, who shouts to the girls in broken Spanish: "There is the Red American you were asking after, eh?" He grins and winks. The Spanish girls blush and turn away, a demur so mannered I can't imagine it outside a nineteenth-century novel. The Dutch man shoots a brash thumbs-up in my direction and clicks his tongue on the side of his cheek. He means well, but however naively, he doesn't understand the indelicacy of his remark. The Spanish girls never speak to me again.

Sleeping in a room of nearly forty exhausted travelers is not easy. When the lights go out at eleven, the sound sleepers, about half the room, collapse into a zany chorus of snores. The rest of the pilgrims are giggling like naughty school-children—the girls, the younger men, the bicyclists, me. The laughter wakes up some of the grouchy men, who shush the crowd, provoking more laughter, waking up more. More shushing. More snoring. More laughter, until the hardship of the day wears down the giddiest and carries us all off to oblivion. We need our sleep. Tomorrow is a thirty-one-kilometer walk to a famous city, Ponferrada, known for the ruins of an enormous fortress built by the Knights Templar.

The new marriage of monkish piety and holy war brutality developing among the twelfth-century crusaders might have made sense in the bloody sands of Jerusalem. Back home, though, such arguments violated fundamental precepts. The words *Thou shalt not kill* don't suggest many loopholes unless you're Bernard de Clairvaux. His mother knew she would bear a great orator when she dreamed she bore a barking dog. As a young man, Bernard had founded the Cistercian order, dedicated to fierce poverty in a desolate sinkhole of French earth, the Vale of Absinth.

Bernard began his defense of the Knights Templar at a conference in Troyes on January 13, 1128. The opponent to this new idea was Jean, bishop of Orléans. He was a notorious sycophant of the king, but there were other rumors. One scribe called him a "public dancer," and another cast aside euphemism, condemning him as a "succubus and a sodomite." His nickname among the clergy was "Flora." His presence at the proceedings may, in fact, have helped.

Bernard de Clairvaux refined his arguments, eventually putting them in a letter entitled "In Praise of the New Knighthood." By killing infidels, he argued, the Knights Templar were doing nothing wrong because "either dealing out death or dying, then for Christ's sake, contains nothing criminal but rather merits glorious reward." In this way, the Templar "serves his own interests in dying, and Christ's in killing!" Which is not murder because "when he kills a malefactor this is not homicide but malicide, and he is accounted Christ's legal executioner against evildoers."

Bernard's words carried the day. The intoxicating combination of monkish righteousness and military ferocity made the knights extremely popular. They assumed the uniform of monks, dressed in white to display their chastity. The code of conduct, or Rule, of the Templars was tough and manly (a feature that would later haunt them). It prohibited the company of women because it is "a perilous thing, for through them the ancient demon denied us the right to live in Paradise." The Rule stated that "none of you should presume to kiss a woman, neither widow, nor maiden, nor mother, nor sister, nor aunt, nor any other woman; therefore the knights of Christ must always flee from women's kisses." Their weapons were painted basic black. Their hair would be cut short, but they grew thick, bushy beards. Violators of the code were punished brutally. An errant knight was forced to eat his meals directly off the floor, and he was forbidden to shoo off the competing dogs.

The appeal of the Knights Templar made them an unparalleled source of fund-raising. A meeting was convened in Toulouse, France, in 1130 just to coordinate the promiscuous, often competitive donations of property and money to the popular order. Hundreds of estate owners throughout Europe willed their lands to the Templars. The most impressive donor was King Alonso I of Aragon. He ceded one-third of his kingdom in Spain.

On March 29, 1139, the pope issued the most powerful decree ever given to an order of monks. The Omne Datum Optimum, or "Every Best Gift," exempted the Knights Templar from local taxes, tithes, and nearly every other financial claim. Their only responsibility was to the pope. The church at last had an army, and now a well-funded one.

The power and the privileges of the Knights Templar, though, soon caused resentment. In Europe the every-best-gift decree infuriated the local clergy. Their greatest weapon against the secular nobles was the edict, or the suspension of church activities—baptisms, marriages, services, etc. Since the Templars were exempt from such bans, they often carried out those offices, at considerable profit, in the teeth of priests' complaints.

Meanwhile, back in the Holy Land, the Knights Templar attacked Damascus in 1148 but were repelled, pursued, and slaughtered. Ibn al-Qalaisi wrote that the corpses of Templars and their horses were "stinking so powerfully that the birds almost fell out of the sky." With resentment stirring at home, defeats such as these provided the local clergy with a rich source of rumor and innuendo. The knights didn't help their case much. In 1154 the Templars captured a Moslem courtier named Nasr, who was fleeing Egypt after murdering the caliph of Cairo. Despite his conversion to Christianity, the Templars traded him to the caliph's four widows for sixty thousand dinars. Before they reached the Nile, the women had ripped off Nasr's limbs and mutilated the remains. Back in Europe, it didn't sound good: a Christian handed over for certain execution in exchange for a purse of silver? This story had an unpleasant resonance.

Over time, the bureaucracy of the Templars grew, and the abundance of detailed amendments to the Rule suggests nasty, often bizarre infighting. One new regulation forbade a brother from leaving the dinner table except for a nosebleed. Another codicil excused from chapel "any brother who is washing his hair." Could the mighty Templars be going soft?

The mission of the Templars was getting cloudy as well. For example, after the Fourth Crusade of the early thirteenth cen-

tury, the Templars were asked by the pope to help combat a
potent heresy in the French region of Languedoc. The Templars—now a century old, all descendents of Holy Land warriors, more Eastern than European in temperament—were
pleased to slaughter the Cathar heretics in the French town of
Béziers. They had only one question: How could one tell good
Catholics from bad? The papal legate Arnaud Amalric
responded notoriously, *"Tuez-les tous! Dieu reconnaîtra les
siens."* It is an answer that is still with us. I have seen it on the
T-shirts of marines on leave from Parris Island in South Carolina: "Kill them all! Let God sort 'em out!"

By the mid-thirteenth century the Templars weren't performing well in the Holy Land, either. Out of the east had
come a new breed of infidel. One witness raged: "Men? They
are inhuman and bestial, better called monsters than men.
Thirsting for and drinking blood, they butcher the bodies of
dogs and humans, and eat them. They wear bulls' horns, they
are armed and squat, with compact bodies; they are invincible
in war, and blood to them is a delicious drink." These were the
Khwarazmian Turks.

Their attack on Jerusalem in 1244 was brutal. Only a few
Templars survived a Holy City consumed in fire. It would be
the Christians' last look at Jerusalem for almost six centuries,
until Napoleon entered.

In 1291 the last bastion fell. Templars began drifting back to
Europe, a land many of them had never seen. Despite total
failure, the Templars returned to their European fortresses and
vast wealth. The local clergy and the secular nobles had their
long knives out for the Templars. A poem written by Rostan
Berenguier of Marseilles at the time spoke of the knights "riding their gray horses and taking their ease in the shade and
admiring their own fair locks." The verses ended with the ominous proposal that Europe should "rid ourselves of them for
good." One writer said that the Templar defeats were not
merely a military matter, but "a judgment of God against the
order which he himself had approved and established." Their
return was not just a decampment; it was a sign from heaven.
The Crusades had been wrong. The common folk plunged into

a dark mood, troubled by self-doubt and wallowing in the self-pity that comes with defeat. Europe pouted, like a scolded child in search of a scapegoat. "It is no accident," writes twentieth-century historian Peter Partner, "that representations of Christ at this time begin to place less emphasis on Christ in majesty and more on the man of sorrows, on the passive Christ." Could the Templars have come in contact with something evil? Might they have wrongly possessed something? Had they done something perverse? There had to be a reason, didn't there?

At the end of any day, groups of pilgrims gather, coalesce, and then diverge with ease. For a while, the amateur historians of the road are myself; Louis, AKA the Frenchman Who Has Walked the Road Eleven Times; Javier, the Spanish Banker; Roderick and Jerri, the Young Married British Couple; and a few Germans. But there are other groups that form. Some are keen on the peculiar traditions of the road—a pilgrim is supposed to pause before a statue or throw a coin off a certain bridge. Others are taken by the physicality of the road. They gather and discuss the intricacies of the backpack. And yet others, like the Flemish, have a more carpe diem approach.

All of us participate in these groupings in some way or another. And in these maneuverings and jostlings, one can feel a kind of low-grade panic. We are trying to assert an approach to the road or an interpretation of it that is in some sense bigger than ourselves. The old vocabulary of the road—that language of suffering, penance, grace, mystery—are terms most of us find uncomfortable in our conversations. There are those who make a show of old-fashioned piety. They assume a public position at every church, praying a little loudly. Or they strike stances of studied pensiveness, make it known that they are writing in their journals, or alert other pilgrims to the beauty of a sunset. They are, in short, annoying: they walk the road with an untroubled confidence in what they are doing. The rest of us are anxious. Madame Debril's words haunt everyone, even those who may not have encountered her. Are you a true pilgrim?

This frantic effort to make the road into something else,

either through history or tradition or endurance or mere
enthusiasm, is tangible. It is a kind of competition. All our discussions are flavored with a subtext of "I know more than
you." At times this competitive edge manifests itself as knowledge—of history, of tradition, of what's around the next bend.
This spirit assumes its most primitive form the next morning
in Rabanal.

As the cocks crow, I pop open my eyes to see the early birds
such as Louis and Paolo packing in the auroral light for the
walk to Ponferrada. Willem, of course, has left hours ago. The
little noises of cinching a strap or stowing a tin cup have sent
an electric message through the room. Eyes are opening all
around, and the fever felt by the pilgrims is one of primal competition. Sleep too late and walk with the laggards! True pilgrims must rise now! Pack! Down a coffee and hit the road!
Within minutes the entire room is buzzing with hectic pilgrims, packing furiously.

This morning the claim to purity, to true pilgrim status,
takes an old, old form. Today's proof will have nothing of history or solemnity or detached silence. I can feel the group
dynamics of the herd gather into a force. It is nothing less than
a race.

I can't resist (partly out of being a guy, partly out of some
vestigial sense of duty). I am stuffing my sleeping bag care-
lessly into its little sack, and within minutes I am seated with
the hostel's British proprietor in the kitchen, crunching toast
and slurping coffee with the others. A stifled hysteria blazes on
each face. Were we bulls, this would be a stampede. But we are
human, sniffing in the air an ancient odor. Breakfast has all the
dignity of "Last one out is a rotten egg."

The rain of the last few days has secreted in these mountains
enough little pockets of water that the insects are overpower-
ing. The cattle in the neighboring pastures swat the air with
their metronomic tails. Throughout the morning's odd blue
light, we pilgrims pass each other and fall back. We look like a
line of hasty cowards surrendering in battle, snapping the air
before our faces with bandannas.

The morning's competition has put us in Ponferrada by

early afternoon, giving us enough time to see the place. The famous Knights Templar castle, set in the center of town on the banks of a river, is the size of ten football fields. The city surrounds and is defined by this beautiful ruin.

"The great mystery of the Knights Templar is buried there, you know," Louis says. I honestly can't tell whether he is serious or not.

"Ask any local," he says.

So I do. At the gate to the fortress is a gypsy and her two children. The town employs her to sell postcards. Admission is free. I ask her if the Knights Templar had hidden anything here.

"The Holy Grail," she says matter-of-factly. "No one has ever found it."

The fortress is a child's dream. Much of it has been destroyed over the years, but there are enough crenellated walls, oddly shaped turrets, storerooms, ammo depots, and the like to keep this tired Hardy Boy roaming for hours. Up a steep, narrow stone staircase, I clamber onto one of the corner turrets. It is a small space, no larger than a good-size room. A few minutes later two young men in dark blue suits emerge from the staircase, dragging a bag of books. We greet each other in Spanish as I notice name tags on their jackets that say "David" and "John."

"Excuse me," I say in English, "are you two Mormons?"

"Yes, how could you tell?"

"Clairvoyance, I guess."

They are missionaries from Utah, sent here to proselytize. They try to give me a book of the words of their angel, Moroni, but I explain to them I am a pilgrim to Santiago. I am thinking: One religion at a time, please. Soon they want to know if I have any inside dope on the castle because they know plenty.

The boys are amateur experts on the Templar castle, and I get the impression that these missionaries play hooky every afternoon and cruise the fortress. (Note to Utah: Not a good idea to send two young men to a Spanish city with a huge empty castle.)

"Have you found the secret passage?" they ask.

"Secret passage?"

"Oh, yeah, follow us."

They escort me to the back end of the wall near the river. Outside the fortress a slender hump, like the top of an earthen pipeline, descends to the river. A caved-in hole in the ground opens into a subterranean staircase. I step inside and walk as far down as the light will let me. Here was the answer to at least one Templar secret. In case of war, the knights had hidden access to the freshwater river outside the fortress.

"Isn't this place neat?" they ask.

"Extremely neat."

From atop another turret, they point to the remaining walls and corner establishments. Templars were said to be enamored with order, the boys explain. Many of the Templar establishments are built in octagonal shapes, suggesting some kind of cabalistic significance. But this fortress seems to quarrel with any attempt to impose order on it. The wall appears to be twelve-sided, each one of different length. And each turret is shaped differently, with unnatural protrusions of stone. The theory, they explain, is that the odd un-Templaresque shape of this fortress speaks some message to those who might understand it. So far, no one has broken the code.

After a while I tire of peering into empty stone bed chambers, ammo dumps, and meeting rooms. At the front gate I stop to buy a postcard from the gypsy mother and her kids.

"Did you find the Holy Grail?" she asks. There is not a trace of irony in her voice.

"Still looking," I tell her.

The king of France at the turn of the fourteenth century was known as an uncommonly handsome man. He was called Philip le Bel, the Beautiful, an ironic epithet for a king of Gothic pitilessness. Because of the French king's constant financial problems, relations between Paris and Rome had degenerated into a ludicrous state. The Beautiful had exhausted all the usual medieval methods for balancing the books. He had stolen property, he had arrested all the Jews, he had devalued his currency. As a last resort, he tried to tax the church.

Pope Boniface VIII was a fat and dissolute pontiff. One contemporary described him as "nothing but eyes and tongue in a wholly putrefying body . . . a devil." The Beautiful himself openly referred to him as "Your Fatuity." But Boniface knew the rules of the game as well.

In retaliation for France's new fiscal arrangements, the pope issued a dictum forbidding the taxation of the clergy.

So the Beautiful closed French borders to the exportation of gold bullion, cutting off Rome's transalpine money supply. To rub it in, he arrested the bishop of Pamiers and charged him with blasphemy, sorcery, and fornication.

So the pope issued a bull condemning the arrest and revoked some of the Beautiful's papal privileges.

The Beautiful burned his copy of the bull in public.

The pope delivered a stinging sermon filled with ominous warnings that the church was a creature with one head, not a monster with two.

The Beautiful issued charges, in absentia, against the pope himself, alleging blasphemy, sorcery, and sodomy.

The pope excommunicated the Beautiful. He compared the French to dogs and hinted that they lacked souls. His nuncios leaked a rumor that the pontiff might well excommunicate the entire country.

The peasants were stirred by such a threat, and the Beautiful quickly grasped that revolution was a better future to them than excommunication. So he acted fast, dispatching an army to Anagni, where the pope was staying. He placed the eighty-six-year-old pontiff under house arrest. The locals managed to save him, but a month later Boniface passed away. Some allege he succumbed to shock at the outrage; other sources say that he beat his head against a wall until he died.

After a pliable pope assumed office, the Beautiful returned to his economic problems. His wife died in 1305, and since he no longer would have to kiss a woman's lips, he applied for membership in the Knights Templar. The permanent knights of the Paris temple may have suspected that his intentions were less than pious and did something almost unspeakable: they blackballed the king.

The following year, the grand master of the Knights Templar, Jacques de Molay, returned to Europe from the Mediterranean in a show of luxury. He was accompanied by sixty knights and a baggage train of mules laden with gold and jewels. Around that time the Beautiful was more desperate than ever to solve his messy state finances: he tripled the price of everything in France overnight. Open rebellion broke out in the streets. Rioters threatened to kill him. He fled to the Parisian temple and begged the knights for protection. It was all too humiliating.

So in the fall of 1307, the Beautiful arranged a state action impressive even in these days of data highways and rapid deployment teams. On September 14 he mass-mailed a set of sealed orders to every bailiff, seneschal, deputy, and officer in his kingdom. The functionaries were forbidden under penalty of death to open the papers before Thursday night, October 12.

The following Friday morning, alert to their secret instructions, armies of officials slipped out of their barracks. By sundown nearly all the Knights Templar throughout France were in jails. One estimate puts the arrests at two thousand, another as high as five thousand. Only twenty escaped. The initial charges were vague, but they didn't sound good: "A bitter thing, a lamentable thing, a thing horrible to think of and terrible to hear, a detestable crime, an execrable evil, an abominable act, a repulsive disgrace, a thing almost inhuman, indeed alien to all humanity, has, thanks to the reports of several trustworthy persons, reached our ear, smiting us grievously and causing us to tremble with the utmost horror." What followed was so foul, according to folklore, that Templar sympathizers cursed the day itself, condemning it as evil—Friday the thirteenth—whose reputation never recovered.

Soon after the arrests, 127 charges were leveled against the Knights Templar. Nearly the entire indictment was fiction, but a few of the charges were quite colorful, and word of them spread quickly. During Templar initiation, the knights kissed each other on the mouth, then the navel (some interpret this to be the penis), and finally (no uncertainty here) the anus. Also during initiation, the novitiates had to spit or piss on the cross. They had to profess worship to a bedizened idol named Baphomet. Finally, they had to submit to homosexual orgies on demand. According to the confession of Templar grand dignitary Hugues de Pairaud, "I would tell [the novitiates] that if they felt any natural heat that pushed them toward incontinence, they had permission to cool it with the other brothers."

The confessions poured out quickly and voluminously from all the Templars, even Grand Master Jacques de Molay, because of an innovation in interrogation, the Inquisition. Already the Dominicans in charge were known by a Latin pun on their cruelty: *Domini canes,* the "dogs of God." The rules and regulations governing the use of torture were recent—Pope Urban IV wrote them in 1262—and they were full of loopholes. Essentially anything was permissible, as long as it resulted in neither "mutilation, incurable wounds, violent effusion of blood, nor death." The Beautiful tested the outer limits of these porous restrictions. His men stuffed rags in the mouths of some men and poured water in their nostrils. They threw knights in pits and left them to starve. They tied them to the rack. The inquisitors hog-tied the defendants' limbs and dragged them up and down hills. They branded them with hot irons. Other knights were submitted to the strappado, in which the victim had his hands tied behind his back and then hanged by the wrists with weights attached to his feet or genitals. In other jails a Templar's feet were rubbed with animal fat and simply set on fire. At one trial a knight arrived on stumps that concluded at his shins.

Not surprisingly, the Templars confessed to everything: homosexuality, pissing on the cross, bum kissing, idol worshiping. One Templar said that he would have "killed the Lord if it were asked of him." When asked why the Templars shrouded their initiation ceremony in such secrecy, one knight replied sadly, because we "were stupid." Which is probably as close to the truth as any answer. The Templars were largely illiterate. Grand Master Jacques de Molay could not read. The library at the Commandery of Corbins was found to house sixteen books. The Templar James of Garrigans stood out as a wonder because he could "write shaped letters well, and illuminate with gold."

The pope by this time, Clement V, was a compromise candidate and therefore politically weak. He realized he had been outmaneuvered by the Beautiful and sought to reclaim his authority by ordering the Templars to stand trial.

Initially it looked good for the pope and his frightened army. Jacques de Molay retracted his confession, and 597 Templars soon followed his lead. The pope successfully delayed the trial with papal paper pushing and blue-ribbon commissions until the spring of 1310. And the French king had no physical evidence for the trial.

But the Beautiful was not one to lie back in defeat. He had insisted that smaller, minor trials of the Templars be carried out at the local level throughout France. In Paris, one such proceeding was presided over by the brother of the king's finance minister and a royal toad. When events began to move in the pope's favor, this judge pronounced the Knights Templar before his court guilty and sentenced them to die—that *afternoon*.

By sundown and before anyone could intervene, 54 men were tied to stakes and set on fire. Observers reported that many of them shouted their innocence from the flames. Even the peasants in the audience, not known for their queasiness at such events, grew sick and scared. More sentences were hastily issued, and some 70 more were immolated. In the frenzy, some dead Templars were exhumed, their rotting corpses strapped to stakes and set on fire for good measure.

This tactic had an effect. The Templars who had retracted their confessions now retracted their retractions and begged for mercy. The pope was in a terrible bind and moved swiftly to cut his losses. On March 20, 1312, he dissolved the Templars and ordered their holdings to be dispersed.

There was still one loose end for the Beautiful. Grand Master Jacques de Molay and one other high official refused to confess. On March 18, 1314, the Beautiful set up two stakes on a small island in the Seine River in Paris. Amid defiant cries of innocence, the last of the surviving unpenitent Templars were burned.

The Beautiful's ham-fisted tactics didn't serve him well for long. The media of the day turned against him. In Dante's *Divine Comedy*, the Beautiful is likened to "the second Pilate" whose cruelty has grown "so insatiate that without decree / His greedy sails upon the Temple intrude." And among the peasants, stories began to be heard. On the day of the arrests, it was said, de Molay had instructed his nephew to take the "treasure" hidden in two hollow pillars that adorned the choir stalls of the Paris temple and flee. And from the flames, de Molay predicted that the menacing king and the spineless pope would soon join him in death, which they did. At sundown, the day de Molay burned, a few men saw monks swim out to the island, paw through the warm ashes, and dog-paddle back to shore with something—some say bones—clenched in their teeth.

When I return to the church rectory in Ponferrada—a catacomb of sleeping rooms—I sidle along the narrow pilgrim's corridor in search of a bed. The place is buzzing with secret conversations to which I am not invited. The doors are built with thin light plywood so that my inquiries begin with a sudden *whoosh*. A naked German man is hopping about on one leg, confounded by the second hole in his underpants. I apologize, and the door slams shut—*blam*—like a rifle shot.

Whoosh: Paolo looks up from a lumpy mattress, disturbed from a nap. *Blam.*

Whoosh: Javier is explaining Marcus Aurelius to another pilgrim. *Blam.*

Whoosh: Ah! The bathroom, and no lock on the door. An unfamiliar old woman undressed from the waist up except for a sturdy bra washes herself at the sink. A hurried apology. *Blam.*

Whoosh: Willem is writing his daily missive beside an empty mattress.

Pilgrim decorum requires that he offer me the available bed, which he does plaintively. I drop my bag. Willem's unease at my arrival causes him to overcompensate by spilling the afternoon's secret. Louis and some select pilgrims will be eating dinner tonight at a special restaurant, a place recommended by one of Louis's many friends on the road.

The evening sky is a gray cast-iron dome. Streaked clouds have backed off high enough to nuzzle among blinking stars. A huge dump at the edge of town is the resting spot of hundreds of storks. At the blast of a truck's horn or a factory whistle, they panic into swirls of flight and swoop over the town. En route to Louis's restaurant, our small band crosses the river beside the fortress. A pacified covey of storks circles slowly before turning on bended wing back to the dump in search of frogs. Willem notes the beauty of their bucket jaws dangling in silhouette. "A hundred babies are being born tonight," he says.

The restaurant is not fancy, rather a workingman's joint with huge platters of meat, a vegetable or two, and cheap prices. The other diners are all farmers or laborers who have come here for the same reason we have. They check us out as if we are new workers freshly arrived in town. We wear their faces and the same worn-out togs. At times we sit at the table in the same exhausted silence, elbows on the table, eyes gazing nowhere, a single fork standing disconsolately in the air.

A bottle of wine or two and our spirits are lubricated enough to resume conversation. Louis is in command. He knows the people, the owner of the restaurant, and the lay of the land. By the end of the evening, Louis is explaining the mystery of the Knights Templar and the significance of the giant castle.

After the destruction of the Templars, legend has it that they brought some great mystery, some object, to be housed here in one of the most sacred and largest of their temples, Ponferrada. Louis states that this particular fortress is unique in that it is the only one that seems deliberately to resist the geometrically ordered plan of most Templar constructions. Each turret, with its curving shape or peculiar corners, perfectly mimics a constellation in the sky. Two rounded turrets connected by a small stone bridge, still intact, are obviously the zodiacal sign of Gemini, the twins. Louis says that on specific days of the year, the towers align with the constellations in the sky. Some say that on those special nights when the mystery of the castle on earth matches the mystery of the stars in heaven, something is revealed.

One theory holds that splendid shafts of light penetrate an oddly arranged set of windows in one of the rooms, pointing to a sacred spot. There, perhaps, lies whatever it is that the Templars kept hidden. One source suggests that the mystery is the store of knowledge the Templars inherited during their time in the Holy Land, the esoteric secrets of the Pyramid builders. Others say that it is the Holy Grail or the Ark of the Covenant. Even others declare that secreted away, somewhere among the stones of Ponferrada, is the very knowledge learned by Adam when he sank his teeth into the apple.

The wine has rendered us all helpless in the wake of Louis's stories. We are pilgrims, anxious to make sense of the mystery of why we put ourselves on this road. A night of mysticism dampens the earlier jokes and observations. The forks resume their abstracted position, wagging in the air, pointing to the heavens. The walk back across the bridge is made in silence. The center of town is occupied by the great meandering castle, a field of darkness ringed by the pale streetlights of the city.

Louis and the others enter a bar for a drink. Other pilgrims have gathered, and the talk is of Ponferrada, the Templars, the mystery. On a wall outside, the anarchists have painted a giant slogan. *Tus pesadillas son mis sueños:* "Your nightmares are my dreams." A bookstore across the street has a window display advertising a collection of books on the Knights Templar. I excuse myself. As I push open the door, a stick at the top rakes across a set of harmonic chimes, filling the room with the tranquil melodies of a New Age shop.

The books look so inviting, dust jackets swirling in creamy brilliant colors, fantastic emblems and personages, and such promises. The secrets of the Knights Templar. The hidden truths of the Dead Sea Scrolls. The true story behind the many (recent) sightings of the Virgin Mary. The revival of paganism. The wanton practices of witches. An encyclopedia of angels. The heavenly octave has summoned from the rear the pro-

prietress. Even in Spain she looks like her American counterpart, a dirty blonde with fallen shoulders, wraparound print
skirt, tank top, sandals, and headband. She walks past shelves
of books and tables of lava lamps and astronomical maps and
glow-in-the-dark rosaries and jars of crystals and geodes of all
sizes. They even sell those eight-balls I used to buy as a child;
shake them up and a message appears. Mine reads "Try
again." Her face is a tired expression of pinched eyes, expansive crow's-feet, and downturned lips, as if she had decoded
the mystical universal puzzle, and the great truth was to buy
low and sell high.

She is counting out a fistful of peseta bills from a cash register, tallying up the day's take in esoteric truth. Capitalism and
mysticism make very awkward companions. I tell her I am a
pilgrim en route to Santiago and am interested in the latest
research on the castle across the way. She jerks her head
toward the dozen books in the window.

"Ponferrada is filled with specialists on the castle," she tells
me. She mentions a few names of locals to whom I might want
to talk. Then she opens one book to a page of fat type and
reveals one theory she finds particularly curious.

The Templars had a secret code to which only the highest
twelve members of the order were privy. In the event of some
catastrophe, such as the near annihilation that took place in
the early 1300s, any one of these surviving members could
come to Ponferrada and just by taking in the architecture
could "read" the stones and know where the great mystery
was hidden. That code turns on the letter T, or Tau, which
signifies the Templars and the cross and is somehow related
to the number twelve, which in turn harkens to all kinds of
associations—master Templars, apostles, months, zodiac
signs. Only one Templar establishment had twelve towers—
Ponferrada.

Scholars studying the fort here have discovered that, just as
Louis said, the towers mimic the constellations in the sky. The
problem is, they are not in the proper order ever to match the
stars in the sky. So this author—she points to a page of out-

lines of towers and connect-the-dot renditions of the constellations—figured out that the towers, taken in the order of their construction, must spell out a code. Some of these towers even have the mysterious *T* carved on lintels or beside doorways. If one writes down the first letters of the zodiacal names of each of these towers, including the signifier *T*, then it spells . . . absolutely nothing.

But then this author remembered that the Templars were drawn to the number 2. For Templars, the symbolism of two as one was powerful, and she proved this by reminding me that the original seal of the Templars was a horse carrying two knights as if they were a single rider. Okay, so look once again at the names of those turrets (in Spanish and substitute "Señora" for Virgo): Tauro Castor, Géminis, Poloux, Libra, Cáncer, Vaso, Señora, Sagitario, Escorpión, Capricornio, Peces, and Aries. And now take the first two letters of each in this order and you form a kind of sentence: *Taca ge poli cava se sale escape arcano.* It doesn't quite match up. But, she explains, one must jiggle with the letters a bit because (I lost her here) something or other about old Spanish and modern Spanish. Whatever, one ends up with this sentence: *En la taca que hay en la "g" de la ciudad, cava, se sale al escape (o entrada) del gran secreto.* More or less, it means "In the room in which there is a 'g' in the city, dig there, and come away with the great secret." The author of this book believes that the Ark of the Covenant is hidden below this special room in a cathedral cave filled with Templar wealth.

"Has the author entered this wondrous cavern?" I ask.

"He cannot enter," she tells me sadly.

"Why not?"

"Ponferrada is a Spanish treasure, registered in Madrid. He has applied to the government for permission to dig below the room, but the officials won't let anyone disturb a national landmark. They probably think he is crazy. So, until there is some change in the government, we may never know."

She screws up her face and snorts in disgust. Bureaucrats.

I peel off the equivalent of ten dollars for the book. But she says it is only seven. The key to the secret of the Templars has been marked down.

• • •

The accusations against the Templars didn't immediately play well in neighboring Spain or across the Channel in England, where the knights were still held in favor. But after the papal dissolution, the monarchs saw an opportunity. In Spain, James of Aragon dispatched an army to occupy the Templar castle of Peníscola. Better to be prudent.

After the settlement of Templar property and wealth throughout Europe, what survived was their story—a splendid drama of political jostling, gems, gold, Crusades, forts, popes, kings, and divine mysteries. The Templar story was so fertile that it eventually became everything to everyone. Voltaire rewrote the story as a tale of ecclesiastical tyranny. For others it became a proof of monarchal oppressions. Antichurch propagandists of the seventeenth century performed the difficult trick of recasting the illiterate Templars into wise philosophers who foresaw the wrongheadedness of Catholic orthodoxy—cunning dissidents trying to work for change from within.

Almost five hundred years after the Beautiful's auto-da-fé, King Louis XVI was executed by guillotine during the French Revolution. It is said that a member of the Freemasons, the reputed heirs to the Templars, jumped onto the wooden platform. He ran his fingers through the king's blood, flung droplets over the crowd, and shouted, "Jacques de Molay, thou art avenged!"

The most lucrative retelling of the Templar story repositioned them as warlocks and mystics, possessors of written secrets, hidden treasures, and powerful relics. This rewriting began in 1531 with the publication of *De Occulta Philosophia,* a sixteenth-century best-seller by the most notorious alchemist and magus of the day, Cornelius Heinrich Agrippa von Nettesheim. In his book, Agrippa had merely mentioned the Templars alongside another group of sorcerers called the Bogomils, whom he alleged had orgies, burned the resulting babies, and made bread from the ashes. A later book mixed up the allusions until it was believed that the Templars had a ritual orgy to impregnate a select nun. After the baby was born, the knights gathered in a circle and roughly tossed the newborn around in a circle until it died. The infant's corpse was later roasted, and the oil from its flesh was used to wax the idol Baphomet.

Scarcely a decade passed without the emergence of a clubby group of brave mystics, such as the Freemasons, who married a new nostalgia for knights with a tincture of their magic (but not enough to warrant charges of witchcraft or heresy). They wore impressive uniforms, and the most convincing of them made good livings peddling elixirs, cures, alchemical formulae, and the secrets of transmutation. They spoke of their allegiance to "unknown superiors" and assumed increasingly orotund titles. One neo-Templar in England was known as the Knight of the Great Lion of the High Order of the Lords of the Temple of Jerusalem.

The exact identity of the Templar mystery was hard to pin down. Wolfram von Eschenbach wrote *Parzival* and connected the Templars with the Holy Grail. Others claimed it was the Ark of the Covenant. Another school said the knights brought back from the Holy Land the mysteries of engineering and that a breach in security resulted in Gothic architecture. Still others traced the game of chess to the Templars. More recently the Shroud of Turin is credited to the Templars. It was once in the possession of the family of Geoffrey de Charney, the occupant of the neighboring stake when de Molay burned.

The Freemasons and other neo-Templar organizations created hundreds of different grades of knighthood, with a fee for each ascendance, new uniform, and chest of badges. The mystery of god was a cottage industry. Secret charters began to appear. One was written in blood, another in a secret indecipherable code. Long, tedious genealogies surfaced, tracing an unbroken line of Templar masters to eras long before Christ. Bombastic constitutions appeared; one spoke of the priories of Japan, Tartary, and the Congo.

Some strains of neo-Templarism faltered. In 1831 one self-proclaimed Templar tried to start a new group centered on the supremacy of three men—Confucius, Parentier the apostle of the potato, and the banker Lafitte. It didn't catch on.

How did Columbus discover America? According to twentieth-century Templar historians Michael Baigent and Richard Leigh, "Columbus himself was married to the daughter of a former Grand Master of the Order [in Portugal], and had access to his father-in-law's charts and diaries."

When these historians approach the subject of the neo-Templars and America, they find connections everywhere. Ben Franklin was knighted the provincial grand master of Pennsylvania in 1734. Later, while in France, he was dubbed the master of the nine sisters and was later accepted into the Royal Lodge of Commanders of the Temple West of Carcassonne. George Washington, Paul Revere, and John Hancock were Freemasons. The philosopher behind the American political idea, Montesquieu? Freemason.

To read the history of America from the pages of Templar-fired imaginations is to learn that our founding was less a revolution than a conspiracy. Of the signers of the Declaration of Independence, possibly a third were Freemasons. Nearly half of the general officers of the Continental army were Freemasons. The minutes for the November 30, 1773, meeting of the St. Andrew's Lodge in Boston contain this significant note: "consignees of the Tea took up the Brethren's time." This phrase is held up as proof that the Boston Tea Party was a Templar soiree. George Washington's appointment as commander in chief was fixed by fellow Freemasons.

According to this strain of thinking, the Templar mysteries had at last found its ultimate expression, the Constitution of the United States. The idea of the rights of man, the precept that power should be invested in continuous offices and not in people, the theory of federalism, and the notion of checks and balances are old Templar methods of bureaucratic organization that date back to the time of Tutankhamen. "Philosophers such as Hume, Locke, Adam Smith, and the French *philosophes* are regularly enough invoked," write Baigent and Leigh of the origins of the American idea, "but the Freemasonic milieu which paved the way for such thinkers, which acted as a kind of amniotic fluid for their ideas and which imparted to those ideas their popular currency, is neglected."

The most visible evidence of Templar control of the American experiment apparently is Washington, D.C., itself. Tour guides may say that the Frenchman Pierre l'Enfant designed the city, but they neglect to add that George Washington himself altered the plan. If you look carefully at the great Mall and the grid streets bisected by diagonal boulevards, you might notice "octagonal patterns incorporating the particular cross used as a device by masonic Templars." For some Templars passing over the capital by plane, a simple glance out the window confirms that the ancient mystery has at last found a local habitation and a name.

After the sun goes down in Ponferrada, the town withdraws. The storekeepers turn out the lights, and bolt the doors. The houses too are dark. The little balconies seem dressed in mourning, lined with flowers colorless in the night light, or draped in the afternoon's laundry snapping the iron rails. From one or the other balconies stare faces of fatigue, a tired housewife, a housebound teenage girl, an old man taking his cigar in the cool air. Ponferrada is in retreat, and the refuges are the bars.

At the dark woody establishment where I left my dinner companions, other pilgrims and more locals have gathered. Above the head of the bartender hang haunches of Spanish prosciutto dripping grease into tiny cups. On a scarred mahogany bar is a setting of small plates, tapas of roasted peppers, ham and bread, Spanish omelet. Outside and in, crowds form at small tables.

"You are an American," says a German pilgrim I have encountered once or twice before. He introduces me to an angry Spaniard who wants to know if the military installation a few miles back up the road is under the control of the American military establishment. Several years ago Spain joined NATO, apparently under some kind of pressure from American politicians. On the road today, I saw several splashes of graffiti that translate "Spain. NATO. Out."

"Is this part of an American spy ring?" the Spaniard wants to know. He rattles his glass of whiskey menacingly. The German nods, a jerk of the head that places him squarely against the Americans. But my mind is filled with secret passageways, cryptic messages, long-lost treasures. I am in a Hardy Boy mood, and these men want to discuss international politics.

"I don't know. I haven't had my CIA briefing this week." I wander over to another table.

I take cover in a group of nearby pilgrims who are lamenting the absence of some of the Rabanal gang who didn't make it this far. The Welsh family and the Flemish group seem to have been waylaid in Molinaseca—literally "Dry Hill," yet famous for its flat terrain, crashing river, and giant swimming hole.

At a nearby table some other pilgrims are speaking with a red-haired man. I grab a beer and step over. He is not a Spaniard, although as the walk moves farther west, red hair is common among the locals. His brogue is Irish. His name is James, and he is a stumpy but well-fed man, distinguished by his powerful arms and buttery hands. I pick up from the conversation that he used to be a priest. The glassy look in his eye, either from alcohol or insanity, is offputting. When I walk up I hear him discussing the Antichrist.

The mystery of god that passeth all understanding is quite comprehensible to James. From his chatter I sense that he is a demented soul who wandered into the orbit of the Templar mystery in Ponferrada and has never managed to escape. As I listen, he explains one of his theories.

The current pope is the Antichrist. James has the proof. Our age is drowning in a decadence not matched since Noah, he says. Everyone nods in agreement. The first pope of this era, Pope John Paul I, was legitimate. But the time for the forces of evil had arrived, so he was killed off and replaced by Satan's proxy, Pope John Paul II. This truth is revealed in an ancient formula. James scratches onto a waxy scrap of bar napkin the words *Vicarius Filii Dei*.

"This is the pope's title in Latin," he says. "It means 'vicar of the Son of God.' It is three words, and this pope is the first one to take a three-word name, Pope John Paul." James looks around, knowing that this is scant evidence to a group of road-hardened pilgrims and longtime locals. He readies his pencil for some of the requisite math.

The formula works like this. Hidden in the pope's Latin title are Roman numbers. He rewrites the title using only the numerical letters, so that it looks like this:

V   I   D
I   L   I
C   I
I   I
V

Which translate into Arabic numbers:

5   1   500
  1   50   1
100   1
  1   1
  5

Add up the columns:

112   53   501

And then add up those three numbers:

666

He circles the digits many times in bold strokes of his pencil: "666." Cocked eyebrows all around.

I mention—sarcastically, I thought—that Ronald Wilson Reagan was the first president in American history to have three names of six letters each. James reaches out to shake my hand. I speak his language.

When I spot Louis across the room, I drift away from James for a while. I want to explain to the Frenchman the marvelous Templar theory I picked up in the bookstore. Everyone in town has one, and now I do too.

Later I amble back to the mystic corner, and James is deep into Templar lore. He has his rap down beautifully and can segue effortlessly from secret numerical codes to eerie modern coincidences. He has an American dollar on the table and is pointing to some of the symbols. And there is a piece of German currency, along with some other documents. A bar napkin is now crowded with algebra. I regret missing the setup. James is explaining that there are modern Templar organizations such as the Freemasons that still transmit the secrets. And I am left to wonder if the mystery of the universe might not have been passed on to the Charleston, South Carolina, chapter of the Shriners. For all I know, those old men in fezzes who drove crazy-eights in go-carts during the local parades of my youth were trying to tell me something.

What was the mystery of the Templars? James asks. Well, it's not what people think it is. It's not the Holy Grail, or the true cross, or the Ark of the Covenant. Oh, no, he says, the mystery is not an object. That is the *diversion*. The mystery dates way back. The gnostics knew it. The desert dwellers of the Holy Land knew it (they told the Templars, in fact). Christ knew it, but there were those before him who knew it. The mystery precedes the builders of the Pyramids of Egypt (how else could they have pulled off such an impossible feat of engineering?). Noah knew it, and so did others before him, because the mystery of the Templars is the knowledge that Adam learned when he bit into the apple.

"Good and evil," says a member of the little audience.

"The Bible is full of clues," James says, clearing another napkin.

I have had enough beers to contemplate telling James that after well over a month on the road, I have my own theory about what Adam learned when he bit the apple. It was the most perverse revelation in history. He learned that the apple was just an apple. Adam *wished* he had learned some secret knowledge. What he learned was far more brutal—whatever he believed about the apple was his own making. According to Genesis, Adam's first postbite revelation occurred when he "opened his eyes and saw that he was naked," both literally and metaphorically. The apple was just an apple. And for learning this, he was punished, cursed to labor and to roam out of Paradise through the fields to re-create the original mystery of the apple. Adam was the first postmodern pilgrim.

But I keep quiet. How could I possibly compete with James, whose patter barely pauses for air? He has the numbers, the specifics, the code. He turns to his napkin, scribbling madly at his figures. He is adding and subtracting, working out algorithms, performing translations; his audience is rapt with attention and appears comforted as he turns words into calculus and back into meaning.

EIGHT
VILLAFRANCA

The morning out of Ponferrada begins with so many good omens; I should know by now that the road signals its pilgrims in perverse ways. I sleep late, so I am alone when I leave for this morning's leg to Villafranca. As I walk, a synopsis of Spanish history unfolds before me. The pilgrim sets off from the medieval center of town and winds through blocks of the Renaissance until the alleys widen into the Victorian era. Now the balconies are elegant and suspended by wrought iron. These are the homes of characters from the naturalistic novels of Galdós—Spain's Zola or Dreiser.

At the edge of town, the postwar public works of Generalissimo Franco wrench Ponferrada into the twentieth century. Towers of colorless concrete with blocky balconies soar at the edges of four-lane frontage roads, the domain of trucks and buses. The yellow arrows are neat swatches of paint, tucked low to the ground in an unsuccessful attempt at being inconspicuous. From the inside of curbs, wrapped around the cylinder of a light post or coyly turning at the corner of a building, they scream out amid the simple fascist gray of this exurb.

The arrows direct me into the rusting industry of the 1940s and 1950s. Moments later I slip into the commerce zones funded by the new money of King Juan Carlos I and his Common Market investors. The arrows thread among newer plants, windowless factories, toy makers, and furniture builders—neat, clean facilities. Eventually homes reappear, and soon enough the streets lose their names and the sidewalks disappear. Yards expand beyond fences into pastures. They are bounded by trees or ditches, holding not only clotheslines and scattered toys, but small apple groves or victory gardens. The paved road breaks up into rubble, then becomes a familiar path of hard-packed dirt and, finally, the comforting view of a pilgrim's day—a ribbon of road traversing fields of peppers and miles of corn, patches of cabbage and melon, then stands of grapes, apricots, and figs, and orchards of cherries, oranges, apples, and pears.

It is late in the afternoon when I enter the town of Cacabelos and I stop for lunch at Prada à Tope, a restaurant suggested by some farmers I passed this morning.

I order a modest meal, yet inexplicably out come heaped plates of vegetables, mashed green items, a casserolelike substance, and a salad. I start to protest, but the waiter shrugs. A few minutes later he returns with a cutting board piled high with meats—a plump turkey leg, joints of lamb, and thin slices of pork, veal, and a boned chicken breast.

I eat, of course, because "no" is just not a word you want to introduce into a conversation with a Spaniard. After the waiter removes my plates, he replaces them with a bowl of quivering flan. No sooner do I push aside the half-eaten dessert than he appears again with a cigar the length of my forearm, flown in from the Canary Islands. He removes from his pocket a cigarette lighter, sets the dial to blowtorch, and puts the flame before my face. I light up. Then a different man arrives with a decanter of twelve-year-old sherry and pours two glasses. He is the owner of the place, and he pulls up a chair. He proclaims his love of pilgrims and tells me my entire meal is on the house. He pours me another glass of thick sherry before sending me back to the scorching dust and the walk to Villafranca. Andrew Boorde, a British traveler who preceded me by four centuries, said of good Spanish sherry that it makes "the brain apprehensive, quick, forgetive, full of nimble, fiery, and delectable shapes."

At day's end, when I catch up with the others, I will tell my story of lunch, probably topping it off with a joke about walking into the hot sun of León province with a mind sautéed in aged sherry. Every night at the shelter is story time for pilgrims. In these stories I am beginning to discern different pilgrim narratives. The first group is the smallest and the least significant. They adhere fiercely to the ancient vocabulary of pilgrims. These few would have no problem describing my free lunch as a miracle. They are an intense lot. One of them saw a statue move. They avoid the rest of us, as we do them.

The most populous school of pilgrim thinking interprets the day's actions through tradition. They insert themselves into the anecdotal customs of the road or make an effort to learn the history of each place. They measure their own actions by what others did and knit the past into their experience. For example, in the mountains between Rabanal and Ponferrada is a place called Foncebadón. Roman soldiers stationed in these parts knew it as the Mountain of Mercury. Pagan tradition encouraged wayfarers to pick up a rock in the valley, carry it to the peak, and toss it onto a pile. Today, a skinny shorn pole topped by an iron cross is embedded into this magnificent heap. Pilgrims adapted this tradition a thousand years ago and made it their own.

For several days Foncebadón was the talk of the shelter. Did you throw your rock? Did you know it was a pagan custom? Did you know the mountain was once protected by the Roman god Mercury, a kind of pilgrim in his own right? How many rocks do you think are up there?

Accounts of these activities fill the tables at supper and become the basis for the ongoing story of our pilgrimage. For the traditionalists, my serendipitous lunch happily confirms the great tradition of unimaginable charity on the road.

Then there is the rest of us, a pilgrim miscellany. We constitute not a school of thought, but a condition. We're anxious, mainly. We're too cautious to discover a deliberate pattern in our luck. We're hesitant about forcing our experiences into a coherent tale. So we end up telling jokes, or sitting quietly, or, like Claudy, drinking heavily throughout the day.

I suspect that these varying approaches to pilgrimage have always existed on the road. I began my walk clinging desperately to history and tradition and never managed to get very comfortable with either of them. When it comes to matters of (pick any of the following) clothes, church architecture, miracles, attitude, mysticism, local customs, I've tried them all on. And I've been shucking tradition, in one form or another, since the Pyrenees. What I'm left with is a kind of pilgrim neurosis.

While I become less and less confident about being here, the others grow increasingly assured of their enterprise. Arrival in any town means locating the rituals, the traditions, the history. This often means going to the church to see the pilgrim sculpture or painting. In another place it might mean finding some site of historical interest or looking at some town's rendition of the ubiquitous statue of James himself. In and around each of these items one finds the stories and traditions, which then become the topics at dinner. So each day and each night provide the pilgrim with fresh but strangely familiar material, which he can comfortably work into the story of his modern pilgrimage.

But there is one aspect of the past that doesn't make it into anyone's conversation: relics. By relics, I mean the bones and objects associated with saints and regarded as sources of divine magic. In the Cliffs Notes version of the Middle Ages, relics have come down to us as one of the great carnival schemes of organized religion. The story of relics is now seen as little more than a centuries-long infomercial in which huckster clergy ripped off a continent of frightened serfs.

I have been avoiding relics the entire trip, as has everyone else. They are, let's face it, embarrassing for any contemporary pilgrim. It's easy to fit much of the ancient pilgrimage into a modern story, but Saint Theresa's index finger—well, gross.

Relics constitute part of that old vocabulary of pilgrimage

that is out-of-date. But somewhere back there—possibly around the time I became aware of the other pilgrims' certainty with their traditions—I became hooked. What interests me now is that relics have become relics of themselves. Instead of being transistors of divine power and wisdom, they are proof of man's foolishness and impotence. Even the clergy is embarrassed today, and they only keep the relics out on display for uneducated peasants and those ubiquitous widows.

During my walk, I have seen, without much effort, the ulnas and radii, the tibias and femurs, and the metacarpals and metatarsals of probably every well-known saint, and I've examined flecks or dust from hundreds of others less acquainted with fame. Historically, it would make sense that relics would flourish on the road; it was an avenue of trade. But relics were also the most concrete manifestation of the need to discover. A pilgrim set out to *find* something on the road, and it's no coincidence that many of the most fantastical relics of the Middle Ages were found on or near the road to Santiago. When I left America, the perennial question was, "What do you expect to find?"

The story of relics is a cautionary tale about the ideology of discovery, something that's on my sherry-soaked mind as I lumber toward Villafranca. Search hard enough for what you are certain is there, and you will find it.

Originally, relics were not body parts, but items, such as the filings of the shackles that once bound a martyr's legs or, say, his handkerchief. Early relics were talismans, called *brandea,* no different in their mass appeal from the bedsheets of the Beatles or the coat of Elvis today. They were items that conjured up the memory and the power of a great person, an impulse still with us, even among the educated classes. Not long before I left America, Sotheby's auctioned off the ashtrays and piggy banks and Tupperware of Andy Warhol for millions of dollars.

The *brandea* were souvenirs of sorts; the shell of Santiago was one. Visitors to Mont St. Michel still leave with a pebble from the base of the island. In the days of martyrs, tombs had hatches so that the faithful could insert their heads to breathe the rarefied dust of a saint's remains.

At first the authorities tried to deter people from infatuation with dead bodies, but this served only to acknowledge the corpses' power, undermining any effort at restraint and investing them with great value. In 1047 Fernando, the count of Carrion, informed his debtor, the emir of Córdoba, not to send him precious metals: "Of gold and silver I have enough already; give me the body of St. Zoyl." Most relics were the entire body of a saint, usually with accompanying documentation.

Nobles began collecting relics, according to historian Patrick Geary, the way the rich today collect art. It was a way to distill wealth into a single physical and portable item. Complete bodily relics were often little more than a few bones and some dust in a sack. But to describe relics so is like saying van Gogh's *Starry Night* is a sheet of linen with smears of oil. The bones were direct physical contact points between the wretched and the divine. Relics translated the confounding abstractions of Christianity into something penitents could hold in their hand. Over time relics became a kind of currency, a substantial part of the economy, a hot commodity.

In 1204 there was a major shift in the commerce of relics when the Fourth Crusade sacked Constantinople. In Eastern Christendom, the collectors were not so picky about a relic being a whole body. They dealt openly in body *parts*. When the crusaders overwhelmed the town, these parts coursed through Europe, flooding the market. The sudden surge of supply forced up demand in the short run and then created all the problems common to inflation.

As long as relics had meant entire bodies, value and supply could be somewhat regulated. Now the possibilities for fraud and forgery were out of control. Relicmongers didn't need to bother themselves with a bag of bones and dust and the semblance of documentation. A simple knuckle would do.

The market boomed since nothing could stanch the growth, not even common sense. When confronted by reports of two monasteries claiming to have the head of John the Baptist, the master logicians of the day concluded that one was his head as a youth and the other his head as a mature adult.

St. Hugh of Lincoln was a zealous relics collector. He wore

a finger ring set with St. Benedict's tooth. When St. Hugh was visiting the Abbey of Fécamp, he asked to see the arm of Mary Magdalene. The abbey monks were horrified when St. Hugh ripped into the cloth wrapping with a knife and struggled to snap off one of the lady's fingers. After that failed, St. Hugh sucked one of her fingers into his mouth and chewed vigorously, "first with his incisors and finally with his molars." When asked to explain his behavior, St. Hugh responded logically. Hadn't he just eaten the body and blood of Christ during mass? "Why should I not treat the bones of the saint in the same way," he said, "and without profanity acquire them whenever I can?"

In Jerusalem, the true cross was protected around the clock by a battalion of 385 deacons to prevent pilgrims from diving at the cross to bite off a few splinters.

Relics were valuable for many reasons. They attracted throngs of worshipers. They raised funds. They created prestige and celebrity. They caused miracles. The demand for them grew so intense that monks took to carrying out raids on each other's reliquaries. Some of these operations were as elaborate as anything an author of a cold war thriller could imagine. The robbery of the body of St. Foy in Agen by the monks of Conques involved a monk-spy named Arinisdus who spent ten years infiltrating the monastery before he pulled off the job. The thrilling stories of the swashbuckling monks on assignment became a literary genre called *furta sacra,* "holy robbery."

In the race to outdo one another in relics, the victor's laurel probably should go to a cathedral just off the road to Santiago in the town of Oviedo. The clergy there were long said to possess an indestructible wooden ark handcrafted by the apostles themselves. It was built in the Holy Land and smuggled into Africa, then Carthage, then Sevilla, then Toledo, and in the eighth century it was moved to Oviedo for protection from the Moors. It was said that an early bishop named Ponce had opened the trunk but couldn't see its contents because of shafts of celestial light emanating from within. By 1075 it was decided the time was right for an inventory, and a host of prominent men were assembled. King Alfonso VI was there, as was Spain's real-life knight, Rodrigo Díaz de Bivar, otherwise known as el Cid. The surviving diploma recording the opening bears the epic hero's actual signature.

The need to discover achieved its high-water mark in Oviedo. Almost no physical item mentioned or imagined in the Bible is missing from the ark of Oviedo. A partial inventory includes

bits of the true cross
a vial of milk from the Virgin Mary's breast
part of the handkerchief laid on Christ's face after death
eight spines of the crown of thorns
several pieces of manna rained down on the Israelites
a large sheet of skin flayed from St. Bartholomew
locks of the Virgin Mary's hair
one of the coins, a denarius, given to Judas in exchange for betraying Christ
several locks of Mary Magdalene's tresses, used to dry Christ's feet
a portion of the rod Moses used to part the Red Sea
a piece of the grilled fish and a chunk of the honeycomb that Christ ate after his resurrection and during his appearance before his apostles
one of St. Peter's sandals
one of the jugs from the marriage of Cana, in which Christ miraculously changed the water to wine
bones of St. John the Baptist
parts of several of Christ's apostles
bones of St. Stephen, the first martyr
chunks of bread left over from the Last Supper

As I enter Villafranca, an old stooped man appears from the bushes. He pulls a live brown snake from a filthy sack. He has the snake gripped just below its head so that its open, terrified mouth looks like a satanic nosegay sprouting from his fist. The tail wiggles cantankerously below his outstretched arm.

"Would you like to touch it?" he asks.

I decline and change the subject to shelter, and he suggests that I stay at the parador, one of the special hotels found occasionally throughout Spain. Sometime during the Franco regime, the generalissimo thought to attract tourists by rehabilitating old castles, châteaux, or any glorious Spanish edifice of tenuous historical interest. Paradors are famous for classy pretensions and high prices. Somerset Maugham is always quoted on the promotional brochures, saying (dubiously), "If you're going to stay anywhere in Spain, it should be a parador!"

When I come upon Villafranca's parador, I can't figure out what was preserved unless it was the first Howard Johnson's in the country. There is a massive parking lot, American in scope, and a flat, nondescript, utilitarian building. It doesn't seem any better than some of the pilgrims' inns, and the prices are quite low. So I engage some cheap quarters.

My room has a comforting familiarity to it. There are two double beds with linens tucked to military specs. A quarter would bounce off the spread. A gleaming gold lamp is permanently fixed on the bedside table. Wickedly, I rev up the air-conditioning. The television set is mounted on a stand jutting out from the wall. I tune in a bullfight. A lengthy bathtub dominates a mirror and tile room charged with the aromas of Crabtree & Evelyn. I fill up the tub, grab the complimentary hotel magazine, and feed myself slowly into a bubble bath of soothingly frigid water. I glance around the room and out the door to my bedroom. I could be in the Kansas City Ramada Inn, but for the enamel abbreviations C and F for hot and cold on the tub's spigots. And the shrieks of death blasting from my television.

Later that afternoon while scouring the main plaza to find a restaurant, I spot three bicyclists wearing shells. They are standing around a phone booth. One boy is slamming the receiver into the phone box while another boy and a girl curse in Spanish. This is a relief to see because I thought only spoiled Americans raged at Telefónica, the country's communications monopoly. But the boy in the booth, named Miguel, tells me that the Spaniards call Telefónica by another name: Franco's revenge.

Bike pilgrims and foot pilgrims don't often have a lot to say to one another. Chances are good we will never see each other again. But these kids are cheerful enough.

"Have you not been to the tent of Jesus?" asks Miguel.

"The tent of Jesus?"

"All the pilgrims are there," the girl says. "He has water and showers, beds and meals."

"Jesus does?"

"You can't leave Villafranca without meeting Jesus."

Certainly not, so I get directions and walk off.

I am not sure how I missed the tent of Jesus since it is just off the path I took into town earlier this afternoon. The place is bustling with the frontier chaos that I have come to enjoy. Everyone is here—the cast of the Flemish film, the Welsh Family with the Mule, Javier the Spanish Banker, Willem the Dutch Air Force Officer, the Italian Man, the Old Dutch Couple, the German Man, Louis the Frenchman Who's Walked the Road Eleven Times, and Paolo the Young Man with Louis. And there are at least twenty or thirty other pilgrims milling about whom I have yet to meet.

A beaming Claudy calls out from the bar. He is swinging a snifter of brandy and orders me a beer before I can decline.

"This is the place," he says, beaming, and sweeps me off for a tour. The tent is a two-room Hooverville hotel built entirely of plastic sheets, used lumber, and bent nails. On one side are pallets and floorboards with enough double bunks or plain mattresses on the ground to sleep a hundred people. The other half is a restaurant and bar. At the juncture of the two main rooms are bathrooms.

Above the slightly raked incline of plastic canopies is an array of lawn sprinklers—precisely the suburban models that slowly spray fans of water back and forth. Japanese pilgrims from last year had something to do with this advance. The continuous flow of water from above keeps the tent cavernously cool when one of Spain's dry winds blows in. The off flow of warmed water collects into side tanks, which is heated by solar panels and is used in the showers.

Jesus is Jesús Jato, a farmer who has adopted all the pilgrims who come through Villafranca. He is a tall, dark, sinewy fellow, with huge fists and fingers liked knotted rope. From his shorts extend bony, misshapen legs with a baseball of muscle at each calf. The phone at his chaotic desk in the tent rings, and Jesús negotiates the rental price of a piece of farm equipment. Afterward he reminds me that he runs the tent off donations and then stamps and writes in my passport: "May the stars light your way and may you find the interior road. Forward!"

"My wife will cook you dinner," he then says. "Tonight is lamb chops. Fifteen hundred pesetas. Take any mattress you find. I will be back in an hour. Drinks are extra."

Jesús jumps into the cab of an old, beat-up truck, turns the key with an explosion, and disappears in a cloud of white dust to negotiate another deal.

The tent exudes a cool breeze and even a slight perfume of shampoos and soaps as miraculous as Ramon's foyer. The rugged plainness is inviting—the solar showers, the makeshift bar, the worn unpainted lumber assembled into long row tables. No two chairs match. All of them rock gently on three legs. The atmosphere is confusing but as warm as a big family. The intersecting fans of water on the plastic roof and the sheets flapping in the dry wind are as soothing as a summer squall. Though it looks haphazard, there is a stately rustic utilitarianism here, as efficient and clipped as the double iambs of the name *Jesús Jato.*

The layout of the tent's dinner tables and benches form an L at the far end from the door. Two long tables extend down the length of the tent, and another turns the corner. Benches run along the plastic walls. Scattered chairs and stools fill in the gaps, creating a stage for the irrepressible Claudy. He is well advanced into a brandy-inspired nirvana. He dips in and out of private conversations at the tables with the demeanor of a polyglot host.

Now he is Spanish, prancing before an audience of bicyclists, trying his hand at sexual innuendo (a difficult genre for the unnuanced flamenco). Now he is Flemish for Rick and Karl, rolling his eyes and clutching his heart melodramatically at the appearance of Willie the Filmmaker. Now he is Esperanto, taunting the oblivious Italian Man with an imitation of the poor man's syntax. Now he is British, entertaining the two Welsh boys, as he often does, with a fresh riddle.

"Three missionaries are returning from a journey with three cannibals," he says. "They come to a river but have only one canoe. The problem is, if the cannibals ever outnumber the other men on either bank, they will eat them. How do the missionaries get the team across?" Claudy places six coins, three large ones representing the cannibals and three small ones representing the three missionaries, on either side of a crack—the river. The boys fall into argument, pushing the coins backward and forward. Claudy breaks into a Randy Newman number about America dropping nuclear bombs on every other country in the world.

As the food arrives, the pilgrims set to their plates. Hot lamb chops, bowls of *caldo gallego* (the regional soup), platters of steaming vegetables. Unlabeled bottles of blood-red wine empty quickly and just as swiftly are refilled. Claudy is losing his audience as smears of oil grow about the lips of the diners.

"Don't you look clean?" Claudy says to me, by way of segueing from his song and dance.

"I took a bath."

"A bath? Are you not staying here in the tent?"

Uh-oh.

"Well, actually, I took a room at the parador."

"The parador!" Claudy crows in case anyone had missed my answer. Suddenly I have taken over center stage, cruising a field of upturned faces. "Parador" is not a word that needs translation into Flemish, French, English, Italian, or German. The word is part of a pilgrim's lingua franca. In Spanish it literally means nothing more than "inn" or "lodge." But it is a word that comes fully dressed in connotation: luxury, indolence, comfort, *baths*.

"Yoo air noot uh twoo peal-gwum," he pronounces in pseudo-Flemish-accented sarcasm. The bicyclists laugh at my plight. They understand this taunt even in English.

"The parador pilgrim," says Wyn, the Welsh veterinarian,

tossing out a phrase that will chase me the rest of the night. He means it in a playful spirit, like Claudy, but its brevity and aptness give it a demeaning force.

One of the boys declares that there is only one way to solve the riddle. "The missionaries must be eaten," he says.

Javier is disturbed. He and I had a rapprochement after Estella and have had an occasional discussion on the road since then. He looks at me with a countenance of true pain, even betrayal. "How could you stay in a parador?" he asks me, cutting through the ridicule with a straight question.

"Javier, it's just a hotel. Not even that good a hotel, to be honest."

"But why are you in a parador?"

"We've all stayed in finer pilgrim hostels than this place, I can assure you." This is not exactly true and not a particularly convincing tack.

The road, Javier once said to me, was nothing more than a dirt path on which we walked. Over time, the road takes up residence within us and becomes a way to something else. Javier, more than any of the other pilgrims I have spoken to, has troubled himself mightily about the literal and metaphorical road.

"A pilgrim has to live off the land," Javier says. Others are listening. "He has to accept the kindness presented to him. He has to carry his goods on his back. A pilgrim is poor and must suffer."

Frankly, I don't feel so good. Renting the parador was done without any thought. I had heard of paradors and had long wanted to try one out. But only now I realize I had surrendered momentarily to the temptations of a *tourist*.

"Javier, I'm just staying there one night."

The German in the corner pipes up, in English, "Then why not stay at a parador in every town?"

I never learned the German's real name. It is irrelevant. He is a remote fellow and doesn't talk much, so his pilgrim epithet never earned any specificity. He was simply the German. He is a big round-faced Teuton with a meaty nose and arrogant cleft chin. He hasn't liked me since we first met. When anyone attempts to speak of the road in language he finds inappropriate, he makes a production of eye rolling and chin scratching. I should have seen it coming. The undertow tugging at our casual conversations is about our pilgrim motive, and it's beginning to seem tangible. It was only a matter of time before it burst through the veneer of aimless banter about history and backpacks and water bottles. Ideas about proper pilgrimage are losing their abstractness and shaping into coherent concepts—and judgments.

"You are missing my point," I say, not only to the German, but to everyone, it seems. "I'm not saying that you should stay in a parador every day. But the road is hard. Makes us into pilgrims. It is hard—and long."

Huh? The words are not coming. I am being crushed. My ideas about the pilgrimage, albeit crudely formed, arrive in my mouth like cotton and come out damp.

The German slices the air with a knife and says, rightly so, "Pahhh." His eyes tighten, and his face assumes the rectitude of Torquemada. This is a man born for auto-da-fé. He shovels a few more faggots beneath my stake.

"Why not take a car and drive to Santiago?"

"But I am not driving a car, now am I?" I am furious, upset, and, quite obviously, wrong. I return to Javier, whose grimace continues to upset me. I try one more time.

"Should a pilgrim dress himself as a beggar even when he isn't? Do we honor the poor by imitating them? That is not piety." I begin to find my voice. "It is . . ." And I search for the right Spanish word for "mockery." I guess *travestía,* and thankfully, I find that it is a word. Javier does not look convinced.

"Only an American would rent a parador," interrupts Torquemada.

The German has no shame. And his nationalistic dig is subtly suggesting: Why is an American here? Why aren't I walking the Appalachian Trail? Rafting down the Mississippi? Hitchhiking the blue highways? I needn't answer. Ad hominem and xenophobia don't play well among international pilgrims.

"Pahhh," I say. I have scored a point.

The German tears into a lamb chop, stripping off a large chunk of charred flesh. His cheeks bulge with meat.

The bicyclist Miguel rises to my defense. He asks, What is the difference between eating in a decent restaurant (which all of us have done) and sleeping in a hotel? No one answers him, and in that silence a nasty judgment is voiced: Who the hell are you, *bicycle punk,* to talk to those of us on foot?

Bicyclists are dicey allies. I might as well side with Willie the Filmmaker, who is traveling by mobile home. I turn away from Miguel to listen to Javier.

"What about the Barefoot Priest with the Blanket? Isn't he the true pilgrim?" Javier asks. He is referring to a priest said to be walking the road barefoot with nothing but a blanket. He has no money and begs for food from town to town. I have not run across him, and I have never spoken to anyone who has actually met him. I have long suspected he was the pilgrim equivalent of an urban legend: if he doesn't exist, we would need to invent him. I would wager that a rumor of such a priest floats across northern Spain every summer.

"Javier, do you really think he is a truer pilgrim than you?" I ask.

"He is true to the tradition. He comes with nothing."

"I respect what he is doing. But it strikes me as extreme to say that the only way to be a true pilgrim is to imitate what we like to think a true pilgrim is. The tradition of the ascetic pilgrim, the beggar, the mendicant, is only one version of what can happen on this walk."

"What else is there?"

I feel as though I'm stepping on solid ground at last. And talking on this level is clarifying, even though we speak different languages. I converse in Spanish with Javier and English with the German, which ought to make our discussion more difficult yet has the opposite effect. The Tower of Babel is not a good place for vagueness or subterfuge. It is extremely difficult to hide out among nuances. Each of us is forced to trim our remarks into brief clear statements. Babel is a fine editor.

"I am saying that a pilgrim must accept the hardship that the road imposes on him. The difficulty of the walk is inherent in walking. We needn't artificially add more hardship than is already there. That, in my thinking, is being a false pilgrim.

We all eat at restaurants. We all have used the telephone. We all have stayed at hotels. I don't believe pilgrims ignored the creature comforts of the road five hundred years ago any more than we should. Each of us assumes the hardship that the road demands of us. That is enough."

A central dichotomy takes shape: suffering versus labor. According to my theory, anyone who follows the road on foot, bike, or horse, but accepts the hardship it imposes, is a true pilgrim. But for Torquemada, additional suffering is essential. My theory has a certain appeal, but it also is shot full of holes. The German finds one of them and plunges his dagger in.

"Can anyone who drives a car be called a true pilgrim?"

"It depends," I answer. Pathetic. The problem with my idea is that it's too expansive and liberal. It allows everyone to be a pilgrim. The German is right. Why shouldn't people in cars, possessed of the right attitude (or whatever I just said), be counted as pilgrims? Yet the German's definition is so narrow that no one is included except, possibly, himself.

I feel trapped and attempt to extract myself by playing to the audience.

"Aren't these bicyclists here true pilgrims?" Miguel and his friends are physically present. It's easy to exclude drivers of cars since there is not one here. Will the German dare to deny the bicyclists even as they sit right next to him?

"They are children, out for a fresh breeze." He lacerates the air with his knife again.

I underestimate this man.

"Are people on horseback true pilgrims?" I ask.

My afflatus returns, however tardy.

"There is a tradition of riding horses," says the German.

"But isn't sitting in the comfort of a saddle a bit more luxurious than biking? It requires less 'suffering' and less 'work.' Why can someone ride a horse but not a bike?"

Jesús's daughter puts a plate of food before me. I cut a large piece of meat from a lamb's bone. It tastes delicious.

"But that is the tradition," says the German, standing his ground.

Expressions of support come my way. Claudy takes up a

position behind me. He has nothing to say (this is not his kind of conversation), but he physically lines up on my side. Rick winks at me and puts his clenched fist over his chest. "We know we are pilgrims," he means to tell me.

The debate continues into the night and past many bottles of wine. The distinctions drawn widen and narrow as my fellow pilgrims struggle to determine just what it is we are up to. Occasionally schisms erupt over the most unpredictable arcana. The bicyclists, it seems, have their own private heresies. On one issue they descend into their own bitter differences and ridicule one another. Some of the bicyclists ride mountain bikes with thick rugged tires and few gears. They actually travel on the tough pilgrim's road, pumping up and down the same stony, stumbly paths we foot pilgrims do. Others are on racing bikes with thin elegant tires and ten gears. They are forced by their superior technology to follow the parallel road of the paved highway.

A dozen standards and distinctions emerge. After a while I escape into the bathroom and jot down a Homeric catalog:

all others v. cars
walkers v. bicyclists
mountain bikers v. racing bikers
short-distance walkers v. long-distance walkers
imposing suffering v. accepting suffering
not spending money v. spending money
tradition v. improvisation
past v. present
walking alone v. walking in a group
Catholic absolutism v. non-Catholic relativism
knowledge v. doubt
certainty v. ambiguity
solemnity v. hilarity

Sitting in the solar john, I run my finger down the list. I am on the right-hand side of every *v* and the German is on the left. The road is honing its distinctions. That first question—Who is a true pilgrim?—is demanding its answer. In past centuries, it was easy: Do you believe that the bones beneath the altar of the cathedral in Santiago are the true body of James the Apostle? No one on the road believes that today. So our walk and our quarrels are about developing a new standard for inclusion, a new kind of faith, if you will. Tonight has focused this question considerably. Is this pilgrimage a sacred task or is it trumped-up tourism?

By the time I return, the conversation has pacified. Here and there is the familiar patter of arguments coming to a close.

"But that's all I have been trying to say all night. . . ."

"Exactly. That really *is* the point."

Jesús pulls up in his truck, exploding to a halt just outside the tent. He is back from his enterprises (probably balancing the books at his investment brokerage agency). He hugs his daughters, who clamor for his generous affection. He pats the younger ones on the head and then shoos them all away.

"*Es la hora para el Rito de la Quemada!*" he proclaims. The Ritual of the Burning, he seems to be saying. How fitting.

We are directed to an ornate doorway of Iglesia de Santiago, a twelfth-century Romanesque chapel up a slight incline from the tent. This church had achieved a moderate fame during the pilgrimage's heyday. It is said that if a pilgrim were ill but made it as far as the Puerta del Perdón (Doorway of Pardon) of this church, then he could legitimately turn back and depart with all the privileges of a true pilgrim. Is this pure "tradition," as the German might say, or is there in it an element of medieval Chamber of Commerce improvisation to put a few maravedis in the town coffers?

The ceremony begins in the blank darkness at the side entrance to the chapel. The moon is obscured by a bowl of clouds, studded at the edges with a few stars. The only other source of illumination is the nearby tent, a giant Japanese lantern. By flashlight Jesús takes his place on the steps at the doorway. We all gather around as if at a campfire. Into a large tureen, Jesús pours streams of colored alcohol from an exaggerated height like a clowning bartender. He speaks about the significance of the pilgrimage with the easy aplomb of a toastmaster at an Elks luncheon. Platitudes follow one on another until he holds up a mason jar filled with a dark, unappealing liquid.

"Every night come the pilgrims," he says, affecting a biblical grammar, "and the *quemada* is prepared. All drink from the same bowl, the same *quemada*. And at the end of each night, always, what is left in the bowl is kept in a jar and poured into the next night's mixture, as it always has been. All pilgrims drink from the same *quemada*.

At the end of this intonation, Jesús withdraws a pocket lighter. After failing on the first, second, and third tries, he finally puts the flame at the appropriate distance from the bowl's contents. Like an amateur backyard grill master, Jesús jerks back as a column of fire hisses to life.

"*Quemada!*" the children shout. Jesús takes a long-handled ladle and parcels the fiery drink into his collection of mismatched cups. Each pilgrim clutches his own small flame. Jesús utters a short paean to pilgrim community. He raises his cup and swallows the burning liquor. Some attempt drinking around the fire. The more cautious blow it out. We all drink together, as the night's question lingers even here. Is the *quemada* the continuation of a tradition or the invention of one?

And later on, the conversation initiated today sporadically breaks out again. I catch the German and Miguel arguing over, of all things, the etymology of Santiago de Compostela's last name. Miguel says that Compostela is a contraction of the Latin phrase *campus stellae,* literally "the field of the star." The German, after boasting that he has university credentials, says the name derives from the Latin *compostum,* meaning "burial place."

Even in this recondite discussion, one can make out the themes of the evening's debate. For the German, Compostela is buried, a grave, a dark, closed place to be dug out and discovered. For Miguel, the possibilities of Santiago are visible, shimmering with light, open-ended.

The fragile theology in this tent is at its crudest when it centers on who's in and who's out. But it's also about the language of discovery versus improvisation. It's the difference between looking for what you know is there and making it up. The German stands clearly on the far side of tradition, of order, of knowing. On the other extreme of the spectrum, I think, stands Claudy, our Dionysian clown. He is too busy plowing through the hilarity and inebriety of each day to give a jot about history.

I want to say that those of us who are troubled by doubt are somehow superior to the German and his allies. I want to make a case for Claudy and drunk pilgrims and bicyclists and eaters of fine meals and sleepers in comfortable beds. But the German will always win these arguments because he has so much material to draw on for support—the reservoir of tradition. The rest of us have only the nub of our developing and feeble tale with few uninspiring details. We've only just started. I want to say that ours is the riskier proposition because we are out beyond what is taken for granted. *Per agrum.* Out past the fields. Pilgrims.

And it sounds good. But in these conversations the German is more often right. Even in this final debate on etymology, I want to jump in to help Miguel. But I don't. I get up and mosey out of the tent. As it happens, I know the German is correct. "The field of the star" is what linguists call a folk etymology. In other words, it was invented. Somebody just made it up because it sounded good.

I want no more arguments tonight. Unnoticed, I slip away from the infinite rhythms of Jesús's artificial rain. The German will be with all the other pilgrims tonight. I will be alone. I have to follow the road I am walking, and tonight it winds just past this tent, through a dark alley, and into the air-conditioned dead end of my parador.

NINE
O CEBREIRO

T he soothing rumble of the thermostat kicks on, and waves of freon-treated parador air drift across my face. I scissor my legs back and forth under crisp, hard sheets. In a morning daze I dream I am among loafing conventioneers with name tags attending seminars. I am back in America, with nothing awaiting me but food and pointless chatter in the amniotic security of a Hyatt Regency atrium. I clench my fat pillow, release it, and stretch into Leonardo's image of noble man. My toes nuzzle into the taut corners of the bed. So comfortable this is, so yummy, so—*krong*—a plunging dagger impales me, and a gob of morning spittle clots my throat.

My feet land inside my boots. I race to the bathroom and stumble over my shoestrings. I pack my kits and instinctively steal a minibar of soap. I stuff papers and notebooks, small bags, and yesterday's stinking shirt into their familiar nooks in my rucksack. I toss it on my back, lace myself in, and race to the front desk. Here is a brand-new emotion, fresh and undifferentiated remorse. Pilgrim guilt. I gotta get out of here.

The morning clerk settles my account, taking his time with credit card checks in New York.

"A complimentary breakfast comes with the room," he says in hotel lobby English. "All you can eat." New guilt is no match for old hunger.

The morning's board is a familiar movable feast. Every conventioneer in Pocatello, Flagstaff, and Lubbock is peering over the same selection. Chunks of cantaloupe and honeydew. Scrambled eggs floating in stainless steel tins heated by a blue Sterno flame. Corrugated fingers of sausage. Paper-thin slices of ham. Bowls filled with plums and pears. Toast! Small boxes of cornflakes. Strips of undercooked bacon marbled with thick veins of fat.

I pile it on, taking two trips to set my table. I untangle an apricot-colored napkin folded into an upright lily blossom. I slurp and clink at a bowl of cereal. I smack my way through a pile of melon balls, sucking the riper chunks straight through my teeth like Jell-O. By the time I notice my neighbors, two tourist families looking at me in disgust, I can't close my mouth. I've slid three sausage links in the pouch of my cheek and presently am stuffing a jellied triangle of toast topped with bacon into the maw. So the road has changed me in some ways.

Out through the plate-glass view of the parking lot, I spy the Flemish, Willie the Filmmaker, his wife, and the owner of the tent, Jesús, trudging with a mule among the Citroëns and Mercedeses. A panic seizes me. I'd rather not be seen among Sterno flamettes and melon balls. I snag an origami lily from another table and rush to the banquet table. I pile a small volcano of meats and bread and plums and oranges into the napkin and cram it into the top of the pack. One German couple has made me an object lesson of American barbarism for the children. Glad to be of service.

"Big trip today, yes," Rick says as I walk up.

My map points us to O Cebreiro, a ninth-century village, still intact, high in the Galician mountains. The road is uphill all the way, following the new interstate cut through the old mountain pass.

"I know the mountains," Jesús says in Spanish with the assured confidence of a local. "The old road has been abandoned since they built the interstate. Today we will find the original route, and mark it for future pilgrims." On Jesús's mule is a homemade wooden saddle, built of busted two-by-fours and broken pieces of plywood—the same style as the tent. Tied to it are torn lengths of yellow plastic fertilizer bags. Jesús says the mountain brush won't accommodate arrows, so we will tie plastic strips into the bush to indicate the direction of the reclaimed road.

I am thinking about the redemptive power of the hard work of the road and about how good it feels to be walking instead of arguing in a tent. My sublime reflection is interrupted when Bacchus gooses me with his staff.

"We are going to find the old Santiago road through the mountains," says Claudy. "No interstate for you, eh? Twoo peel-grim."

At a bar on the edge of town, we stop in for a final drink. Claudy and Rick order their brandies. Willie makes weird circumnavigations about the barstools. It is his way of condemning Rick's decadence. Karl and I drink several *cafés con leche*. Jesús announces that there are only a few villages on the way. We all buy bottles of water and strap them to our packs.

On the outskirts of Villafranca just past the dilapidated electrical station, a white corrugated concrete road lurches straight up and disappears into distant mountain clouds like an infinite driveway.

"Ho," says Rick.

"Brrrrrrr-eeeepppp," cries Karl to the mule, and slaps the beast amicably on the rump. Karl worked with mules in Belgium and speaks their language. Jesús withdraws a huge long-necked bottle of mysterious liquid and pours a pint straight down his throat. He yodels the official local cry.

Nothing like an acute angle to quickly silence an enthusiastic crowd. Immediately we are forced to cut back and forth,

like deer ascending a steep hill. Willie is dressed in his usual—
pale blue, short-short jogging pants with built-in underwear.
His crotch is a Euclidean tent of belongings. More disturbing,
though, is that his wife has adopted this habit. They are both
wearing the equivalent of bedroom slippers. Jesús, acting on
Galician instinct, stays away from them.

Willie's tiny daypack holds his videocamera. His plan today
is to film the pilgrim's reclamation of the medieval road to the
top of the first mountain. Then he will descend and drive his
mobile home to O Cebreiro to meet us in the evening.

From time to time Claudy fills me in on the continuing soap
opera, which has always come across as opaque since it is performed in Flemish. A few days back, relations between Rick
and Willie broke down. For the nonce, Willie speaks directly
only to Karl. This makes our morning conversations simple
but comically complex. Whatever Willie has to say must go
through Karl, then to Claudy, who speaks English, then to me,
because I speak Spanish, and at last to Jesús. This morning's
excursion is the pilgrimage in miniature.

The road is a garbage dump for Villafranca. To our left it
shears precipitously into uninhabited scrub canyons streaked
with landslides of burned stoves, open refrigerators, stripped
cars, and burst bags of paper trash. An hour later the road
assumes a cinematographically rustic look. Willie bolts up the
hill, popping his slim hips like a speed walker, to film the same
old shot of trudging pilgrims, now locally colorized by the
mule and the leathery Jesús.

I ask Claudy to ask Karl to ask Willie what the story line of
his narration will be. I am trying to be friendly, but I am also
curious. Willie has nothing but miles of footage of the Flemish
grunting and stumping. Word seeps back that Willie will not
adulterate his film with narration. The images will speak for
themselves. Claudy shrugs at me as he explains Willie's answer.
From time to time Claudy enjoys learning an Americanism. I
teach him a new one: putz.

When the road levels out a bit, old farmers wielding scythes
appear in the slanted fields. Babushkaed crones in black togs
stuff grasses into outsize gunnysacks slung over their backs.

Every view frames a Brueghel painting. Willie shoots some picturesque B-roll. A clutch of houses appears, called Dragonte.

Jesús ululates outside a gate, and a small gray man with a blank face appears at his door, an American gothic translated into Spanish. We are introduced to José. He has an odd smile, a feeble wrinkle that suggests he's out of practice. His smile comes on like a switch—click—and then disappears. He invites us into his bodega, a half-underground hut poorly lit by a square dimming bulb. When José steps to the back, maybe twelve feet away, I can't see him. The timber is black from age. The moist air is dank but feels cool and refreshing. Around me on the hard dirt floor are kegs of wine, cheese wheels, and mounds of potatoes. Many of the potatoes have sprouted long green fingers groping for the door, a desperate attempt at escape. José twists a small spigot on a red wine barrel and fills cups. Willie grabs the first one, downs it, and asks for more before everyone else is served.

"This is how a rich man eats cheese," Jesús announces. He takes a wedge of José's sheep cheese and carves out the soft creamy belly. He pops it in his mouth.

"This is how a poor man eats cheese." He skins the rock-hard rind, throws it away, and bites off a piece of the toughened edge.

"And this is how a pilgrim eats cheese." He slices off the stiff hide of the rind again, but this time he gnaws at it.

Willie missed this photo opportunity because he was engulfing José's cheese (eating like a rich man). So he asks Jesús to repeat the story, which he does. But the lens cap was still on, so Jesús does it yet again—all the while it's so dark that each of us is little more than a flash of cheek or Cheshire-cat grin. Willie films away.

José continues to refill our cups and carve us wedges of cheese until we are stuffed and drunk. When he passes a plate of cakes, Willie scarfs down the helpings before even his wife has a piece.

Claudy looks at me inquiringly.

"P-u-t-z," I remind him.

• • •

The misty road out of Dragonte climbs up through tall scrub, drops down into a stream, and pitches up again past a field. The brush is high and wet, a temporary shield from the warming sun. At each possible intersection, Jesús halts and ties a yellow strip to a shrub. He drinks more from his bottle. Then he whacks the mule.

"Oooohhh-aaaauuuuu," he howls.

"Brrrrrrr-eeeepppp," adds Karl.

The mule lumbers into motion, and we proceed. About an hour later the path takes us around and up a bald hill covered only in flowering heather and broom, as if we have climbed out above the tree line. At the top, for the first time, a distant view of Galicia's mountains rises before us. Willie gleefully makes a honking noise signifying pleasure and aims his lens at the pacific horizon. Three mountains over, each one higher than the last, is a communications tower. Jesús tells me that O Cebreiro is just beyond the tower.

"We will make it by sundown," he says confidently.

Jesús unscrews a tin of fishlike substance and offers around bits of blackened scaly sea meat on a shard of bread. Everyone declines except, of course, Willie. After snacking, Willie sends word through the grapevine that he's had enough and is turning back. Jesús tells me that in thirty minutes or so we will link up to the marked road. He intends to call his daughter and drive down the mountain. Jesús asks me to offer Willie and his wife a ride down with him.

I explain this to Claudy. Rick understands it, and the three of us entertain a foul plot. We *won't* tell Willie, thereby forcing him to endure several hours of thigh-trembling, knee-buckling descent.

Then Rick says that Santiago wouldn't appreciate this unpilgrimlike attitude and that there's no reason to punish the innocent wife. We all reluctantly agree and spill the news. Willie's face brightens so much at the prospect of a ride in a car that we all immediately regret our virtue.

Jesús offers me a swig of his drink. I throw back a swallow. My nostrils flare. My eyes widen. I feel the tender flesh of my interior cheeks dissolving, but I swallow. Jesús is chugging colored grain alcohol. We're all lit from José's bodega, but for the first time I notice Jesús's bloodshot eyes. His pupils are pinpoints, and his eyeballs no longer make contact with the soft skin of the socket. He is completely stinko.

Forty-five minutes later the road takes a deep, wet slide. The mule walks sideways and brays its contempt. As do we. A trickle of stream water dampens the road. Our boots are slathered with mud. Willie and his wife follow literally in our footprints, trying to keep their bedroom slippers dry. Toward the bottom of this gulch, the road levels out and the tight undergrowth disappears. We are in a forest of ancient chestnut trees. The canopy of cool shade makes the woods majestic and magical. Each tree is crouched at the trunk, massively thick, sprouting convoluted tumors of bark the size of basketballs. In the distance another house appears and then a small village, Moral de Valcarce. Willie is relieved since the town means that he is minutes away from a ride.

Then again, maybe not. The only accessible roads are ox paths, all paved in squishy sheets of bovine and ovine dung. The village smells of fresh shit, quite piquant in the late morning. Parked at the front door of each house is an ox, who welcomes us by evacuating his bowels in a small explosion. At the occasional post is a tethered cow who also seems genuinely excited by our arrival and speaks oxen. Scrawny dogs howl at our approach, scampering along and then slip-sliding in an impressive 180-degree halt. Chickens flit along the surface of the shit, screeching an unconvincing claim of ownership.

Let me say this about shit. I have spent months walking through all manner of it. To tell the truth, a pilgrim comes to like shit. I know this sounds like an acquired taste, possibly born of necessity. But shit, of the rural variety, can have an attractive odor. I am not including humans; don't even want to talk about it. But ruminants, horses, rural dogs, and chickens produce tons of dung along the road. And I welcome it because the wafting perfume of manure is an olfactory signal of pending rest. It means animals, which means people, which means shelter, which means coffee and water and food.

A pilgrim's appreciation of shit, however, has not been achieved by Willie the Filmmaker or his wife. They tiptoe with the deliberation of soldiers in a minefield. The rest of us happily plow through. Sliding down one street, we pass an open barnlike area just below a house on stilts. Inside, a middle-aged housewife and her two sons, about ten years old each, are standing in a shed impressively full of shit. They appear to be raking it, possibly grooming the place for show.

The woman looks to be in her forties, although I suspect she is in her twenties. She stares at us in fear, which is actually shyness. She has on green slacks and a white tank-top T-shirt. Just beneath her armpits, one can see the supporting strap of her bra. All of her clothes, even her undergarments, are filthy with dirt. Yet I can see her beauty, ruined by labor but still visible in her bashful green eyes. Jesús says hello and explains that we are pilgrims.

"We haven't had pilgrims in many years," she says coyly.

"My friends and I are marking the old road so you will have more pilgrims in the future," he says.

She is happy at this news. She brushes her hair out of her eyes and shuffles about, embarrassed in the presence of so many men. She wipes the shit off her sons' faces. As if she had temporarily forgotten her manners, she lets out a yell and disappears. She returns with two bottles of wine and stacked glasses.

None of us has been sober this morning. Willie, naturally, is first to the bottle.

Suddenly the Flemish are in a rumpus, talking excitedly and pointing at the woman because the slogan on her T-shirt is in their language. It also happens to be in English. There is a picture of a car and beneath it a meaningless Madison Avenue oxymoron: "The only unoriginal." Willie is overcome by the coincidence, and somehow this sets off many ideas for him. He draws his camera from his tiny daypack like a sword and starts filming. Our presence is hard enough on this painfully shy woman. Willie closes in with the camera, working his way around for an artistic arc shot, and swoops in close to her shirt.

It is bunched up just at the Flemish words. Without so much

as a howdy-do, Willie yanks out her shirttail and begins pulling it down over her pants. He tugs at her shirt around her crotch and then smooths the fabric flat up to her neck. He touches her breasts. The woman stands at extreme attention, like a patient enduring some unspeakable medical exam. She turns her head sharply to one side, in the direction of Jesús. It looks like a cry for help.

Jesús speaks rapidly at me. I don't understand his words, but I do understand his meaning. I turn to Claudy, who understands, and he wails at Karl in Flemish. But our chain-letter translation takes too long. Willie is turning off his camera now, absolutely oblivious of our anxiety. The young woman stands frozen. We are speechless, and the thick fog of our languages has made us incapable of saying a word. We stand as stiffly as she, resorting to the crinkled smile of José. It's the best we can do to say we are sorry.

In these mountains the business is cows and oxen and sheep, so naturally the road out of Moral and deep into the woods is nothing but an endless trench of manure, freshly dampened by morning dew, then thinned by a trickle of stream water and the natural humidity of this forest. The banks are crumbly and wet and laced with aggressive brambles. The only painless route is straight through the trough.

Jesús has graciously allowed Willie the Filmmaker's wife to ride on the mule. This is a dubious luxury, sitting upon an A-frame of plywood and two-by-fours. On an incline, the mule stumbles and takes the age-old precaution. It pitches its burden to the ground. Willie's wife flies off the mule, but not before her gym shorts catch a nail in Jesús's homemade saddle. The entire backside of her shorts is ripped out. The valuables in her crotch spill into the muck. We are embarrassed but stare. One of them is a spoon.

Willie is angry because after two hours of treacherous walking, the village with the phone and the car ride has not appeared. Jesús mumbles that it will be soon. We help Willie's wife, who has a few bruises and below the waist now wears nothing but a blue polyester loin flap.

In another chestnut forest—it's probably around one P.M.—we stop for a rest in the shade. No one has food, and we're all a little weak. Rick produces a candy bar and breaks off a piece for everyone. Jesús turns the key on another can of sardine parts. I look through my pack for a plum or pear and discover my breakfast cache from the parador.

Genuine jubilation breaks out as I unfurl a cornucopia of fruit and sausage, bread and cheese. Willie pops over and sits beside me. When I pass a portion of food for his wife, he takes a bite before handing it on. I hope Saint James won't think poorly of me when I am driven to beat his brains in with a rock.

Not far up the road, the chestnuts reveal an unnatural geometry, a rooftop, and soon another remote village. Villar is nothing more than six houses on the path, all red roofs with white walls listing with age. A pink man and his pink wife open a door and greet us. His face is a perfect circle, completely bald, topped by a beret that shuffles from side to side but never falls. Willie lets it be known that he wants me to ask the man if there is a telephone.

"Of course," says the man, almost offended. "The last house on the street has one, but it hasn't worked for several months."

Claudy reminds me that we almost sent Willie back down the mountain with a lie; instead look what splendid horrors virtue produced.

"Saint James," says Rick.

Jesús and the pink man are talking animatedly around the mule. Their Spanish is fast and colloquial, but enough words finally come through. Jesús is trying to sell the mule for the equivalent of $400. The pink man will offer nothing more than $150. He pries back the mule's baggy lips, points at her receding gums, and scoffs at Jesús's claim that the animal is young. He walks around the animal's backside and sizes up her hips. Too narrow, he says, not a good worker. They both argue until the pink man starts swearing and curses Jesús as a typical *gitano*. It means "gypsy." I realize that we are not marking the old road, but accompanying Jesús on a business trip.

Meanwhile Willie has climbed a cherry tree and snapped off an entire branch. The pink man cries out that he sells cherries for a living and calls Willie many bad words. Willie ignores him while he plucks, eats, and spits.

I offer to buy some in order to keep the peace (such an American). I don't know the going price of cherries in these parts, so I give him about five dollars in pesetas for a small bag. We are instantly restored to his graces, and soon his wife emerges with a tray of exquisite coffees. We drink three pots. The coffee is so tasty, I am again thinking American. These beans will make me a fortune back home. When I ask her where she gets her beans, she returns with a regular coffee can. The trick is her secret ingredient, and she holds up a bottle of lethally potent *guapa*. So we get tanked yet again.

The road out of Villar pulls a sharp U-turn and then twists back again to a major intersection of dirt roads. The three mountains and the communications tower are as far away as when we began. Jesús hunkers down beside a rock, taking his compass reading in private, as he prefers. He points to the rightward path.

This doesn't make sense because it's due north. The road always moves west—the path of the setting sun—and its arc is unmistakable. Due west is down an old road to the left. Besides, the path on the right appears freshly cut. But Jesús invokes the privileges of local color, chugs some more from his long-necked bottle, and insists we follow him. The sun doesn't *always* set in the west, I console myself; it's a deceptive guide-post. The road descends sharply for an hour and then halts in a massive quarry shimmering with quartz.

We reclimb the entire road to the top, and Jesús takes another private compass reading. He points to a curving narrow swath. This looks to me like a cow path that rambles among the contours of least resistance. Man cuts wide roads that tend to go straight. But I am overruled.

After a half hour of downhill twisting among sharp, stiff shrubs, the path dissolves into a meadow flung like a spread over the mountainside, a beautiful place for a cow.

I sense a mutinous mood among my compadres. Jesús crouches to take another compass reading. I tiptoe closer and peer over his shoulder. Jesús is mumbling strange words while dangling a string from his forehead. Attached at the end is a pink stone set in gold. The stone circles around until it settles into a back-and-forth pendulum motion. Jesús rises (a bit startled by my presence) and points away from the sun and declares it to be west.

Gitano, I think, means gypsy.

I point in the direction of the setting sun. Jesús consults his stone again, this time publicly. He points into the setting sun and sheepishly confirms, "West." Now that that is settled, we climb back up the mountain to the intersection where three hours ago I had first suggested we turn left. I have had my fill of local color for the day and am not alone. I could teach Jesús a new word now. A French word. Coup d'état.

Finally and inevitably, a fresh breeze full of omens—manure, mainly—shuffles through the trees. The road widens into a well-walked path, and soon we are threading our way through the seven o'clock rush-hour traffic of Sanfiz de Seo—oxen carts, skittish sheep, ambling herds. The road on the back stretch was as brutal as any I've been on. Willie and his wife are smeared with crap and mud. They are scratched and bleeding wherever flesh is visible. Willie's clothes are shredded as well, so both of them are practically naked. Willie hasn't said a word or shot a frame since lunchtime. Perhaps he has learned something about pilgrimage. But probably not.

Jesús has been guzzling from his bottle all afternoon, having lost his leadership role to an ugly American. He's been singing slurred lyrics in a subdialect of Gallego. Without our usual siesta and nap, we pilgrims are exhausted. Our gait is a stumble. We rhythmically shift our packs to find one unused muscle, but there is no comfort.

At a bar, we lumber to a table beneath a curling Bruce Springsteen poster, next to . . . the telephone. Jesús has no trouble working Telefónica, which confirms all my suspicions about him, the telephone company, Spain, and the ongoing conspiracy of the universe. Over a round of lukewarm Cokes, we sit in catatonic bliss, waving away hundreds of flies with our bandannas. The mule pokes its head through the open door and swishes its tail in empathy.

When Jesús's friend arrives in a huge American-built Wagoneer, Willie races out to get the best seat. Rick, Claudy, and I are crammed in the rear well with our knees in our faces and our gear on our laps. Claudy translates a message from me to Willie: Remember, Willie, Americans only really do one thing really really well. Kill people.

We agree to return to the tent, and tomorrow Jesús will drive us here to resume our transmontane quest. At the tent I have a glass of wine, which transforms me into a moron. I drift out back among the mattresses, collapse somewhere, and suffer turbulent nightmares until I awake late in the morning, to a real one.

Claudy bought the mule for $150. By the time I intervene, it is too late. Jesús has filled out a sheaf of papers that purport to comply with the fantastically complex Spanish law regarding the movement of pack animals. Spain's equine stock is infested with something called *peste del equino*, "horse plague." By law, movement of such animals into the rest of Europe is forbidden, but even in Spain there are restrictions from region to region.

"Claudy," I plead, "this mule cannot even carry our packs. What is the point?"

"What do you know, American?" inquires my Dionysian friend.

Meanwhile Rick has stumbled onto some nuns somewhere who have sold him an ancient cape and floppy hat and dozens of shells. With his long gray beard and skinny frame, he now looks like a textbook medieval pilgrim. Despite my best efforts, we retreat into cliché.

At Sanfiz de Seo, we untether *our* mule, who spent the night there. The morning walk is tedious and slow. Claudy has named the mule Ultreya, an ancient pilgrim cry that means "Go West," or "Westward-ho." And that's the last attention

Ultreya gets from its new owner, who gambols ahead, singing "Love Is in the Air." The noble Karl takes the reins since he speaks mule.

In Greek mythology, all the stories of Dionysus take place at night, where the riotous drinking hellacious fun-loving deity parties with his frenzied maenads and rutting satyrs. Curiously, there is no body of lore concerning Dionysus during normal working hours. I know why. By day Dionysus is a pain in the neck.

In early afternoon, about an hour past the last village, Villasinde, the arrows and markers die out just under the communications tower. O Cebreiro is still a valley and a mountain away. But there is no road. Claudy and I set off on a reconnaissance. The bald mountain's slope is deceptive. Claudy can walk twenty feet ahead and disappear from view and out of shouting range. I look back and cannot see Rick or Karl. When I try to approach the tower, it gets farther away. Voices float in the breeze. We are lost on a bare hilltop.

When at last I find Rick and Karl, we triangulate our location using the tower, the interstate far below, and the distant peak of O Cebreiro. According to my calculations, if we just keep descending this magical hill toward the northwest, we will come to the town of Herrerías, which will put us back on a marked route to O Cebreiro. Claudy materializes among some shrubs. He has a complicated plan but is voted down.

The knee-high shrubs scrape at our legs. The bristles are tough and vicious. Soon the shrubs rise to chest level, and we raise our arms in the air to accommodate locomotion. The hill pitches down, down, sharply. Rick has lit out ahead, blasting through the brush and crying out in anguish. Somehow I have Ultreya's tether. The shrubs give way to some bamboolike plant, lined with spikes and monstrous puff balls. Every step blows open a suffocating cloud of green dust. I open my knife and hack my way forward.

We also have to contend with big condo-size anthills. Since none of us can see through the thicket and spore clouds, one step sends ants into pandemonium. They crawl up my legs and feed at the thread lines of blood coursing down into my socks. But I can't care. I am trying desperately to stay with the others. Five feet in this stuff and visibility ends. I hear Claudy scampering by and yell at him to help me with the mule.

"You fucking brought us this way," he explains.

Tempers are short.

A sheer four-foot drop-off sends me collapsing into more thicket, twisting and falling until my pack hits the ground. I am turtled, unable to maneuver my carapace.

"Claudy, you motherfucker, come back here and help me."

"You're the fucker."

Rick calls out, "Fuck you both, eh?"

That hurts. Et tu, Rick.

Ultreya is stuck. As I lie on my back, the mule stares down at me from the ledge. Its dull, weary eyes and baggy lips compose themselves into an expression of idiotic superiority.

Karl, then Rick, appear to help me. The mule, in keeping with its internationally notorious reputation, will not budge down the four-foot steep. I cut some sticks, squash some brush by sitting on it, and fashion a makeshift plankway. The mule is not impressed by my ingenuity. So we are reduced to cartoon tactics. Karl and I pull the rope, while Rick pushes the hindquarters.

"Brrrrrrr-eeeepppp," says Karl. I, on the other hand, speak to the mule in Anglo-Saxon. Ultreya brays fiercely, which I understand as a translation of my own words. At last the mule stumbles forward, hee-hawing menacingly. The beast falls and then scrambles to stand. Karl trills sweet intimacies.

Claudy has worked his way back, offering his late hand. The four of us chop and hack for twenty more minutes. There are curses, and Rick suffers another attack of claustrophobia and dashes off yelling. Claudy shouts curses at him and damns me for this route. When a chestnut tree appears, the area beneath is clear and open. As I walk in, Claudy calls me a son of a bitch. He says we'll never find Herrerías, and he shoves me in the chest. I stumble back in an explosion of curses. He rushes me, his invective reduced to pure syntax—"Fuck ya fucker, ya fucking fucked up." We shove and shout, never exchanging true blows. Rick steps over and Claudy pushes him. The bearish Karl intervenes. I swing at him in rage, inexplicably, since Karl could put his thumb on my head and handily force me to take a seat.

After Karl has restored the peace, Claudy collapses to the ground and plunges both his hands onto piles of unshelled chestnuts, which resemble spiked golfballs. Claudy bolts up, bleeding and crying, flashing his stigmata at me since obviously I am to blame. Rick laughs, but it's a bit premature. This sets Claudy off on a new round of colorful Flemish curses.

When Karl finds a small path leading away from the tree, we set off in a sullen silence. A half hour later we walk straight into the backyard of a house. Uneasily we slip around the side, click open the front-yard gate, and step into the street. A car zooms up and screeches to a halt. A man stops and says in Spanish, "Are you pilgrims?"

"Yes."

"Welcome to Herrerías." And he drives off.

According to the maps, O Cebreiro is a three-hour climb from Herrerías, straight up. But it seems like nothing. The road is wide and treeless, filled with big stones mortared with the morning's manure, dried by the afternoon sun and good for uphill traction.

As the road ascends, the temperature drops, and soon it's almost freezing. The church of O Cebreiro is Roman and dates from the 900s. The local architecture still favors the Celtic stone quarters that predate the Romans. Here, centuries ago, a fallen priest celebrated mass and watched the bread turn to quivering, bleeding flesh and saw the wine thicken into hot blood. The chalice and paten of this miracle are enshrined in a high-tech bulletproof glass vault outfitted with special gas sprays and monitors to track the silver's fragility. Apparently the miracle is decaying.

After dinner the priest invites us to sleep in one of the authentic Celtic *pallozas*. They are perfectly circular stone buildings roofed by a cone of straw woven tight enough to keep out the rain, which falls night and day this high up. Our *palloza,* home to barnyard animals when pilgrims aren't around, has no fire or heat.

"O Cebreiro is where the Holy Grail is buried," says the priest, trying to engage us with some local color and another anecdote from the annals of pilgrim tradition. "O Cebreiro was the origin of the Parzival story. Many pilgrims come here to look for the Holy Grail."

"You'll have to find someone else to do the work for you," says Rick in an unusual burst of sacrilege. "We're too tired to go looking now." As we all laugh, the priest leaves in a scowling funk. We each immediately stake out a bit of stone arc and scramble into our sleeping bags on the straw floor. I smell shit nearby, extremely nearby. It's old shit, that's certain. And if my new powers of discernment are not mistaken (and I would bet money on them now), it is pig shit and of pretty good quality.

"A hard day," Rick says into the inky darkness.

"Yes," says Karl, surprisingly.

"I am glad you are here," Rick says to no one in particular.

"We have a long way to go still," someone says. The silence is filled with unspoken thoughts—a moment quiet as prayer— and then broken by sighs, grunts, and snores.

TEN
ARZÚA

The following morning, the path down from O Cebreiro warms with each kilometer, and that's about all that can be said for it. The landscape is tedious. The Flemish and I climb quietly up rounded hills amid rocky soil covered in a morning mist, unchanged since creation. The towns here are as useless as they were when eighth-century Moors took one look and turned back. In the twelfth century, the powerful archbishop of Santiago Diego Gelmírez bestowed a few benefits on the valley west of O Cebreiro because of its location on the final leg of the journey. That was the last time the distant power brokers of Spain paid attention to these parts.

By midday the tiny villages of Alto de San Roque, Hospital de Condesa, and Padornelo slip by as quickly as they might in a car. Old men guide their ox-powered carts down the street to the fields. No EEC tractors here. All the young people have moved out. The buildings are wired for electricity. But the presence of technology is mockery. Except for lighting, no one can afford appliances. These little towns are dying, but they've been fading for so long that they no longer notice the passing centuries. As they did in the Middle Ages, the old women gather at the town fountain to wash clothes in the early warmth of the sun.

Alto del Poio can only boast of a ruined pilgrim establishment. Otherwise, the guidebook says, *"Hoy existen cuatro casas, modernas"* ("Today there are four houses, modern ones").

Fonfría del Camino still can claim the attraction found in its name—a cold-water fountain. The literature speaks of a time when the Hospital de Santa Catalina here greeted every pilgrim with "fire, salt, and water." The days of such largesse are gone, as is every stone of the hospital, carried off a few centuries ago to make sheep pens.

The open-ended plot line of the soap opera of Willie the Filmmaker takes a worthy twist this afternoon. We climb a steep short hill, and the ridge above is crowded with activity. Tripods are set. People are milling about, careful at the crumbling edge to catch a peek. Cameras roll as we labor up the twisting path. At the top we discover that Willie the Filmmaker has been joined by another Flemish man, obese, jolly, and rich. He drives an enormous mobile home with sitting room, bedroom, and kitchen. It is far superior to Willie's. And he has come with very sophisticated video equipment. So a dash of free-market competition has been introduced into the play for our pilgrim affections. The result is satisfying. The Fat Man has a grill fired up and is roasting sausages. Cold drinks are packed in ice. Lawn chairs are set around the smorgasbord for our comfort.

Claudy giddily tells me that Willie is in a state of panic. He is broke (and miserly anyway). He has already had a fight with the Fat Man and is now fretting that this guy is stealing his idea. This fresh intelligence restoreth our pilgrim souls.

A nearby bar, named Refuge of the Pilgrim, is just across the field. In fact, we are picnicking in its parking lot. I retreat for a coffee. Inside are dozens of motley pilgrims, all awkwardly dressed, shells at the neck, yet small identical packs strapped to their backs. Obviously, all are worn out from the day's walk. On half of them baggy lips dangle; their faces are blank with fatigue. A dozen weird stares follow me to the bar.

Pilgrims are a breed of loners, afflicted by a set of problems unknown to outsiders. Like southpaws or fly fishermen or Roosevelt Democrats, pilgrims feel an uncommon glee at a chance encounter with others of their oppressed group—people who can empathize with the difficulty of membership.

I nod and grin as I move among them, touching my shell as if I were communicating the special code, our secret handshake. I say hello to a young man, but he makes a strange face. A grin broadens unnaturally wide, and his eyes well up with tears. When I step up to the bar, another young fellow extends his head like a turtle and makes a gawking expression. He withdraws suddenly, and several others shuffle away with him.

Pilgrim fatigue, I know, can lead to truly strange behavior—a half hour of catatonic abstraction, sleeping standing up at a bar, weeping after a single beer. I forgive them their peculiarities. Some days the secret code just doesn't work. Again, I say hello to a young girl at the end of the bar. She sticks out her tongue, laughs, and runs off to her friends. From the bathroom, a tall blond man emerges, checking the last inch of his fly. When he detects my presence, he bolts straight for the bar.

"Are you a pilgrim to Santiago?" he asks in Spanish.

"I am."

"How long have you been here?"

"Uh, just a minute. Are you with these pilgrims?"

"I am their guide."

"I can see from their faces that it's been a hard day of walking. You all look insane with fatigue."

"They are not tired or crazy, señor," he says sharply. "They are retarded." It is an indictment that comes off practiced, even enjoyed for its easy righteousness. "They are good walkers and can put up with anything you can."

Apologies and explanations rush so quickly to my lips that not a sound escapes. My mouth hangs open, unable to clear the congested traffic of regrets.

He gathers his troupe and heads out the door. A few

untamed smiles flash back at me. The girl sticks her tongue out again and waves her hand furiously in the air.

As I say, the tug of human companionship begins to pull fiercely at a pilgrim after nearly months of blissful solitude. The events at Jesús's tent clarified the formation of two camps. And the friends and acquaintances that have been made try to stay in contact. For example, the Welsh family had rested at Jesús's tent for a day and then planned to follow our yellow plastic strips into the Galician mountains. Poor fools. They might be dead now.

We left a note at the hostel in O Cebreiro for a later rendezvous down the road in Triacastela. But once there, I find no pilgrims, although I did stumble upon a representative of the august councils of European unity in a cafe on the edge of town. The man's name is Dirk or Derek or Dreek or some variation. He has the bespectacled look of a promising functionary, broad square-frame glasses that say "I am open to new ideas." He carries a sheaf of papers and resolutions, reports and recommendations.

Dreek is part of the team from Brussels behind the future promotion of the road as a continuing symbol of European unity. He speaks English, but it is the narrow dialect of transnational bureaucrats. It is a language, taught by Berlitz, which favors a thesaurus of buzzwords and phrases sadly familiar: incentive, supply, demand, motivation, genuine excitement, bottom line, broad-based plan, publicity campaign.

When I tell him that it might be difficult to convince modern tourists of the joy of walking a thousand kilometers through rough territory that lacks amusements, at times even electricity and food, he is untroubled.

"Hey, I hear what you are saying. We have a plan here for promotion."

He spreads his papers and shows me the plan. I recognize part of it. Along the road, I have seen modern billboards that simplify the complexity of the road into digestible journeyettes. Their insignia is the shell, turned on its side and streamlined into a fan of lines intersecting at the left. The lines are the roads of Europe symbolically joined in Santiago with the idea of continental unity. He lets me in on a big secret. In a few years headquarters is going to begin a publicity sweep featuring a cartoon character as mascot. He withdraws a small button and hands it to me.

On it is Peregrín, a figure composed of triangles, playfully arranged into the shape of a human being. Peregrín's floppy pilgrim's hat hangs so low that his eyes jocularly peep out of the top. He is toting a gourd on a staff, and his triangle feet are set in the reckless abandon of skipping.

"Next year, man-sized Peregríns will tour Europe," Dreek says. "In costume. We will sponsor contests and get maximum media exposure. We have already assisted in the opening of offices in several countries to serve as clearinghouses of information for the modern pilgrim. We have contracts in selected towns on the route in France and Spain to open pilgrim gift shops. It's a comprehensive, broad-based plan."

I don't resent Dreek and his plan. The road has never been without one, the first being the early propaganda that Charlemagne himself walked to Santiago and discovered the body of Saint James. The *Codex Calixtinus* of Aimery Picaud is a broad-based plan. It was the product of bureaucracy—Cluniac and Augustinian monasteries—whose pan-European organization would make Brussels's look like a couple of county agents. Some of the collapsing stone houses on the road were gift shops five hundred years ago. My medieval predecessors were quite fond of buying miniature jet carvings of pilgrims, statuettes of Saint James, maybe a decapitated Moor. Such items are now priceless. Even the execrable Franco gave money to Santiago at the end of the civil war and twisted the revitalization of the road into a victory campaign.

I remember a casual remark by Francisco Beruete, the head of the arrow-painting group in Estella. I had stopped by his house to talk. He asked me my motive for walking the road, and I told him I didn't know. He appreciated my honesty and said, "It doesn't matter, really. Pilgrims start the road for all kinds of reasons—history, outdoors, religion, culture, architecture. They may fight it all they want, but when the pilgrims arrive, they realize they have all taken the same trip."

"Dreek," I say, "let me give you some free advice."

"Shoot," he says, and winks.

"Your plan will fail."

"Oh, I don't think so," he says with practiced confidence.

"Trust me, Dreek. I am an American. Public relations is my second language."

I translate myself into Dreek-speak.

"The bottom line is this. Your plan is good, decent. But it has its downside. We live in an age of image and celebrity. This is a draw more powerful than amusements and capitalism. You are not going to attract great numbers of pilgrims by offering cartoon characters and inexpensive baubles. The key is celebrity."

"What are you saying?"

"What I am saying is nothing new, really. The road has been walked by a number of famous people, either in legend or in fact—Charlemagne, William the duke of Aquitaine, King Louis the Seventh of France, Saint Francis of Assisi, the Cid, Saint Brigid, the painter Jan van Eyck, Ferdinand and Isabella, even Pope John the Twenty-third in 1954."

"Yes, so what you are saying is—"

"What I am saying, Dreek, is Julio Iglesias."

"To walk the road."

"Precisely. I would wager that, historically speaking, the road was jammed not long after each of those famous people walked to Santiago."

"What a great idea! I will make a list."

"Try for some political heavyweights, Dreek, preferably non-Spaniards. It will broaden your reach. I think Maggie Thatcher could use a good pilgrimage, maybe two. How about that inexplicably popular band, Abba? That will attract the youngsters. And you might get a fallen angel. Are there any famous criminals in Europe who have recently finished their sentences? A penitent criminal would be ideal. And don't confine yourself to Catholicism, Dreek. Drive the road and you will discover that it is covered with atheists and Protestants,

Jews and Asians. Broaden your broad-based plan, Dreek, and television coverage will come without even trying."

"This is genuinely exciting. What is your name again? Can I get your address? I would like to correspond with you later." Dreek gives me the button of Peregrín, which I pin to the strap of my pack.

When I meet up with the Flemish and tell them of my conversation, they accuse me of selling out the pilgrimage. I don't know. The road has been manhandled by everyone from Charlemagne to Archbishop Gelmírez to Queen Isabella to the generalissimo. The cons and schemes come and go. I'm with Beruete. No one who endures months of walking through northern Spain will mistake the trip for a visit to Euro Disney. The road can take care of itself.

Had I brought along my seer to read the entrails of a chicken, I suspect the auspices would be gloomy. As if Dreek weren't an ominous enough introduction, the Triacastelans have a dark history. The three castles of their name vanished inexplicably a thousand years ago. I suspect the culprits were the locals, who have plagued pilgrims since our history was first written.

The Santiago "tradition" associated with Triacastela, thankfully in decline, was to force each pilgrim to carry a huge chunk of limestone on his back ninety kilometers to Arzúa. There it was smelted into lime for use as cement in the twelfth-century construction of the cathedral of Santiago. One author of the history of the road speaks of the cathedral being held together as much by the sweat of pilgrims as with mortar.

Literature from the 1400s shows that the Triacastelans charged pilgrims a toll—strictly forbidden by a succession of Spanish kings.

By 1682 the Triacastelan hospital (now gone, not a trace) took up the practice of charging two reales for pilgrim funerals. I suspect a lot of pilgrims died here since they were worth more dead than alive.

The only "historical" building that survives in Triacastela is a four-hundred-year-old pilgrim *jail*. It seems too Freudian that the locals would take such care to preserve this building.

On the wooden planks forming the doors are the pathetic carvings of French names, no doubt belonging to pilgrims waiting for someone, anyone, to loan them some bail money. Also among the names are crude depictions of a gamecock, apparently an old French symbol for "yearning liberty." Triacastela is a medieval speed trap.

By the time I join Rick and Karl at an outdoor café, the soap opera has turned violent. This afternoon Willie returned to his caravan after shopping in Triacastela and found it kneeling like a dying elephant, two of its tires slashed. Willie suspected Claudy, decked him with a punch to the jaw, and threatened to kill him. Karl had to intervene. Claudy peaceably withdrew to cope with the better-tempered Ultreya and find some free pasture. Later Willie also called the Fat Man an "amateur" and shoved him to the ground.

Even Karl is upset by day's end and has ordered Willie not to leave the area of his beached caravan. We are sitting out on the main street at a cafe table. So from time to time Willie emerges and bellows curses down the street but never crosses the invisible line drawn by the bearish pilgrim.

Karl is worried because he and Rick are slated for their weekly phone call home this evening and an interview on the radio. Rick explains that they will have to discuss Willie and the Fat Man and are concerned about what to say. They are politicians, after all. So we huddle and discuss "spin control," Flemish city council style.

Rick and Karl figure out a convincing ruse to avoid the topic, but Karl wants me to do him a favor, in the name of Santiago: take Claudy away from them for a few days so he can try to cool things off. The road does temporarily split in two at Triacastela and rejoins two days on. One way leads into pure wilderness broken only by a sixth-century Benedictine monastery at Samos. The other follows the rural road. We flip. I am going to Samos.

When we discuss Willie's slashed tires, none of us believes that Claudy could have done it since he has been with us throughout the day. That leaves the Fat Man, conclude Karl and Rick. But I have my own theory, and I tell them the history of Triacastela.

The waiter is a hatchet-faced man with an aspiring mustache, who whines that he has to balance his books and wants payment now. He presents us with a bill for several rounds of coffee and a couple of plates of food. It's for eighty-six dollars.

Morning in Triacastela arrives not upon rosy fingers or amid dew-dappled grasses, but on a wind so foul that Claudy and I awaken in our hostel amid coughs. Have a thousand sheep been flogged into convulsive flatulence? Is an errant pilgrim being burned at the stake? Perhaps Willie is behind it. Claudy and I make no investigations but strap on our packs, untether our mule, and head off to Samos.

On the way out, I see a poster plastered to a wall that declares Triacastela to be "the pearl of the Oribio." The Oribio is a cloacal rivulet that barely trickles beyond the parish line. Triacastela's epithet seems as parochial as any I've seen, and I'm from South Carolina, "home of the first lampshade."

Shaking off the dust of the pearl of the Oribio, the road winds up and down among tranquil hills. Ultreya takes no time in detecting the absence of the strong hand and yodel of Karl. It behaves like a child set loose from its parents and placed into the care of a frightened baby-sitter. Our mule zigzags back and forth across the road. Ultreya brays and drools and runs at the nose intolerably when we suggest walking straight. To Ultreya, the road is not a linear passage but wild temptation. Long turgid stalks of something that smells like licorice, a species of anise, grows in the ditches. It is the asinine equivalent of catnip. The two- or three-hour trip to Samos takes up most of the day.

Claudy is in no mood to help. My polite and restrained requests for assistance are met with a lounge-lizard descant:

When I was just a little baby.
I didn't have many toys
But my mamma used to say,

Son, you got more than other boys.
You may not be good-looking,
And you may not be too rich,
But you'll never ever be alone
'Cause you got lucky lips.
Lucky lips are always kissing
Lucky lips are never blue
Lucky lips can always find a pair of lips
   or two.

Ultreya seems nonplussed, possibly offended at the mention of said lips. I laugh mildly at first, which Claudy mistakes for appreciation and seizes upon with the tenacity of a child. By the time we amble into the valley of Samos and the top of the monastery appears amid the trees, I am in a brown study of regret: I should be walking alone.

I trundle into Samos with Ultreya's lead line hoisted over my shoulder sailor style. I pull her into town like dead weight. Several once blank synapses have been permanently branded with the opening stanza of "Lucky Lips."

Claudy is depressed, possibly at the forced exile from his Flemish friends or because of my own dark disapproval. His solution is to drink the rest of the day. The village is in the middle of seasonal fiestas, and at early evening everyone assembles on a field beside the ancient monastery for a traveling fair. A wretched imitation of an American rock band has taken the stage. The lead singer is an obese man misshapened by decades of Spanish cuisine. His costume is knickers, a sawed-off T-shirt, and a psychedelic tam-o'-shanter. Swags of shamelessly visible fat rock 'n' roll to the beat of "Eleanor Rigby," "Satisfaction," and "MacArthur Park."

Claudy follows me like a dog as I use every trick I know to lose myself in this crowd. He is staggering drunk by the time the band begins. With the help of shots of Carlos Primero, the morning's song has become to him a multilayered joke so dense with strata of humor that he can barely blurt out a line before being engulfed by hilarity. To me, the song has broken down into linguistic phonemes, atomic packets of sound

unmoored from their meaning like a single word repeated to
the point of senselessness. Even here, the words cut through
the cacophony of the fair and hammer on my eardrums like
nails. I remember reading of laboratory orangutans subjected
to repetitive sounds over a period of time. Eventually they ate
their fingers.

At one of the food booths, I strike up a conversation with a
man on vacation. He is a professor of American literature at a
university in Barcelona.

"I specialize in modern American fiction," the professor
says, "specifically Jewish and southern writers."

"Who does that leave out, Joan Didion?"

A face lurches beside us and bellows, "I didn't have many
toys," before crumpling away in the darkness.

"Right now," he says, "I am teaching a course on Bret Eas-
ton Ellis. His novel *American Psycho.*"

"Why?"

"It's the most talked about subject in America."

"It's just one of New York's periodic publishing scandals," I
argue. "Dime a dozen. We have a couple every year."

"Precisely," he says. And he explains that while Europeans
hold to some fraudulent standard of "greatness," only Americans have revealed the true arbiter of the sublime: PR, scandal,
hype.

The band strikes up its version of Madonna's "Like a Virgin." The obese man sings. As I try to argue with the professor,
the troupe of retarded pilgrims appears beside me. The young
girl who yesterday stuck her tongue out at me has motioned
me to dance. How can I decline? I start pitching back and
forth in that sad WASPy gyration that is to dance what Spam
is to smoked Virginia ham. And the professor shouts on.

I want to attempt a rebuttal, but his view sounds oddly convincing way out here. American culture is a Walpurgisnacht at
this fair. The band's rendition of the Carpenters' "We've Only
Just Begun" is unnaturally loud and riddled with head-banging
electric guitar riffs. If Dante were to consign all of American culture to one circle of hell, our circle would resemble this scene
with a third-rate Spanish band playing America's worst music.

A lumbering figure crashes between me and my dance partner. "I may not be good-looking . . ." Two bloodshot eyes sink
to the ground and crawl away.

I turn my attention to the only redemption at hand, my
dance partner. I whip myself into a dancing machine, and she
responds in kind. Her friends and then others join in the erupt-
ing chaos. We become a band of howling, drooling, gyrating
maniacs. The keening vocalist competes with the roars from
our twisting throng. Some are retarded, some are pilgrims, all
momentarily indistinguishable.

The evening before, Claudy and I had discovered a bit of paradise for Ultreya. Behind an abandoned house was a modest
glade of anise sprouts on the banks of a flowing river. This
morning the sound of our approach is recognizable. Ultreya
stirs from a couchant position and stands for our arrival. Our
mule trumpets hee-haw blasts crackling with excitement. The
banks are shorn of anise, a flat terrain of stubble. When I untie
Ultreya to begin the day's walk, the mule nuzzles several of its
dampest orifices into the nape my neck.

By coincidence I came across a book yesterday afternoon
during a discussion of mules with one of the monastery's laymen. *Horses, Asses, Zebras, Mules, and Mule Breeding* was
written a hundred years ago by two British military men, W. B.
Tegetmeier and C. L. Sutherland, "late of the War Office." In
its pages the authors proclaim the mule's greatness: "Sure of
foot, hard of hide, strong in constitution, frugal in diet, a first-
rate weight carrier, indifferent to heat and cold, he combines
the best, if the most homely, characteristics of both the noble
houses from which he is descended. He fails in beauty, and his
infertility is a reproach, but even ugliness has its advantages."

Mules, I had forgotten, were man's first attempt at genetic
engineering—a mix of the European horse and the African ass.
Although ridiculed as a beast with "no ancestry and no hope
of posterity," the mule has certainly worked out better than
some of our other hybrids—the toy poodle or baby corn, for
instance. But the mule was, in fact, a dangerous creation. Its
unnatural endurance turned war from a local phenomenon to

a regional one. On the other hand, it made food production more efficient. Leisure may owe its origin to the mule.

A mule requires work and effort, and I am slowly coming to understand her. (Today Ultreya assumes a gender.) She is a little society all unto herself. Ultreya wants to eat and rest as often as possible. And I don't want her to. So we gradually work out the fundamentals of a social compact.

As we leave Samos, Claudy teaches me by his own thoughtless error. He takes the lead line and walks twenty feet ahead, leaving her to meander from side to side in a zagging wake. When the mule slows down, which is often, Claudy barks orders at me from the front.

"Beat her, eh? You're not helping."

"Claudy, I don't think we can just pull her. We have to walk with her."

"Uhh. You fucking Americans always want to tell everyone everything." He yanks the rope and jerks her head forward.

I resign myself to my position. I walk alongside Ultreya, whispering apologies for Claudy's behavior. When a car approaches, I nudge her closer to the side of the road. And she responds. There is a twinkle of understanding in her eye.

Every hour or so I suggest we let her take a few minutes to feed on roadside dandelions, buttercups, or the wheat that grows through the fences. At a river I let her drink. In exchange for this privilege, I walk beside her, pulling her bridle when she speeds up and slapping her rump when she slows down.

Eventually we do come to terms and work out a language. I carry a long thin stick balanced in my left hand. It runs the length of her body. When a car approaches or she speeds up, I rattle the stick in front of her face, a sign to move to the left and slow down. If she starts to flag, I twist the stick the other way and give her a good switch on the rump, speeding her up. This contract works so well that Claudy disappears up the road, thrilled to be free of his duty.

At the top of a hill, where the road curves sharply, a rolling wave of thunder peals through the trees. I snap Ultreya sharply in the face, but she is so startled by the roar, she freezes. A

truck rumbling at fifty miles per hour is taking the bend recklessly and hugging the curve tight. Instinct lays out my options
in a half second: I am stuck between a mule and a moving
truck, and I must move one of them. I throw a low body block
into Ultreya. My shoulder digs into her belly, and I push off
the edge of a ditch with all my strength. As the truck blasts
through, its horn a piercing siren, Ultreya tips sideways down
into the ditch. The weight of my pack propels me over her
back and to the other side of a thin trickle of oily water.

The truck is gone. Claudy is sprinting back up the hill to see
if we are dead. Ultreya bolts to her feet and stands still. A
length of snot fires from her nose. Rattling her head, she stares
dead ahead. She reaches deep into her genetic past and summons up her most elegant posture: the picture-perfect equine
profile. I drop my pack and whack her in the rear. Taking her
bridle in hand, I speak directly to her left eye, a soulful but tentative eye.

"Listen here, dammit. When I give the command to move
left, you move left. Do you understand? I thought we had a
deal. Okay, fine, here's the new deal: You listen to me, or you
die." I cock my foot to kick her in the ribs. But I pull up short.
I grab her bridle firmly and rattle her head with considerable
force. "Do you understand? That's the deal."

Claudy appears at the top of the hill.

"And you! I have had enough of your crap." He stands at
attention and speaks not a word. I should kick *him* in the ribs.
"You're the one who brought this mule on the road, and now
you want to run off."

"No, no—"

"Shut up. Here's the deal for you. You walk in front of us
and call out when a car approaches. When we get to Sarria,
we'll work something else out. But for now, your job is up
front, looking out for danger."

Claudy turns abruptly and takes up his position. The rest of
the day is spent in solitude. Claudy does not sing. No one
talks. Ultreya is blissfully compliant. Claudy and I may still
have to work out some terms, but my mule and I understand
each other faithfully.

"Mules," said the book, "so nervous from having been ill-treated that it is not safe for anyone ignorant of their nature to go near them, by kind and at the same time firm treatment, as a rule, become perfectly quiet and tractable."

My private terror about the road is coagulating into a rich panic. Maybe Karl was right. We should lose Claudy. Maybe I should lose them all and return to the proper image of the road—alone. This companionship, while comforting, is fouling my intent. Instead of freedom of thought and movement, the road has quickly become bogged down in a crude version of the world I left behind—a morass of responsibilities, concerns, people, mules. After I get to Sarria, I have decided to slip away from Claudy, Ultreya, the Welsh, everyone.

In the midafternoon Sarria rises out of the slanting sunlight like an oasis. The old village winds itself around in circles on a central hill, and modern plaster houses and shops spill down its sides like architectural trash.

Near the top beneath an oak tree, Rick and Karl cry out from the shade. The two caravans are parked side by side, and a crowd has gathered, shouting in Flemish.

In our absence, the priest from Rick and Karl's home of Keerbergen has arrived, along with half a dozen Flemish villagers. For a day there was peace and decorum. But now not even the presence of a man of the cloth can stifle the two filmmakers. A huge dent has appeared in the side of Willie's van, and the Fat Man is blamed. As Ultreya and I enter the circle of shade, the priest is standing between the two cinematographers, arms outstretched like a traffic cop. To the side their two wives stand a yard apart, bent at the waist. Their faces hang in the air like masks, only their mouths move, and from them issue gruff barking noises—Flemish charges, countercharges, and spittle.

Rick and Karl run and cling to us as if we were the police. They needn't say it: Please never leave us again. And there is more disturbing news. The throngs have slowed their pace and bunched up. The towns are brimming with pilgrims, and new ones are showing up on the road all the time.

At the Brothers of Mercy monastery, which runs a hostel not

far from here, a crowd of some fifty pilgrims is hanging around out front. The brothers refuse to open their doors until six o'clock, according to their rules. But the sun is burning, and one of the new pilgrims has *one* leg. He is lurching about on crutches and shouting obscene Spanish at the monks. He threatens to have them excommunicated.

In the mob I come upon the British couple, Roderick and Jerri, and later the Welsh family. We all conspire to leave with the Flemish in the early morning to outwalk the rabble. We all wear faces of desperation and fear, as if we were refugees trying to outrun our pursuers.

That night I sleep in the monastery's hostel. It is crowded wall to wall with warehoused bodies. At three in the morning one pilgrim gets violently ill and the dead air thickens with the stench of closeted sick. I move to a grass field outside and lie awake until my friends assemble, and we slip away into the coming dawn.

As we make our way to Portomarín, I hear the lugubrious chords of the "Song of the Volga Boatmen" ringing in my ears. The walk is punctuated by sprays of warm drizzle. On stretches of hard-packed earth, patches of dampness recede almost visibly in the hot sun. The yellow arrows appear haphazardly. One of them is a banana peel, splayed in the mud, pointing into a fuggy tunnel of wet trees. The road is so populated now, the ground is churned into a hot, sloppy muck.

Portomarín lies at the other end of a long modern bridge over the Miño River. In the early part of this century, the government built a dam upriver. Out of respect for this ancient pilgrim town, the main street's granite arcades and the fortress-style church were removed to higher ground and rebuilt stone by stone. Because of seasonal droughts (which occur every season in this part of Spain), the Miño is a standing thread of water, a thin line of glass framed between two parched red slopes. The ghostly streets and foundations of the old town visible on the banks give the arriving visitor a phantom sense of place. By the time we climb up to the city itself, we eerily know where to go.

Behind the church, the pilgrim's hostel is under construction, an old sunken house with punctured walls and no door. Workers toting Sheetrock and boxes of tools come and go. At the front door of the pilgrims' hostel, I see the leader of a group of students I had met in Sarria. He grins superiorly, which sets off some suspicions. It is peculiar that he should be here. We woke in the early hours and left long before he could have. I nod a hello.

In the bunk room, I find Val and Wyn, who arrived a few minutes ahead of me. They pull me over into a conspiratorial huddle. The schoolteacher, it seems, is traveling by car. He motored in this morning and "claimed" all the bunks for his students, who are walking leisurely. He has already claimed the kitchen by placing an empty pot on each eye of the stove.

This is petty behavior, even for pilgrims.

The schoolteacher steps into the doorway and crosses his arms. I don't think he understands that we are traveling with Dionysus himself. Claudy blows past the teacher and scopes out the problem. The invincible Claudy can outpetty any miserable high-school lecturer. Claudy rips apart his pack, brashly laying items on just enough beds to save them for the others who are minutes behind us. He slaps an arm around the schoolteacher and escorts him to the door. When Karl, who has been limping lately, and Rick arrive, Claudy asks the schoolteacher in broken Spanish if he intends to steal bunks from this old man and his crippled companion. Intuiting their role, Rick and Karl assume the faces of the damned.

The Welsh boys scamper past Claudy.

"And these little children?"

The pilgrimage takes on a decidedly different complexion now. Traveling alone is impossible. The operative metaphor of the lonely drudging hermit has given way to the stratagems of Clausewitz. It may be petty, it may be juvenile, but at stake are the basic necessities. So, it's war.

That night Claudy hatches a ridiculous scheme. He wants us all—including the two mules—to start walking at two o'clock in the morning for the next day's trip to Palas del Rei. Everyone but myself and Roderick and Jerri decides to go. When we awake at a reasonable hour, the neighboring bunks are empty. By midmorning a sea of pilgrims oozes out of Portomarín. On top of the occasional hill, the view is medieval. Broken strings of people inch their way forward. When the path veers near a paved road, bicyclists pass by in huffing packs. At a small village the bar is closed, but when word spreads of the sheer number of us, the owner appears and cranks up the espresso machine, breaks out the bread, and opens boxes of *magdalenas*.

At the edge of Palas del Rei, we come upon a priest standing in the road. He is directing the traffic of pilgrims.

"There is no room left in Palas del Rei," he says as our band approaches. "We are asking if you wouldn't mind sleeping in the field at the athletic arena. Follow this road down the hill and you will see it on the left."

The priest tells us that he has diverted nearly two hundred pilgrims away from Palas del Rei since he was dispatched out here this morning. Forget sacred, pilgrims are now a municipal problem.

"Did you happen to see a group of pilgrims, one man with a long gray beard?" I ask.

"The ones with two mules?"

"Yes, they are the ones."

"They just came through, about an hour ago."

"An hour ago," Roderick bleats with glee. "They must have got lost."

The athletic arena is a massive building housing a basketball court. On one side is an empty meadow of crabgrass, on the other a soccer field, and then a public swimming pool. Scores of people are flowing from place to place. Encampments are set out. Fires burn. At scattered tubs, men and women and children rinse their socks and shirts in thick, filthy water. Walking sticks have been spiked into the ground with lines stretched between them. Wet clothes flutter in the day's final blast of heat. Several locals have driven trucks out here and have set up mobile shops, selling food, drink, and trinkets. Before an oil drum set over a fire, an old woman is boiling *pulpo,* octopus, until they are finely pink Medusan heads. The trucks are surrounded by hagglers, who are claiming that the prices are too high for sacred pilgrims. The locals aren't moved.

Coming through the fence is like blending into a world of gypsies. The camp is broken into settlements: The old men from Holland. The five young German men. The man with one leg and his rough gang. A group of school girls from Valladolid. The retarded pilgrims. The two Dutch couples. The Italian man is here, a world unto himself. And, of course, our group. We locate Val and Claudy and the others by asking after them in the new nomenclature. Pilgrims' epithets are useless now; there are too many people. So we go by our tribal names. I ask after the People of the Mules and am directed to the grass field beside the building.

"Hey, you are not true pilgrims," Claudy proclaims as we walk up.

"Really," says Roderick.

"Oh, you missed an exciting night. Walking by the light of the moon. It was transforming."

"Really."

"We had a perfect time. We didn't have to walk with all these people."

"Really."

"We got in early and claimed this great spot."

Soon, though, the boys start giggling.

"It was dreadful," volunteers Val. "Freezing cold, you see. And the first turn we took was the wrong one. We spent the whole night in the forest with one dim flashlight, holding on to one another's sleeves, trying to find a path where there wasn't one. We didn't regain the road until morning. Frankly, we were terrified that you might have passed us."

By late afternoon the world of this pilgrims' camp is settled and circumscribed. Inside the basketball court, groups have taken shape and marked territory. The foul-line key is occupied by the girls of Valladolid, and despite the indoors, they have strung up their tents. Other groups have scattered as symmetrically as cows occupying a pasture, putting in beneath the bleachers or marking a spot along the wall. In the grass outside each door, a fire burns.

In the bathrooms normally reserved for visiting basketball teams, boys and girls and men and women strip naked, wash, change, and clean. The intense work of the walk has burned off the libido of even the most adolescent among us. Young girls in panties and bras take sponge baths at the sinks. The men spend their time at the urinals. Others are naked, but there is nothing to it.

I try to peek. Some vestige of my sexual self wants this to be an erotic experience. But the image of a young girl in her skivvies scraping crisps of dried mud from her shins or pinching bugs from her hair doesn't light a spark. One of the old Dutch men is in the middle of some peculiar ministration that requires his pants at his feet. When he suddenly attends to his ankles, he moons the room.

At our campsite, Val is talking to an old Spanish man of weathered good looks. Augustín is in his sixties, a former merchant marine who had spent his life at sea. Not adjusting well to life on land, he walked out of his house a few weeks ago because he "missed the sea." His thick mane of white hair is wrapped pirate style in a blue bandanna, set off by a handsome smile of perfect teeth. He wears blue jeans, a green cotton shirt, and a sailor's peacoat, which he sleeps in. On his arm is a tattoo of a dagger, its sharp edge grown dull with age.

Out of trash Augustín stokes a magically long-lasting fire to cook dinner. He has thrown his coat on the ground. It's his way of joining our group. By dinnertime our tribe has grown yet again. Wyn has befriended a young Spanish engineer, his delicate wife, their two young sons, a fifteen-year-old daughter, and a girlfriend.

Out on the edge of the soccer field, groups are gathered around fires sparking from paper and green wood. Soft songs in Spanish and German and Dutch float from site to site. As I work on supper, I catch bits of Augustín's early evening ghost story for the kids. It is a horrifying tale that culminates in a woman who eats her young.

By early evening the fires are dying on our side of the camp. Inside the court, the songs have degenerated into improvisation. Across the cathedral space, homemade lyrics answer back and forth, telling an episodic story of the road, a song about blisters and dogs and weather and loneliness and bad food and wrong directions and dry fountains and heavy packs, and finally, as always, sleep.

Our sights today rest on Mellid, a mere fourteen kilometers through accommodating terrain. But *everyone* is heading to Mellid. By the time we pack and set off on the day's walk, we are cast amid the flowing crowd. Five minutes later we tie our mules to lampposts in front of a hostel and gather inside at a long wooden table for coffee and omelets. We agree to a lengthy breakfast so that the Welsh boy Adam can rest. He was up all night with a stomachache. After an hour and some, Adam descends. He is blanched and tired. His hair is knotted. His walk is tentative. True pilgrim that he is, he has agreed to press on.

The road out of Palas del Rei dumps us briefly onto an interstate. A yellow arrow at a large highway bar points to the right, indicating a narrow beaten path disappearing into the woods.

On the interstate, Adam grows dizzy and falls. I suggest Adam ride Ultreya, but he can't take the bumpiness. Wyn heaves his heavy son into his arms. Exhausted and pathetic, Adam drapes himself across his father's chest. His head is limp on Wyn's shoulder, and he is weeping.

Val insists that we all walk on. She will stay with Adam in Palas del Rei and catch up with us in Mellid. That would certainly have been the solution only a week ago. But not now. We are bound together now—the People of the Mules. So we stand around the parking lot of the last bar in town, debating our options.

A Mercedes careens around the corner, shooting past the restaurant, and suddenly brakes. It whines into reverse, twisting into the parking lot. Out jump a tall man, his wife, and a young boy. He walks straight up to me.

"Hello," he says to me in unaccented English. "Are you American by any chance?"

"I am."

"Is your name 'Jack'?"

"Why, yes."

"I have just returned from Santiago. My father is Willem, the Dutchman."

"Oh, yes." This news stings a bit. I know the pilgrimage is not a race, but we're still a week shy.

"Willem will be staying there for a few days before taking the train home. He hopes he will see you there. He told me to be on the lookout for a giant red American on the road." This description of me must disturb Willem's son, since he towers over me by a good four inches.

"Tell me," I ask, "did Willem really walk twenty-five kilometers a day for three months in your hometown in order to practice for the road?"

"Yes. My father is very efficient."

"He is a true pilgrim," I add magnanimously.

I make introductions, and we all step into the bar for more coffee and food. Once Willem's son understands the difficulty of our situation, he happily agrees to drive Val and Adam ahead to the shelter in Mellid. We ceremoniously put up a fight, but he insists.

Saint James.

Henry David Thoreau explained in *Walden* that he kept three chairs in his house, "one for solitude, two for friendship, three for society." Thoreau was wise to keep his idea of society limited to three. Our society numbers fifteen, and if one includes the mules, and we do, the scales tip at seventeen.

Those days have settled into rituals—stoking fires, cooking meals, handling the animals, corraling the children, dealing with Claudy. And, of course, incidents occur. At Mellid we were turned away from one pilgrims' hostel, and Augustín exploded in rage at a clergyman. We had to stuff half of us in the single hotel room Val had rented so Adam could sleep off his illness. The rest scattered for the night.

By suppertime, Augustín disappeared. I found him the following morning sleeping on a park bench. He made some excuses, but I suspect the old mariner sampled some of the local female talent. Despite Augustín's cantankerousness, he's one of us, and no one could imagine cutting out of town without him. He can find combustibles where there aren't any, and he has an enviable talent for coaxing roaring fires from thin air. By night he becomes our storyteller, although his tales always involve elders devouring youngsters.

The next day, when the engineer's wife turns her ankle, I load her onto Ultreya. By afternoon responsibility for her has drifted to Val, who is steamed. A meeting between Val and me gets ugly. She accuses me of permanently inviting the Spaniards into our group with the offer of Ultreya and then abandoning them to her because she's a woman. She's right, of course, so I agree to work more with our wounded, and things are patched up. Throughout such crises, temper tantrums erupt from Claudy with a certain regularity, about every morning, noon, and night, I'd say.

But the routine tensions within our clan can't compare to the anarchic competitions among the tribes of pilgrims when we enter a town in the late afternoon. In Arzúa—several days shy of Santiago—the panic is visible. Groups range through the streets, looking for the best quarters. The guidebook lists five pilgrim hostels differing in capacity and amenities. Augustín suggests we set up temporarily at an athletic facility on the edge of town and then send reconnaissance teams throughout the city to see what else is available.

The Spanish engineer and I are dispatched to one hostel described in the book as having a panoramic view, an open meadow, kitchen, beds, and swimming pool. When we arrive, the loathsome schoolteacher is standing at the front entrance like a gendarme.

"All taken," he says brusquely. We both shrug, privately happy because the place is grotesque compared to our gym. It is parked on the side of an interstate. The "meadow" is an overturned bowl of dust. The roots of the snatches of grass are exposed like stuck spiders. The pool is slightly larger than the cab of a pickup truck and has washed so many clothes that it is a brown milky color.

By the time we return, Augustín has finished a shopping spree and volunteers to cook tonight. We have slabs of steak, eggs, a variety of cheeses, baskets of apples and plums, juices and colas for the children, magnums of wine, and a sack of baguettes. Out back on an unused street facing a forest, Augustín has already built his kitchen and laid in a night's supply of wood with three chunks of a broken beam, our Yule logs. Our grill is a slotted manhole cover pried out of the gutter.

By nightfall two new girls and a few other pilgrims have been invited for dinner. Augustín fills the air with the aroma of steak and eggs, lamb, and potatoes wrapped in tinfoil. Every adult has a glass of wine in his hand, and the children are plied with sodas. Augustín passes around the fresh fruits and stuffs a baguette in every fist. The old mariner pronounces a toast before dinner and then recites a poem. The Welsh children sing a song in English, and the Spanish children return the compliment in their language. Augustín has another story for the kids; again the theme is parental cannibalism.

A truck inches down the back street and stops since our party takes up almost both lanes. Augustín strides to the cab window, cocks an elbow on it, and chats amiably. Presently the truck driver parks, and our missing guest joins us for a plate.

For a moment, the labor and resentments of the day melt away into wine, darkness, song, and laughter. The night above is clear. The Milky Way, for which this road is also named— the Vía Láctea—stretches a blurred canopy above us. Chances are that some of the pilgrims who preceded us camped right here as well, looked up at the same jet sky spangled with lights, and dined with the same intensity.

The hard work of our day and the sweat and toil it took to get us into this cul-de-sac make the intellectual question of the road—who is a true pilgrim—gloriously irrelevant.

A pilgrim is out beyond the fields. He is stripped not merely of the accoutrements but of the assumptions of his society. A pilgrim is cast back upon first principles and then forced to make some sense of the lunatic impulse that propelled him down this road. Our little tribe has grown over time, beginning in León. Were we to walk for another year or ten years, I can imagine our rump society metamorphosing into a real one. Before I left America, I assembled a file of notes. I had intended somewhere on this road to make some withering comparisons between the vivid metaphors of modern science and the dead language of ancient religion: Our modern theologians are astrophysicists. Saint Thomas Aquinas had his exhaustive explanation of the universe, *Summa Theologica*, and Stephen Hawking has his "theory of everything." Even the religious notion of mystery has been translated into the scientific idiom as "complexity."

Since the big bang theory gained acceptance, scientists have struggled to conjure bracing metaphors for their new vocabulary. I have in my notes a collection of attempts to describe the universal essence: "cold dark matter"; "a great wall"; "supercluster"; "the Zeldovich pancake"; "superdense loops of matter"; "opaque plasma"; "extremely faint wrinkles"; "subtle broad ripples of wispy matter"; "gigantic bubbles"; "meatballs"; "spongelike topology." I wonder how many extremely faint wrinkles would fit on the head of a pin.

In my reading, I found that the mythographer Joseph Campbell believed that the language of science could rescue the desiccated metaphors of religion: "Not the neolithic peasant looking skyward from his hoe, not the old Sumerian priesthood watching planetary courses from the galleries of ziggurats, nor a modern clergyman quoting from a revised version of their book, but our own incredibly wonderful scientists today are the ones to teach us how to see; and if wonder and humility are the best vehicles to bear the soul to its hearth, I should think that a quiet Sunday morning spent at home in controlled meditation on a picture book of the galaxies might be an auspicious start for that voyage."

I think my small tribe might advise Mr. Campbell to put down his Time-Life picture book of quasars and buy a pair of boots. Haltingly, uncertainly, we have created something.

Were we to try to pin down the fragile sense of ourselves that has emerged, it would be about as useful as defining the amiable laughter that animates our nights (staccato puffs of oscillating air, I believe).

But perhaps some part of it can be seen in none other than Saint James himself. He has become a new man for us. In the Gospels, he was a toady. In eighth-century Spain, he was a simple reflection of Christ himself, dead and resurrected. By the height of the Moorish conflict, he had taken up sword and shield, an ur-Knight Templar, as cunning and as cruel as any Saracen.

During the Renaissance, there was an attempt by the backers of the freshly sainted Teresa de Avila to have her named patron saint of Spain. This attempted coup d'état fired the imaginations of James's supporters, chief among them Spain's famous writer Francisco de Quevedo. His defense: *A Sword for Santiago* (still required reading in Spanish grade schools after four hundred years) re-created James as a kind of elder statesman, national patrician, and kindly grandfather. The Age of Reason then reduced him to an addled and quixotic senior citizen, but James survived until he had another revival in the nineteenth century. Not so long ago, Franco straightened the bent arm of our patron into a fascist salute.

Our Saint James is a reimagined man, and vastly different from the stoic Romanesque statues or the bloodcurdling Gothic icons. Saint James has always been the protector of pilgrims, and this James is on our side, too—an impish fellow, capable of sly laughter. Were we to carve him in marble, our James would have the cocky posture of Michelangelo's *David* and a slim Caravaggian smile with a hint somewhere, possibly in the eyes, of the ambiguity of this undertaking. In short, a modern James, willing to wink at our ruses and praise our occasional virtue.

Were we to walk ten thousand miles more, our inchoate world might cohere into a lasting one. We have our own songs and dances, our inside jokes, our stories. A simple hierarchy of responsibility and set of daily chores have already taken shape. I imagine Augustín's tale of cannibalism told over and over again, getting mixed up with our opinion of Madame Debril, who in our new story gets eaten. In time we would have our creation myth, a tale of conflict with an older generation, then death, consumption, and rebirth.

We would find a language, always inadequate, to revive these moments in ceremony. The image of two mules might become to our descendants as significant as cows to a Hindu or as lambs to Jews and Christians. Our robes would be simple, and at the neck would be a shell. Each costume might feature a dark tunic that fits over the head and flows down the back. Theologians would explain that it is a symbolic representation of a backpack. The oral readings would tell a story of hardship overcome by common action. Or there might be a parable of a confidence man hoodwinking strangers. The exegetes would interpret it as paradox and fill it with meaning. This story, they would say, uses irony to inspire readers to virtue, just as Buddha's mischievous smile actually signifies solemnity. The young in the tribe would question the elders for clarification. And the old men and women would explain, in a language not yet written, that this ceremony, these robes, these sacred words, point back to a time when their ancestors set off on a long journey, and after suffering and hazards and quarrels, they found in a thing as plain as an apple or a piece of bread, awe, humility, and mystery.

ELEVEN
SANTIAGO

The word *tourist* comes from the French word meaning "circuit." It is among our chief insults on the road. I've leveled it at others and had it heaped on myself. In the language at large, it is a mild word, yet nearly all its shadings are vaguely insulting. Even as an admission, the sense is humiliating: "Oh, I'm just here as a tourist." The tourist lacks something vital in travel—a sense of caprice, spontaneity, adventure, the open-endedness of life without a schedule. The tourist has none of those. He's treading on the circuit.

On the spectrum of travel, the safe and tedious tourist anchors the far end. At the other end is the true traveler, the one who first blazes the trail—Marco Polo, Christopher Columbus, James Cook. In the path maker's wake come others who are nearly audacious. They are still considered true travelers. After Columbus opened the transoceanic route, the names of Cortés, Balboa, and Magellan followed, although maybe we can't remember precisely what their specific accomplishments were. Over time, though, a journey that once was difficult and audacious becomes routine. The anonymous merchants come. And the trail becomes more well known than the travelers. Not long after the fifth-grade quiz on Balboa and Cortés, I believe I was required to memorize "major trade routes." More people follow until the pleasure seekers set sail in luxury vessels. And finally the discount fares kick in, and the great unwashed swarm the route on package tours with specified hotels and guided visits to famous monuments, many of which commemorate the first person who did in suffering what the tourist is doing in comfort.

We pilgrims want to believe that we are not tourists. But by whatever definition you want to use, pilgrims are tourists. Pilgrims are the lowest of lowbrow travelers, a subspecies of tourist, the most degraded hybrid there is. Our itinerary is a thousand years old. Our route has been walked millions of times. Far from being the first, a pilgrim is in fact the opposite. With each step, we are precisely the last person to cover that patch of ground. And a few minutes later even that lame distinction will vanish, our footprint trampled by a crowd of schoolchildren, or a mule, or robust senior citizens from Holland.

Trying to romance the road to Santiago is a lost cause, and all efforts to attempt any such thing ended provinces ago. A pilgrimage resembles nothing so much as a forced march. We have resigned ourselves to it and are relieved only by the comedy of our burden and the relaxation that comes with each evening. Daytime is work and sweat, and a whole morning or afternoon can pass without a word. It's the quiet familiarity of friends at work, like old pals on the assembly line. Daytime meals pass amid the grunting communications of a family, and our duties are carried out by rote.

The morning after Arzúa, we resume our daily ritual—a train of wounded pilgrims, beat mules, grousing children, and sullen men who are scarcely disturbed when we encounter an enormous problem. Not far out of town, the Spanish government has cut the initial gorge of an interstate straight through a hill, probably to accommodate tourists.

We pull up at the edge. Far below is a red muddy canyon. A set of jerry-built stairs—scrap lumber bound with nails and bale wire—drop straight down before us. Across the way, another set snakes up the other side and leads to the continuing path. Normally such a disaster would require a half hour of theories and solutions, a vote, and then a moment to assuage Augustín or Claudy or whoever's idea was vetoed.

But this afternoon we barely pause. Everyone knows what each must do and performs his or her (or its) task without comment. Wyn and Claudy walk the compliant mules laterally through the woods until the slope affords easy passage for the animals. The Spanish engineer, Augustín, and I carry down the packs. We clamber back up and help the others down.

By the time our band reconvenes on the other side, we have what now passes for conversation.

"Whoo, shit," says Claudy.

"Yeeeoooo," says Augustín.

"Hooooo," I say.

"Heee-haaw," says Ultreya.

"Okay," says Val.

And we walk on.

Arca is the last stop on the road, a mere nineteen kilometers shy of Santiago. The small hostel there is an abandoned house with no running water, airless despite shattered windows, and no furniture or beds. At the front door is the schoolteacher. He has become a regular apparition at day's end, a combination of grim reaper or camp guard. An unctuous greeting is his way of saying that the place is "claimed." We tie up the mules in a nearby yard and push past him without the slightest courtesy or concern.

Within hours the house is overflowing with pilgrims. Since it is a warm and pleasant night, we bail out for a neighboring meadow, along with sixty or so others, and unfurl our sleeping bags on the ground.

This evening is nearly silent. Tomorrow all this will end. The air is slightly regretful. No one bothers with a fire. Meals are eaten from pried-open tins, and chunks of baguette are passed around. There is anxiety about arrival in Santiago. Will it all become blindingly clear tomorrow?

Three medieval musicologists from Belgium named Peter, Martina, and I didn't catch the third one's name melt into the crowd at the hostel. They have studied the road and its medieval music. In English and Spanish they explain the significance of their work and their instruments. The hurdy-gurdy is the centerpiece, an instrument that is to the medieval road to Santiago what a lute is to college Shakespeare productions. The hurdy-gurdy is a fat violin whose bridge is a cylinder of sounding board that is cranked while the other hand fingers a set of keys that press the appropriate strings. It is a complicated Rube Goldbergian instrument, and to look at one is to understand why it died out. The hurdy-gurdy sound is a sad, enduring drone. Throughout the night the trio sings pilgrim ditties in Latin, French, and Spanish, occasionally harmonizing the hurdy-gurdy's groans with the sighs of a small pipe or the muffled skirl of a miniature bagpipe.

The lead musician, Peter, is a serious man. He wears sandals and has an array of crystals and turquoise dangling at his neck. When he introduces the music, he speaks solemnly, assuring us that the simple melodies are rich in texture and meaning. He sings an ancient pilgrim hymn and then loosely translates the words:

> *Herru Sanctiagu*
> *Got Sanctiagu*
> *E ultreia*
> *E suseia*
> *Deus adiuva nos*

> *Señor Santiago*
> *Great Santiago*
> *Come on, let us head west.*
> *Come on, let us keep moving.*
> *God help us.*

Peter says these words with such respect, in the crisp enunciation of a scholar, that the pilgrims erupt in laughter. There is a rarefied, exquisite hilarity to that last line, and we pilgrims are rolling around on the ground venting it. We can't explain it, except that we've spent so many days in bowed solemnity that we no longer refrain from shattering someone else's piety with our laughter. We're certain that pilgrims laughed at that line when it was written a thousand years ago. We know we're on to something. Maybe it's taken all this time to achieve this small moment. It's a strange sound that undulates across the meadow, a paradoxical and complex guffaw. There is suffering in it, like the suppressed laughter heard at a funeral. But it's a fresh laugh, and new—our laugh. The musicians are annoyed as the hilarity infects its way through the crowd, across the gulf of languages, a guess-you-had-to-be-there laughter, and Peter and his friends haven't been there.

The next morning the herd arises and moves out. Through the woods, onto highways, then along a treacherous stretch of interstate near an airport, back among trees, across a small brook, we march—*E ultreia! E suseia!*—into Lavacola.

This last village before Santiago has its own rich tradition. Here, in the old days, the pilgrim washed himself to prepare for the appearance at the cathedral. Actually the guidebooks are quite circumspect about this ablution. In the footnotes of the more scholarly books, though, the truth is revealed. In Lavacola the pilgrim went to the river and scrubbed his behind. In the crude hygiene of the Middle Ages, this act constituted the highest honor one could pay. But we cannot find a river, and Lavacola has lost all its medieval charm, being nothing more than a knot of bars and fast-food restaurants. All that remains of this old tradition is the town's fine name, blunt in that medieval way. *Lava* means wash (as in lavatory) and *cola* means tail (as in colon), literally "ass-wipe."

A few kilometers farther along the road, the path works its way upward and then opens onto a broad hill. From its height the pilgrim can see for the first time the city of Santiago—the glorious skyline dominated by the twin Baroque towers of the cathedral. This hill is called Mons gaudii in Latin, Monjoie in French, Monxoi in Gallegan, Monte del Gozo in Spanish, and, in English, Mount Joy. Santiago is a mere gambol away.

According to tradition, whoever is first to arrive here is called "king" of the pilgrimage. When Guillaume Manier arrived here in 1726, he wrote: "I advanced on ahead by a league, all alone, so that I could be the first to see the towers of Santiago. . . . Upon seeing them, I threw my hat in the air, making known to my companions, who arrived after me, that I had seen the tower. All, upon arrival, had to agree that I was the king."

For this honor, Manier continues, "my companions gave me, as their king, a nosegay," for which Manier bought his companions "several bottles of wine to fete them in recognition of my little bouquet."

In the Middle Ages, this race to the top of the hill was taken so seriously that the victors incorporated their new titles into their real names. Several scholars of the road allege that the commonness of the names King, König, Leroy, and Rex date from this practice.

The monk Domenico Laffi arrived here in 1670 and wrote: "Upon seeing Santiago so abruptly, we fell to our knees and began singing a Te Deum, but after two or three verses we could not sing even a word because of all the crying."

The architecture of this hill has waxed and waned through the millennium. In the twelfth century, Santiago's archbishop Gelmírez built a small chapel, which disappeared long ago. In 1495 Herman Künig encountered a beautiful cross of stone and a cairn of cobblestones. An anonymous fifteenth-century Englishman saw four columns of stone and reported in verse that the tradition of arrival granted the "king" a hundred days of indulgence:

> *By a chapell shalt thou go*
> *Upon a hull hit stondez on hee*
> *Wher Sent Jamez ferst shalt thou see*
> *A Mount Joie mony stonez there ate*
> *And four pilerez of ston of gret astate*
> *A hundred daiez of pardon there may thou have.*

On the top of Mount Joy today there is a small gazebo, built a century ago as a pilgrim rest stop. But the open breeziness of the structure was filled in with white concrete several years ago when the pope spoke on this hill, security reasons. In fact, an entire forest that once grew here was shaved off, cut bald, to accommodate the enormous crowds. Huge water tanks were installed to hose down the fainting masses. These rusting tanks and a plaque authenticating the pope's visit are all that remain of that day.

Whatever powerful emotions a pilgrim struggles to summon at Mount Joy are muted as he tries to negotiate his way to the city. Tradition again reports that pilgrims would run down the hill and into the city. But surrounding modern Santiago is a beltway of interstates, and the city planners left pilgrims out of the design. We bunch up at the edge of the four lanes complicated by exit ramps, medians, and cloverleafs. We scan left and right, right and left, waiting for the buzzing traffic to open a small window of opportunity.

"There, now! Here it is!"

"No, wait!"

When a brief break does appear, a crowd of frightened pilgrims lumbers across the highway, their packs chunking from side to side, hollering words and phrases in all the languages of the world, none of them translations of the ancient cries "Ultreya" or "Santiago."

Closer to the center of town, the medieval precincts of Santiago appear, and history once again embraces the pilgrim. The labyrinthine confusion of these ancient streets breaks up the groups of pilgrims until we are—either by accident or choice— alone. The arcaded medieval streets still bear their ancient names—Las Platerías, the street of the silversmiths; La Azabachería, the street of the jet merchants, the artisans who carved ebony souvenirs centuries ago. The restaurateurs and the pedestrians point and smile in the right direction. Down one street and then another until the city opens onto a magnificent square dominated by the cathedral.

I have seen a hundred town plazas in Spain. There isn't a city or a village that is without one. They come in all sizes, from the simplest bricked square with a bent leaking pipe for a fountain to the gorgeous park and cafés of Pamplona. They all seem a rehearsal for Santiago. In an essay entitled "Watching the Rain in Galicia," Gabriel García Márquez wrote: "I had always believed, and continue to believe, really, that there is no more beautiful square in the world than the one in Siena. The only place that made me doubt its authority as the most beautiful square is the one in Santiago de Compostela. Its poise and its youthful air prohibit you from even thinking about its venerable age; instead, it looks as if it had been built the day before by someone who had lost their sense of time."

Saint James's feast day is Spain's greatest holiday. People from all over the country make the trip to see pilgrims by day and the extensive fireworks by night. Tomorrow, King Juan Carlos's son, Felipe, the prince of Asturias, will make an address in the cathedral. The plaza is filled with milling crowds, children with balloons, trinket salesmen, visitors from all over. After so much work getting here, a pilgrim can't help but fancy that it is all being done for his benefit. There are whispers among the crowd. I am being pointed out and gawked at.

"Look! It's a pilgrim!" The children stare, and I see myself for the first time as they do—a dirty, ragged man with untrimmed beard, a pack and stick. Taking up the central location of the plaza is the long sought after cathedral. Its two outrageously Baroque towers are garish and loud, fooling the pilgrim into thinking that a similar cacophony awaits him within.

But the Baroque frontispiece was built in the eighteenth century to protect the precious twelfth-century stonework that once faced the natural elements. Just inside the doorway is the tympanum of the Romanesque church—called the Portico of Glory—mortared with the sweat of pilgrims from Triacastela. A set of five columns supports three symmetrical arches. Scholars bicker endlessly about this sculpture. Is it the most beautiful example of Romanesque architecture in the world? Or does that superlative belong to Chartres or Puy? Or is it transitional Gothic? Well, you decide, pal, and be prepared to die thereby.

Arrayed across the top of the central tympanum are the traditional twenty-four musicians of the Apocalypse. They form a human halo around the Romanesque figures below. The men are about to strike up the final song proclaiming the end of the world. Two of them toward the middle are fingering a hurdy-gurdy. These sculptures are the work of a twelfth-century genius named Master Mateo. The precision of the pieces is so accurate that when modern musicologists studying the hurdy-gurdy tried to construct a replica of the forgotten instrument, they climbed a ladder to the top of this tympanum and used the amazing detail of this stone replica as a guide.

On the center column, shouldering the weight between the musicians and man, is a life-size statue of Saint James himself. He seems well dressed for a Romanesque sculpture. The folds in his cloak are remarkably smooth. His face wears a slight smile (maybe even mischievous). His left hand rests on a staff that looks like an old man's cane. For the first time that I have seen on the road, he is seated. But his toes point down and his knees are bent. He looks as if he is either about to sit after an exhaustive trip or possibly to stand in honor of my arrival.

At this central column, a few tourists and several standard-issue, babushka-wearing, multisocked, thick-black-dress, wooden-shoed Little Old Spanish Widows have gathered. A guide is explaining the stories of the Portico of Glory and the traditions. There are many, but the one with which I am presently struggling commands that the pilgrim approach the statue of James on his knees. How embarrassing. I had long ago vanquished tradition, so I decide I will simply pause silently, with WASPy self-restraint.

In the Middle Ages this small space where I stand was one of the most sought after pieces of real estate in the world. For as many as five centuries it would have been impossible to get near the Portico without a fight. And there usually were. Hundreds of people camped out beneath the statue of James. Women gave birth here. Pilgrims cooked meals in steaming vats. Fires blazed. Every night was an orgy of quarrels and fights. According to the letters of one Saint Bluze, there were so many pilgrims of so many nationalities crowded in here that stabbings and murder were commonplace in the church. After a while, the functions of the cathedral broke down because the authorities routinely had to contend with the elaborate ceremony of reconsecration. In 1207 Pope Innocent III wrote a quick blessing exclusive to Santiago. A mixture of wine, ashes, and holy water scattered briefly would now do the job.

It was at this place that the Spanish philosopher Miguel de Unamuno wrote, "Before this Portico, one must pray in one way or another: one cannot make literature." And it was here that the Cid, St. Francis, van Eyck, kings and queens, and millions and millions of fellow pilgrims collapsed in gratitude.

Heavy is the hand of history.

Down I go. The tourists step back in a murmur. The guide goes silent, out of respect, as a way is cleared for me to the column. Emotions overwhelm me. Tears squeeze from my shut eyes and run down the dust on my cheeks. A widow weeps with me. The whispers I hear flatter me. Whatever they may be saying, I hear them talking of me, as a true pilgrim—a dirty, ugly, filthy, smelly pilgrim. It's a queer kind of celebrity. Yet every pilgrim wants some sense of confirmation from without. This small group has witnessed my arrival and was momentarily moved by it. But it's not as pure as that.

As I inch my way toward the column, there is the unexpected thrill of victory—an athlete's high, the Olympic buzz of coming across the finish line, hands up, breaking the tape, the body suddenly limp with accomplishment. That part of me wants to jump up, stuff my fist in the air, and scream, "I made it. I did it." And then look into the crowd to find the face of the one person who believed in me all along and see him clench his fist and shake it in congratulation. Obviously this part of me will star in the TV movie version of the walk, *Santiago: Walk with Me, Talk with Me* (based on a true story).

Even here, minutes away from completing my pilgrimage, an air of fraudulence lingers. I had expected a purity, a clarifying wind of revelation. Instead the tourists unsheathe their cameras and illuminate my already soiled epiphany with the strobe of flashes. This clenched face and furrowed brow now bowing before the statue of James—is this mine, a performance, or both?

The pilgrim wants confirmation, and I know there will be other opportunities to get it. The cathedral is practically a gauntlet of confirmation.

On the other side of James's column is a self-portrait in stone of Master Mateo called *Santo dos Croques,* literally "the head-banging saint." Tradition holds that visitors bang their heads against Master Mateo's to receive his wisdom. This custom is especially popular among students at the University of Santiago on exam night. It is not technically part of a pilgrim's obligation. But I am not one to turn down a little wisdom. I gently bang my head.

Afterward the pilgrim walks to the high altar at the other end of the church. Situated above the table is another statue of Saint James, this one gilded, his cloak encrusted with jewels, and bathed in amber light. A small doorway on the side points the pilgrim to a narrow passageway behind the statue where the pilgrim may hug Saint James in thanks. In the Middle Ages the pilgrim customarily put his broad-brimmed hat on Santiago's head before embracing him. Cosme de Medici visited here during the pilgrimage's heyday and noted that from the front, the statue changed its headgear so often that Saint James seemed to be trying on new hats day and night. My shell clangs loudly against the gold as I give him a hug, promised to so many on the road, *un abrazo por el apóstol.*

The exiting staircase reveals an arrow that points to another chamber down below. As narrow as the last, the passageway opens onto a small, low-ceilinged room. Behind protective bars lies a small silver coffin, large enough to hold the body of a child. Within it are the bones of Saint James.

There are several other pilgrims here, and we stare awkwardly. All these traditions have accrued over the centuries, each of them attempting to give to the pilgrim a sense of accomplishment.

The bones of Saint James were long the source of the pilgrim's popularity, but the story associated with them ran its course. Belief in the bones petered out in the nineteenth century, and the authorities didn't know exactly where the bones were anymore. So the church authorized an archaeological dig beneath the church's flat stone floor.

Initially the work did not go well. In order to accommodate the church's activities during the day, the excavations took place by torchlight at night. Digging beneath the floor stones in the location where Saint James's bones were said to lie, the workers were teased by findings of bricks and masonry from the appropriate eras, but nothing else. Eventually the dig progressed to a space beneath the apse. One of the workers, Juan Nastallo, was digging late in the evening of January 28, 1879. In a deposition he reports: "I prayed to the Virgin of Sorrows that the body of the apostle appear. At that exact moment, Canon Labín [the head archaeologist] arrived. . . . I removed the two bricks with the trowel and there appeared various bones contained within a box which exuded an odor that I have never smelled before. I immediately lost my sight for a half hour and I nearly fainted when, with the help of my companions, I was carried out of the hole. I remember well the sanctity of the oath I had sworn, and I declare by all and confirm the commotion that I experienced and the most gratifying odor I perceived. I know too that Canon Labín, who had suffered a serious migraine headache, was cured at that precise moment. I, instead, on account of the commotion, suffered my ailments for eight or ten days."

The church brought in other scientists to confirm their authenticity. The bones were anatomically assembled and surprisingly there were enough for three skeletons, not one. This was interpreted to mean that Saint James was buried with the remains of his two original disciples. But which bones belonged to James?

As it happened, a church in Pistoya had long claimed to have a small piece of Saint James's skull—the mastoid process, to be precise. Could it be? One of the three skulls in the find *was* missing a chunk. When the two parts were finally united, they fit, according to the church, like two parts of a puzzle.

The news of this discovery provoked celebrations in Spain. Even Rome, so belligerently disinterested in Santiago's legitimacy in recent centuries, was excited. Science, the ancient enemy of faith, had confounded itself, and confirmed the beliefs of the ages. On November 1, 1884, Pope Leo XIII issued a formal declaration, filled with unambiguous glee. "Thus," it reads, "the doubts that these bones existed have vanished."

But the gloating was short-lived. In 1900 a church historian, Monsignor Louis Duchesne, wrote *The Ancient History of the Christian Church*. He has little to say about Saint James. He mentions the bones and then asks: "Why was that identification made? We have not the slightest idea. But ecclesiastical authority supported it, and we must in kindness suppose with good evidence—at least in its own opinion."

As I stand looking at the small coffin containing the bones, in wander a few other pilgrims. Then two nuns follow. The only conversation is an exchange between the two sisters. One says that the carvings on the ancient silver coffin are quite lovely. The other agrees and adds that the coffin is also remarkably shiny.

Rick grabs my arm to remind me that there is some paperwork we need to complete. At a side door on the outside of the church, the pilgrims are ordered to line up to receive a diploma. This is the final confirmation that the church grants. The pilgrim signs his name to the rolls, presents his stamped passport as proof, and is given what is called a *compostellana,* a grand parchment written in Latin.

Apparently, handing out *compostellanas* is, among clerical duties, just a notch above cleaning the chapterhouse with a toothbrush. By the time I reach the front of the line, a young, handsome priest invites me to sit in a chair. He asks a series of questions as enervatedly as a bureaucrat in the unemployment office.

"Name?"

"Hitt."

"Eeet?"

I spell it for him.

"Full name."

John Thomas Leonard Hitt.

"Very long." He is troubled. Maybe my full name won't fit.

"What was your motive for walking the road?"

He doesn't bother to look at me until I answer.

"To discover my motive."

"That is not an appropriate answer." He turns his papers around so that I can see that the three correct responses are religious, cultural, or historical. I don't remember which one I checked.

Later that afternoon we pilgrims file by the appropriate window to pick up our diplomas. Mine is made out to Joannem Thoman Leonardum Hitt, and I carefully stow it in a safe corner of my backpack. And that is the last the church has to deal with us, or we with it. If we look for confirmation of our act, it won't be here, in history or tradition or art. We'll have to improvise.

Outside, the conversation turns to celebrations, party dates, and gossip. In the streets, we pilgrims—even those who never once met on the road—know who we are. We stand out in the densest crowd. Our shoulders are broad, our waists are small. I have taken to glancing at a man's belt. Is there a new notch cut into it?

Our haggard look and Li'l Abner build is a confirmation of our status.

On the first night, the gang of Flemish pilgrims and their fellow villagers gather at the Sostel Hotel. Many others, even pilgrims I never met, wander in. The party spills into the streets, and there is glorious news all around. I hear the final chapter of the Willie saga. Somewhere past Mellid, a horrific fight broke out. Each filmmaker stoned the other's caravan, smashing windows and splitting the aluminum siding. Even the kindly priest, says Claudy, lost his temper and told them both to "fuck off." The priest smiles; he's happy to be on our side.

From time to time I see Willie's caravan, dented and listing, prowling the side streets of Santiago, an uninvited guest.

For three days the parties rage. Stories are told and retold until they feel comfortable enough to tell to strangers. The only common aspect of these confirming tales is that none of them takes place here in Santiago. They all occur somewhere back up the road when the days were hard and the nights were spent in solitary wonder or orgiastic drunkenness. But in the next day or two, the celebrations thin out. In the streets the pilgrims grow fewer, and eventually those of us remaining realize that some have left, never to be seen again. One languid afternoon, I bump into Rick on a side street. He is walking with his wife, who had recently arrived to take him home. His wife is a colossal and merry woman, a Venus of Willen, all curves and luxuriant body fat.

"I have many children," Rick says by way of explanation. After introductions, the encounter is awkward. The tidy world we had created is over. Our time together has become something else now, something with a beginning, a middle, and now an end. It is fragmenting, and it is strange to feel it do so. We are sorry, almost ashamed, when we see one another. In the broad daylight and normalcy of Santiago, the past season recedes quickly and seems almost a hallucination. We are strangers again and have little to say. The pilgrimage is being broken down, packed up in the boxes of our little stories for safe transport back home, either to the world we left behind or, more likely, the next one we will inexorably begin making.

By the third day, Rick and Karl are gone. Javier has returned to his bank in Pamplona. Wyn, Val, and the two kids sold their mule and have left for St. David's, Wales. Ultreya has taken up residence on a farm at the edge of town. Claudy is scarce, having hooked up with a Spanish girl. I see him briefly on the street one day, and he tells me he's moving to León to live with her. It becomes increasingly difficult to spot the other pilgrims. New clothes have been bought. We have shaved and gotten our hair cut. Several days of warm showers, comfortable sleep, good food, Rioja wine, long conversation, television programs, and newspaper dispatches are turning us back into ourselves.

I stayed a week in Santiago, and by the end I didn't know a soul.

Before my noon train to Madrid and a plane to America, I spend a final morning in the cathedral. At the Portico, the twenty-four men of the Apocalypse have remained as I had left them. Which is surprising because this orchestra is carved unlike any other sculpture I saw on the road. Most Romanesque and Gothic sculptures of this theme always depict the men sitting formally and seriously. But Santiago's men, scheduled to play the final symphony, seemed strangely unconcerned with their momentous task. They are chatting and joking and laughing with one another. Even the more sober statues on the columns don't seem so sober. A tall life-size statue of Daniel is grinning at somebody—no wait, Daniel is clearly ogling Esther across an archway.

Master Mateo's work is beautifully subversive. Among the musicians, groups of two or three have their heads tilted toward another, whispering. Others are rosining their strings. Still others are tuning their instruments. According to the traditions of religious iconography, these men are about to begin the melodies that signal the end of the world. This is the grand theme, noble and solemn, yet Mateo has carved a private human moment. The men are smiling, laughing, as if they were on to something, cracking private jokes. The guild of musicians captured here casually fooling around is set not merely to end the world, but to start a new one.

When Master Mateo carved this sculpture, he used as his inspiration a story from the Revelation of St. John. The critical verse (5:9) reads: "And they sang a new song." Man invents his truths and then clings to them so stubbornly that he will shape the world around him to conform to them. The tenacity to believe is the greatest folly, said Erasmus. Yet he concluded that it was our only hope.

For a long time god was this belief, and we furiously confirmed his existence. On every mile of this road, the proofs still stand, although sustained now mainly with government funding. A thousand years ago, from this belief but also from crude political calculation, financial desperation, and military necessity, the pilgrimage emerged as a journey to truth. What one finds on the road may not be what god wrought, but it is what man wrought, and, for a time, it was the best we could do.

At the statue of James, a short line of tourists and Spanish widows wait to take up the special place before it. Ever since the journeymen who hoisted this stone in the 1170s set it straight with a plumb line, the pilgrims have knelt here and with their flat hands touched the column beneath James's bare feet. So many have done so that the marble seems to have gone soft. The old stone is worn smooth in one place, about an inch deep, in the perfect shape of a human hand. With my new pants and shirt and fresh-washed face, I have no privileges now. No one notices me. So I take a place in line. One cannot make literature here. When my time comes, I put my hand into the stone and pray.

Afterword

Not long after leaving Santiago, I found myself marooned in a barn in Connecticut. Every morning, I cleared away the late-night cobwebs on my desk, set down my thermos and wrote a book. I spent most of my day puzzling out a soap opera of scenes and scraps of notions and flyaway phrases. All of this action happened inside the barn, if not in my head. And then, as lunchtime approached, I'd step back into the world where gas bills are paid, my wife existed, and the hissing radiator needed to be bled. After a year or so, the life inside the house seemed strange, bordering on fictional.

The narrative flow inside the barn moved at the glacial pace of a few hundred words a day and toward a known end. Out there, the whole thing was full of mystery and seemed comically fast, zipping along at the slapstick speed of a Chaplin movie. So I hardly noticed when my wife quit her job and entered medical school. Then a child appeared, adding a new caliber of noise to the house that made me forget about the pesky radiator. Then, it seemed a few weeks later, another daughter appeared.

By the time the book came out, I had fully re-entered the Einsteinian time warp that most folks live in and found that I had two kids—in the full commotion of being one and three— plus a wife whose medical residency had begun, which meant she would be off on her own trip for about the next three years.

Being alone in a house, choreographing the physical needs of an infant and a toddler (and without a book to write) introduced me to a new kind of solitude, one that even a consummated pilgrim could barely imagine. The social scene on the road to Saint James, looking back, suddenly felt as crowded and elegant as a fund-raiser at the Metropolitan Museum of Fine Art.

I literally don't really remember much about that time. Not a lost weekend, but a stretch of years, a really nice chunk of time, nearly half a decade. Imagine passing your entire college career in nothing but a blur. Maybe that's not so hard. But my point is that my entire world shrank into something roughly the size (and intrigue) of a bus station waiting room in a small Kansas town. Most of the days passed working out small details of logistics. Timing always seemed to be off—wide awake with nothing to do at 4 A.M., nodding out in a chair just before lunch. The coolness of the light coming in the windows seemed perpetually late afternoon, Edward Hopper directing. Visitors were cause for celebration and bunting. The FedEx guy became my pal. A cup of coffee every morning at my local java stand was my only holiday. The one dependable indication of human life was the ebb and flow of some watery, fecally, milky liquids.

Nights that rambled into late hours amid whispers in a pilgrim's hostel were instead spent at the side of a crib, cooing a simple matchstick narrative of pirates and trolls, until the hard oak of my floor woke me at 4 A.M. with a tough reminder that somewhere in this place was a bed. When I thought about the wide-open terrain of the pilgrim—with its oxen-like pace and afternoons devoted to mulling the meaning of the "plateau" as both a metaphor and as an afternoon's conquest—the entire experience had become a thing in my life as long ago as Mrs. Newton's sixth-grade math class.

Into this, my hermetically sealed universette, sometime around 1997, fluttered an unexpected note as if dropped out of the talons of a messenger owl. It was from Claudy, the Dionysian hero of this book. He was living in Belgium. He had found the internet since our days in Santiago. He wrote that it was filled with "genuine opportunities" and other revenue-enhancing potentialities. The odor of spam wafted from every email. The virtual pilgrim had found a home designed precisely for someone with his particular gifts. Though the details of what actually got done on the internet were always vague, the end result was clear: He was flush and would love to take some time out of his international itinerary for a visit to New Haven.

Up went the bunting, and soon enough the cinematic scene of the eager host standing alert and anxious at the train station played out with all the Hollywood moments. The big hello. The meaningful embrace. The immediate chit-chat about food and time. One of my kids was sleeping in a box in my closet so we had a long talk about hotels. Then off to lunch at my favorite Basque restaurant in town which made great tapas, particularly a red pepper thing involving—but we never got there. One of my various digital devices pinged with the news of a sick child.

"Not a problem," Claudy said, bragging a bit about his new effortless life. "I can work anywhere on the internet." I dropped him off at the hotel and swam back into my tiny warm liquidy world. When he called later in the day, I had the child sleeping at home and then there was the other one to pick up from day care after which I would be consumed with a complex regimen of feedings. After two more fractured and hobbled days, it became clear from Claudy's disappointment that he had a vision of what his visit with me should be and things weren't matching up. I think he expected me to be the way he had once known me, as a boon companion who'd happily drop a day of my life to help him decide which of a village's nine taverns served the best Ribera del Duero.

Claudy was here for three days and every time we got together—it was bizarre—obligations intervened and I'd have to run off. As Bismarck once said of history, life just kept on happening, one damn thing after another. I could sense his disappointment at the constant interruptions and demands so I arranged for a quiet supper.

Now, having children is like moving to a foreign country where you only know a dozen words of the language. It's a private place, where most of what happens involves this weird relationship between a helpless quasi-lingual person interfacing (literally) with an omniscient overseer. There are pleasures in it; in fact there can be a thousand of them in the course of an afternoon that absolutely spangle the day in fairy dust. The problem is that by some perverse factor of genetic engineering, at the chromosomal level, the only person who can experience this sensation is the overseer. People dwelling in the quotidian exurbs that rumble at the periphery of this little happy bubble seem perversely bored.

Most of my life, I cheerfully endured my friends with their children and their inane stories always involving drool or lost teeth or inappropriate repetition of Daddy's vulgarities in front of grandma. Then I entered the bubble and discovered the pleasure. It took me a while before I figured out that I was the only one actually having this experience and that the strained smiles I was seeing were just people politely shining me on. My stories suddenly sounded just like everyone else's, and soon enough I sensed that I had become that annoying friend telling his painfully mawkish stories about junior's Einsteinian development.

With Claudy in town, this basic perception was finally coming home—hard. My fleeting pleasures were of no interest to him, through no fault of his, but of mine. I hadn't yet figured out a way to tell the story of having children. There was a similar sense when I returned from Spain. No one wanted to hear the diary version of the walk—the day-to-day home movie tedium of where and when and what. Like the pilgrimage, children's stories can't be told in real time, even though as parents we're hopelessly moored to it. I had to look harder at the moments and think like a writer. Where were the good bits that would be great stories for anyone, not just me? This is the difference between diaries and writing, between bad pilgrim accounts and good ones, between boring kiddie tales and bits of incandescence.

But I hadn't got there yet. I was still frustrated that my friend couldn't appreciate how overwhelmed I was with the minutiae of maintaining my children's lives and the difficulty of it all. My life shuttled between two extremes, awe and exhaustion; then there was Claudy who just wanted to go somewhere and have a beer.

My arrival at the local sushi joint was confounded, of course, by the unrelenting curse of this visit. The baby-sitter fell through and there was no choice but to bring along my little ones to a sushi restaurant and hope for the best.

I say "hope for the best" because that is the eternal optimism of the novice parent who actually believes against all evidence that a six-month-old will not cry in a public place and that a three-year-old will sit still during the most tedious conversation. Claudy had arrived at the restaurant all well-scrubbed and light-hearted. I sledge-hauled my gear along with my unkempt self into the place as if preparing to set up base camp for some later strike toward the summit. When I asked him to pass me a bottle out of a bag, Claudy fell into a stiff manner in handling the thing as if tweezering a hairy insect in high school biology class. It was times like these that all the lines of all the performances of *Cat on a Hot Tin Roof* I had ever seen came drifting back from memory, and I realized there was no escaping my lot as a grubby breeder lost in that witless world of milk and shit.

The night of drinking and debauchery that Claudy so desperately sought never came, and in the morning he had left. Apparently, the ease of the internet is no match for the complexity of diapers.

It was at the sushi bar, in the full throat of my excuse-making and apologies, that I started riffing for the first time about how children were a lot like the road itself. They were just there, never not there, always making small but inexorable demands.

On the road, there was no stopping. Sure, you could rest a day or two, but the push was always forward. Any pilgrim who spent a week lounging in a village would become suspect, eventually branded a tourist if not a weirdo. Children are like that. If I were to take a break from them, then it would have to be for a movie, or an evening dinner at a restaurant with my wife, and it wouldn't really be a break because there would just be more details regarding the logistics of baby-sitter retrieval and drop-off, prefabricated kiddie dinners, laid out jammies, preselected bedtime literature, a thought-out choreography to ease parental departure out the door with a minimum of keening, as well as a printout of emergency numbers including Bruce and Kay next door, the good folks at 911, the theater's house phone, the cell phone, the wife's pager, and, just in case, here's a flare gun.

Every break in the forward momentum of child-rearing, like the road, meant only that we were eventually heading back into the moseying stream of things. Back onto the narrow of the road, back into the necessary regime of conducting the little ones through another day.

Is that what Dionysius or Zorba wants to hear? Hardly. For Claudy, the revelation is the thing. The details of getting there are tedious and annoying. They are literally pathways to the greater goal—the end-of-the-day dropping off of the packs, the kids are in bed let's screw, the big celebration, the grand epiphany. The road itself is merely the means to a more glorious end, not to be considered as anything but a virtual location, a whole like the internet, where the genuine opportunities that lie waiting are never described with as much zeal as the manna that falls from the sky like magic.

Not long after Claudy departed, a book arrived in the mail. A publisher thought I might be interested in reading Shirley MacLaine's new book about her walk on the road to Santiago. The picture of the New Age former movie star on the cover with her head down and a big hat obscuring her face lent the impression that this book was filled with fugitive notions of the divine, shrewd secrets earned on a hardscrabble path full of rocks and stones.

But subtlety is not exactly the adjective that describes MacLaine's revelations. First, she has them as promiscuously as a medieval relicsmonger. Hardly a page goes by that some enormous vista, absolutely life-impacting, isn't peeling open like time-lapsed photography onto the page. She channels ancient pilgrims and medieval princes and has sit-down interviews with them. Saint James speaks to her as well as does, for some reason, Olaf Palme, the Swedish prime minister assassinated in 1986. Epiphanies crowd her account and great revelations are propounded so easily that eventually one wishes for nothing so much as the boredom of the road as relief from so many gigantic truths. For MacLaine, revelation doesn't occur as a flutter in the peripheral range. Rather, the great Emperor of Europe, Charlemagne, walks right up to remind the author of the time they made love. (I'm not kidding.)

This is the plague of even noncelebrity Santiago literature. Every pilgrim's temptation is the need to encounter a brand new truth, preferably one that's panoramic, cinematic, and ecstatic. Like the tidy endings of airport novels or the neat package of lessons learned that close so many movies, they are more literary devices signifying the expectations of the genre than the truth of what happened. Pilgrimages are all about finding a good chunk of chorizo, cool water, a café con leche, some manchego, and fresh bread, as well as blisters, food poisoning, a warm blanket, the rare clean bathroom, and toilet paper that doesn't qualify as grade C sandpaper. The essentials, really, food and shelter—milk and shit.

In the midst of all that work, wrangling the details of life stripped down to that essence, some tiny thing appears. It might be a funny line, a moment, a chance encounter, a thought that gives you the power to see yourself as you really are, there in that awkward surreal place. It's what Eliot meant when he wrote in "Little Gidding": "We shall not cease from exploration/And the end of all our exploring/Will be to arrive where we started/And know the place for the first time."

It's the best one can ever expect from all revelatory experiences, whether it's taking hallucinogenic drugs, walking a pilgrimage, or having children. You want instant epiphany? Try war. You'd be hard-pressed to read any war journal where the big questions aren't answered quickly and dramatically. It's not hard to understand the meaning of life after watching the guy you shared breakfast with get his leg blown off.

Yet even the best of these—Tim O'Brien's *The Things They Carried*—plow straight into the onerous details of Bismarck's one damn thing after another.

It took me a long time to figure out how to tell stories about my kids. The ones worth telling are those small moments when their sharp eyes cut through the callus of the general assumption. My younger daughter has a surreal gift for word association. One logy afternoon as we all zoned out zigzagging up and down the chilly aisles of our local Super Stop & Shop, she started complaining bitterly. She said she wanted to get out of this place, the "Stupid Stupor Shop"—a dadaism that has forever changed how we think about getting the groceries. Or my older's moment when she asked me who Martin Luther King was one January 20th morning. I explained his idea of racial equality and she said it sounded a lot like Jesus's "Do Unto Others" line. Yes, I agreed, it did. Sitting in a crowded coffee shop near Yale, she looked up and matter-of-factly asked, "So, did they kill him, too?"

The private pleasures of having children require some work if you are going to get past the kiddie pics and the grandma stories. Like the road to Santiago: Stay mucked up in the details and keep your eyes peeled for the occasional gem. Saint James is not much of a saint if you're shopping for ecstatic epiphany. You can go to Teresa de Ávila or Francis of Assisi for that. James is the man of details, of the road, of gear, of schlepping through.

In the popular depiction of Santiago, all over Europe, he's typically seen as a pilgrim with a simple expression on his face—determination sometimes, often just sheer exhaustion, but curiously never revelation. In most statues, it's hard to detect any emotion other than that of unaffected purpose, a tired man toting his equipment. He's wearing his cape, gourd, shell, hat, and stick. We look at that image today and read those details as the emblems of the sacred pilgrim, but for most of the previous millennium, Santiago the icon was just a guy carrying his stuff, the way he might well appear today on the cover of *Outside* magazine: sleeping bag (cape), canteen (gourd), sunscreen (hat), and dog-protection device (stick). The shell is the only pure symbol and even that has the improvised feel of something picked up off the ground.

Maybe if Santiago had come later in that first millennium we would have had a different image altogether. Imagine a Bernini version of Saint James. He would probably be shown fully arrived in Compostela, his long ZZ Top beard touching his bended knee. He would be slightly bowing his head, as if at some altar or cathedral door. His face, partially obscured by his hat, would appear consumed with the overwhelming power of receiving a great MacLainean truth.

But James is never depicted that way. He's the most ancient and post-modern of icons. He's the patron saint of the pilgrim in the midst of small things—the swashbuckler exploring for adventure in a suburban den, the warrior looking for bravery on a frontage road, the traveler discovering excitement on the way to the Super Stop & Shop. "God is to be found among the pots and pans" goes the proverb. Santiago lives that creed in his image, always trying to remind his alumni that when the road picks up after Compostela, the only thing that changes is the gear.

About the Author

JACK HITT is a contributing writer for *Harper's* and *GQ*. He also writes for *The New York Times Magazine, Outside,* and *Mother Jones,* and contributes frequently to public radio's *This American Life.* He lives in Connecticut.